MW00620139

EXERCISING SPIRITUAL AUTHORITY

EXERCISING SPIRITUAL AUTHORITY

DALE M SIDES

Liberating Ministries for Christ International, Inc., Bedford 24523

Printed in the United States of America

ISBN 1930433549

The scriptures used throughout this book are quoted from the New King James Version of the Bible unless otherwise noted. Any explanatory insertions by the author within a scripture are enclosed in brackets [ ]. Any words in boldface within a verse indicate the author's emphasis.

Scriptures marked KJV are from the King James Version of the Bible. The King James Version is in the Public Domain in the United States.

Scriptures marked (WEB) are from the World English Bible. The World English Bible is in the Public Domain.

Contents

Author's Forward and Dedication vii

Introduction 1

Part I—Spiritual Authority and the Makeup of Man 5
Chapter One—The Realm of Spiritual Authority 7
Chapter Two—Who Am I? 21
Chapter Three—The Spirit Nature of Man 37
Chapter Four—Exercising Spiritual Authority over the Soul 55
Chapter Five—Exercising Spiritual Authority over the Body 65

Part II—Diligent Discipleship 73
Chapter Six—The Authority of a Disciple 75
Chapter Seven—The Authority to Re-Present Jesus 87

Part III—Spiritual Warfare 113
Chapter Eight—Overcoming the Power of the Enemy 115
Chapter Nine—Closing Portals of Demonic Entry 141

Part IV—Our Authority to Re-Present Jesus in Character 165
Chapter Ten—Developing the Character of Christ 167
Chapter Eleven—Re-Presenting Jesus on the Earth 191

Part V—Our Authority to Re-Present Jesus in Power 205
Chapter Twelve—Receiving the Holy Spirit and Speaking in Tongues 207
Chapter Thirteen—The Utterance Gifts of Interpretation of Tongues and Prophecy 225
Chapter Fourteen—Receiving Spiritual Information and the Revelation Gifts 237
Chapter Fifteen—Spiritual Faith 259
Chapter Sixteen—Gifts of Healings and the Working of Miracles 279
Chapter Seventeen—Other Ways God Can Heal 293

Epilogue 303

Appendixes 305

Appendix 1—Operating the Gift of Faith to Fulfill Your Ministry 307

Appendix 2—Exercising Spiritual Authority to Strengthen Church Government 311

Appendix 3—Exercising Spiritual Authority over Personal Finances 317

Notes 333

Index 351

Author's Forward and Dedication

For over 20 years, I have been privileged to teach live classes around the world on the vast and multi-faceted truth of spiritual authority. Now it is my honor to present it to you in a written format.

Exercising spiritual authority is built upon our foundation—the Lord Jesus Christ. He is the One who gave it to us; and, in a practical sense, it's all about who He has made us to be through His life, death, and resurrection. When we break down the Greek word for "exercise" (*exousia*) to its prefix and root, its literal and practical meaning is, "what comes out of you when you know who you are."

Exercising Spiritual Authority reveals who we really are—spirit beings living in physical bodies who possess souls. It provides lessons on how to live as bold Christ followers who have been given authority to occupy the domains appropriated to each of us by the Lord. It was not written for spiritual sissies but for those who are serious about taking ground for the Lord Jesus Christ and fighting against the spiritual kingdom of darkness.

To all who are under His authority I say: You are not the Man, but you can be the Man's man!

I dedicate this to the Man.

> *For there is one God and one Mediator between God and men, the Man Christ Jesus.* *1 Timothy 2:5*

Introduction

> *To open their eyes and to turn them from darkness to light, and from the power [exousia, authority] of Satan to God, that they may receive forgiveness of sins and an inheritance among those who are sanctified by faith in Me.* Acts 26:18

Acts 26:18 shows the commission that Jesus gave Paul on the road to Damascus; but I believe it is a commission given to all who love the Lord and that He has also supplied each of us with the ability to carry it out.

If you desire to walk in God's power so that you can be rescued and help rescue others out of Satan's kingdom and into God's, then you will love the truths in *Exercising Spiritual Authority* (ESA). Out of all the scriptural truths the Lord has allowed me to teach over the years, and even around the world, my favorite remains what you are about to read in this book. ESA provides a scriptural foundation to overcome the evil one and be victorious in this earthly life—and to help others do the same. It is from this vital starting point that many of my other books, studies, articles, and classes available at LMCI.org have sprung. Thus, it is long overdue to put this foundational teaching into a book so that it can be an accessible primer in the hands of those who choose to live with authority for their King.

Once we make the choice to follow Jesus, it soon becomes apparent that a spiritual battle is unfolding. Not only does Satan want to stop us from walking in the power and freedom of our new nature, but he also is determined to keep us from reaching others with the liberating truth of Jesus Christ that would set them free as well.

In this battle, we will feel weak at times in our corruptible flesh and limited understanding. The Bible says that we can only know in part right now (1 Corinthians 13:9 and 12), yet it also tells us that the Holy Spirit has given us everything we need for life and godliness.

> *Grace and peace be multiplied to you in the knowledge of God and of Jesus our Lord,* ***as His divine power has given to us all things that pertain to life and godliness****, through the knowledge of Him who called us by glory and virtue.*
>
> *2 Peter 1:2–3*

His divine power has given us *everything* we need for a Godly life, including a way to overcome our enemy so that we can do the things He has called us to do.

ESA contains biblical truths of who God has made us to be in Christ and how we can overcome our enemy regardless of human weakness. This book focuses mainly upon the realities of the spirit realm rather than the physical, because our battle is a spiritual one. Not only can we gain a proper perspective of who we are as spirit beings endowed with God's power, but we can also discern our enemy's true size. Isaiah 14:16a KJV says, "They that see thee [referring to Lucifer] shall narrowly look upon thee," meaning that once the devil's façade is stripped away, we will have to squint to see how small he really is.

Because of what Jesus did, all born-again believers have His super-spiritual power resident within them. He even promised that we would be able to do the same works He did (and greater) in John 14:12. Therefore, unless we have reached the point where we are walking in the same power as Jesus did in His earthly ministry, we should be seeking a greater understanding to get there. The Holy Spirit is faithful to open up our spiritual eyes and take us into deeper revelations of the authority Christ has given us for our lives and ministries *if we will ask Him to.*

As you read and study *Exercising Spiritual Authority*, I pray that the Lord will reveal what it means for you individually as well as corporately, according to your place within His body. May your eyes be opened, so that you can turn from the authority of Satan to God.

We were born into captivity under the thumb of a tyrant; and until we received Christ, we remained under the authority of that cruelest enemy. In our fallen condition, we were dominated by our bodies and captivated by sin. But once we entered that covenant relationship with Jesus Christ, our spiritual eyes were opened and we were given the ability to turn from darkness to light. *To the degree that we exercise the spiritual authority we have been given, we will dispel darkness and bring light to ourselves and those around us.*

PART ONE

SPIRITUAL AUTHORITY AND THE MAKEUP OF MAN

Chapter One

The Realm of Spiritual Authority

God[1] has foreknowledge. He knew perfectly well what was going to happen when He created Adam and Eve in His image (spirit) and gave them authority to tend and subdue the beautiful world He placed them in. He knew that the masterpieces He designed to bring His heavenly will to the earth were going to disobey and lose their spiritual connection with Him. But because of His foreknowledge, He had formed the plan of the ages—to send His Son, Jesus Christ, to redeem back for mankind what was lost through their fall. The heavens declared it, the Scriptures confirmed it; and now we witness the fruit of it: *He has given us the ability to walk in His kingdom power and exercise spiritual authority.*

Through Jesus' death and resurrection, those who believe on Him would be given the same authority that was originally given to Adam and Eve. They would be able to subdue the enemy's mayhem and regain ground for the Lord Almighty. The devil would fight against them and perpetually endeavor to rule the world with chaos, but he would only be legally allowed to have the ground they would surrender to him.

It's kind of like the childhood game we used to play called "King of the Mountain (or Hill)." The hardest part was getting to the top of the mountain, but once you got there it was not as difficult to maintain your authoritative position. The good news is that Jesus already did the hard part for us so that He could *start* us at the top of the mountain as "kingdom enforcers." He already gained the ground for us, and now it's up to us to keep that ground by standing within the grace of God that put us there.

Jesus told us in John 16:33b NLT that there would be trials and sorrow in this life, but He said to take heart because He had overcome this world. And now, because He overcame, we can overcome as well.

> *And he who overcomes, and keeps My works until the end, to him I will give power over the nations.* *Revelation 2:26*

The Greek word for "power" in Revelation 2:26 is *exousia*, which is more appropriately translated "authority."[2] One of the prerequisites for reigning with Him is to wisely steward the portion of authority that He gave us. The way we reflect His overcoming attitude in our lives is by exercising that authority and spiritually fighting for what He legally gained for us.

Our love for Him will be a strong motivating factor to beat back the enemy's attacks and hold that ground so that others can be set free as well. Another significant motivating factor will be the desire for reprisal against the enemy, similar to David's motives for taking down Goliath.

Any of us who have been through trying times knows what it feels like to be sick and tired. Once we reach the point of being sick and tired of being sick and tired, the Godly response will be to jump into the spiritual fight, determined to glorify the One who gave us the weapons and armor to overcome.

God is the source of all authority. The words "Almighty God" in the Bible are translated from the Hebrew words, *El Shaddai*, which mean "Lord God Almighty."[3] Truly, He is just that—He is the One who created the world; He is the One who created the universe and made everything we see and even the things we cannot see (Colossians 1:15–16). He is the One with all authority, thus He can apportion authority to whoever He chooses; and He has chosen to give it to His Son and, subsequently, to those who would believe on Him.

God has given each and every one of His children authority over the evil kingdom, and we should be biting at the bit to tap into His amazing power. However, if we do not know that we have this authority, we will not even consider jumping into the spiritual fight. We will continue to be pushed around and bullied by the enemy and barely eek out an existence that's full of frustration and defeat. As Christ followers, we need to learn all we can about exercising our spiritual authority so that we can live the way He intended us to.

Our Sphere of Authority

God has not put everything in the universe under only one believer's jurisdiction. He has given each of us a specific portion of His kingdom to steward—a certain sphere of authority delegated uniquely to each of us according to His will. However, what He has delegated specifically to us, He expects to be stewarded properly. In a sense, He is testing and grading each of us as stewards of what He apportioned to us.

What He puts under each of us should be claimed to its fullest degree, no matter if it's 30-, 60-, or 100-fold. Whether you were given five talents and made ten and someone else was given two and made four, when the two of you stand before the Lord, you will both be judged by the same standard. When that day comes, all of us should long to hear Him say, "Well done, good and faithful servant" (Matthew 25:21 and 23).

Kingdom Enforcers

As we walk in God's power, we demonstrate before the entire spiritual arena that we are His kingdom enforcers—that we are sons and daughters of the Most High. To the degree that we exercise the spiritual authority He gave us, we are the rulers of this planet.

Luke 4:6 shows another spirit being who has authority.

> *And the devil said to Him, "All this authority [exousia] I will give You, and their glory; for this has been delivered to me, and I give it to whomever I wish."* Luke 4:6

This verse clearly states that the devil also has authority that was given to him. The word "delivered" is the word *paradidomi* in the Greek text, which can be translated "surrender, yield up or give (up or over), and transmit."[4] When Adam disobeyed God in the original paradise, he consequently transferred his God-given authority to the serpent, the devil. However, Jesus won this authority back through His life, death, and resurrection; and when we receive Him as our Lord we can then also walk in that authority.

> *Then Jesus came and spoke to them, saying, "All authority [exousia] has been given to Me in heaven and on earth."*
> Matthew 28:18

> *But as many as received Him, to them He gave the right [exousia, authority] to become children of God, even to those who believe in His name.* John 1:12

God gave all authority to Jesus; and now Jesus, as the head of His body, gives it to whomever He chooses.

We have the awesome privilege to walk worthy before Almighty God because of what Jesus did for us on Calvary. One of the ways we can do this is by believing His Word that tells us we can do the same things He did—and even greater.

> *Most assuredly, I say to you, he who believes in Me, the works that I do he will do also; and greater works than these he will do, because I go to My Father.* *John 14:12*

Do you want to be a hero for God? Do you want Him to be able to boast on you, as an earthly father would, because of the things you do for Him and the way you live? Our desire to be His kingdom enforcers should be borne out of our love for Him and because we long to bring Him glory for what He did for us.

Is God in Control?

There is a reason authority has been entrusted to us. Some say that God could snap His fingers and accomplish all His will without us, and I would have to agree with them. The Lord God Almighty can do whatever He chooses, but He has chosen to bring us into partnership with Him in those areas He delegates to us.

One of the paradoxes positioned throughout the Scriptures is the question of what God is in control of. Some will adamantly declare that He is in control of everything in every situation, but I believe this blanket statement only serves to generate confusion.

We may think that He is unlimited in every way, until we begin to ask finite questions like, "If a man jumps off a building and dies—was God in control then?" At this point, we could easily run into a doctrinal quagmire. Someone could argue that God knows the end from the beginning (Isaiah 46:10); therefore, He actually took that man's life since He did not intervene in some way to prevent his death.

God is the master builder (Hebrews 3:4) and the master planner. He is the one who put everything in its order and set the laws of the universe into motion. He also put restrictions in specific places to allow events to evolve according to His master plan.

We can catch a glimpse of our part in that master plan from Ephesians 2:10 where it says that "we are His workmanship, created in Christ Jesus for good works, which God prepared **beforehand** that we should walk in them." When we exercise the authority He gave us, we will produce those good works that He foreordained us to do, all to the end of bringing to pass His ultimate purpose.

A Worthy Opponent

Another interesting reality concerning authority is found in the book of Judges.

> *Now these are the nations which the LORD left, that He might test Israel by them, that is, all who had not known any of the wars in Canaan (this was only so that the generations of the children of Israel might be taught to know war, at least those who had not formerly known it), namely, five lords of the Philistines, all the Canaanites, the Sidonians, and the Hivites who dwelt in Mount Lebanon, from Mount Baal Hermon to the entrance of Hamath.* ***And they were left, that He might test Israel by them, to know whether***

> ***they would obey the commandments of the LORD**, which He had commanded their fathers by the hand of Moses.*
> *Judges 3:1–4*

God gave us an opponent worthy enough to prove us. When we discuss the sovereignty of God, we must take into consideration that He is the One who created Lucifer who then fell and became the devil. He did not create Lucifer to commit sin, but He knew that he *would* sin and has used him to that end.

> *You [Lucifer] were perfect in your ways from the day you were created, till iniquity was found in you.* *Ezekiel 28:15*

There is a reason God put the devil on planet Earth. He wanted him to be punished for the sin of stupidity, so He created us as spirit beings with the potential to subdue Satan and his evil kingdom on the earth. As spirit beings, we have the ability to connect to both the physical and spiritual realms, to walk and talk with our God, and also to exercise the spiritual authority He gave us.

The devil will have a fitting end according to Revelation 20:10 where it says he will be tormented day and night forever in the lake of fire. God could destroy the devil at any time, but the reason He is waiting until Revelation 20:10 and allowing him to continue is because of His perfect plan. Part of that plan is to purify and prove us to see whether we will stand under pressure, or if we will complain when we are overwhelmed, or what we will do if our neighbor gets hurt. Will we walk in obedience to His ways and respond with His love or will we revert to our fleshly, selfish, old man nature? All of these situations "work together for good to those who love God, to those who are the called according to His purpose," as Romans 8:28 and 29 tells us.

And we know that all things work together for good to those who love God, to those who are the called according to His purpose. For whom He foreknew, He also predestined to be conformed to the image of His Son, that He might be the firstborn among many brethren.
Romans 8:28–29

Ultimately, God wants us conformed into the image of His Son; and in difficult situations we can choose to obey Him and be refined through the process. Our earthly trials provide opportunities for us to rise up and believe His words—to engage in the spiritual warfare that He talks about in Ephesians 6 where it says we are not wrestling against flesh and blood but against spiritual entities. Our love for Him and His people will give us the courage to engage in spiritual warfare—to charge a machine-gun nest, drop a hand grenade into the middle of the enemy's camp, blow up the enemy (all in the spirit realm, of course), and rescue those who are being held captive. It's much easier to grasp spiritual authority once we gain this imagery of warfare.

Our time on this planet is a test. We will be tested on love, compassion, forgiveness, and our stewardship over physical and spiritual things, among other things. Within the stewardship of spiritual things is the authority He has given us. Will we let the devil steal it? Will we whine, moan, and cry, or will we be like Jesus? By the sovereign will of God, He suffered the cross and despised the shame—yet He never opened His mouth; He never complained one time when He was under the most intense assault anyone could ever experience.

He [Jesus] was oppressed and He was afflicted, yet He opened not His mouth; He was led as a lamb to the slaughter, and as a sheep before its shearers is silent, so He opened not his mouth.
Isaiah 53:7

> *Looking unto Jesus, the author and finisher of our faith, who for the joy that was set before Him endured the cross, despising the shame, and has sat down at the right hand of the throne of God. For consider Him who endured such hostility from sinners against Himself, lest you become weary and discouraged in your souls. You have not yet resisted to bloodshed, striving against sin.*
>
> *Hebrews 12:2–4*

> *For to this you were called, because Christ also suffered for us, leaving us an example, that you should follow His steps: "Who committed no sin, nor was guile found in His mouth who, when He was reviled, did not revile in return; when He suffered, He did not threaten, but committed Himself to Him who judges righteously."*
>
> *1 Peter 2:21–23*

This is why God allows the devil to remain and use the authority he usurped from Adam—to prove us and refine us so that if we respond the way Jesus did, we will turn out looking like Him.

Spiritual Aggression

Whether it is war or a football game, no one ever wins by constantly playing defense. The only reason for defensive plays in a competitive sport is to gain the offense. A team does not continuously play defense to keep the opponent from scoring. They play defense just long enough to get the ball, and then they begin the offensive plays to score points for their team. *In the spiritual war we wage in life, the way to gain the offense is by exercising the spiritual authority Jesus gave us.*

Many Christians only play defense, meaning they wait for something to happen before they get motivated to do anything. They may begin praying at that point, but they should have been operating and moving in spiritual warfare before anything bad ever surfaced.

In fact, we should probably redefine what "bad" really is. Bad is when we are not aggressive in the spirit realm to prevent or thwart attacks of the enemy; it is when we are only playing defense. We, as Holy Spirit-filled believers, should be playing offense the majority of the time (if not *all* the time), because we can know the enemy's plans before he moves. One of the promises that Jesus gave concerning the Holy Spirit was that "He will tell [show] you things to come" (John 16:13b).

Limitations to Our Authority

There are certain things that are not within our authority. For instance, we cannot by our authority command Jesus to return to earth. The following verse shows another example of a factor we cannot control.

> *No one has power over the spirit to retain the spirit, and no one has power in the day of death.* *Ecclesiastes 8:8a*

There is a time that has been appointed for us to die (Hebrews 9:27); or, as the saying goes, "Our number is up." Someday our bodies will corrupt to the point where they can no longer sustain physical life, but we are still responsible to steward them to the best of our ability until that time. We may be able to slow down the aging process, but eventually our earthly tabernacles will fail us. We also have the authority to retain our spirits; but when that appointed time of death comes, we will no longer have that authority.

There are certain areas of authority that we alone have the right to exercise over ourselves; and we either take advantage of that right or we give it up. Even as God is sovereign, so has He given us sovereign control over our will. This means we have the responsibility to make moment-by-moment decisions either to submit to His ways or to our own—to His thoughts and purposes or to our own thoughts and purposes. While we are here on earth, the fruit of our decisions will be evidenced in our lives as either corrupt fruit or good fruit. Ultimately, we will be judged for the decisions we made in the stewardship of all aspects of our lives.

Man's Jurisdiction

> *What is man that You are mindful of him, And the son of man that You visit him? For You have made him a little lower than the angels, And You have crowned him with glory and honor. You have made him to have dominion over the works of Your hands; You have put all things under his feet.* *Psalm 8:4–6*

"Man," in Psalm 8:4, means mankind—both male and female. The Hebrew word for "angels" in verse 5 is the word *elohim* and should have been translated "God."[5] God did not make men and women lower than the angels. God made mankind *a little lower than Himself.* God made man like Himself to rule; God rules in heaven, and He placed man on earth to rule.

However, this does not mean that we are to rule over each other. A problem in many churches is the doctrine of the Nicolaitans which is mentioned in Revelation 2:6. The root word for "Nicolaitan" literally means "victorious over the people."[6] This can refer to ministers who pervert genuine authority and seek to dominate people. People who love to dominate others are prevalent in the world systems, causing problems that have led to death and destruction. Sadly, there are Christian leaders who do the same and have caused spiritual death and destruction in the church. God has *not* given us authority to "lord it over" people (Mark 10:42 and 43; 1 Corinthians 9:18; 2 Corinthians 10:8). It is witchcraft to dominate and control other people.

> *Then God said, "Let Us make man in Our image, according to Our likeness; let them have dominion over the fish of the sea, over the birds of the air, and over the cattle, over all the earth and over every creeping thing that creeps on the earth."*
>
> *Genesis 1:26*

God made mankind lower than Himself but higher than the angels. He gave man authority over fish, fowl, cattle, oxen, and demons—these are all a lower form of life. Even though that authority was taken away from mankind through Adam and Eve's sin, Jesus fulfilled it within His uncorrupted human body. He never allowed it to be taken from Him through sinning. Then through the sacrifice of His perfect blood, He cleansed us of all our sin (Hebrews 9:22–26; Revelation 1:5) and gave us back that authority so that we could represent Him here on earth.

> *Therefore we are ambassadors for Christ, as though God were pleading through us: we implore you on Christ's behalf, be reconciled to God. For He made Him who knew no sin to be sin for us, that we might become the righteousness of God in Him.*
>
> *2 Corinthians 5:20–21*

Our spiritual authority is in the spirit realm (Matthew 10:1). This is what Adam was designed to do—to be fruitful, to multiply, to replenish, and to *subdue* the earth (Genesis 1:28 KJV). The subduing of earth was not limited to the Garden of Eden—it was the whole earth. Adam was the authoritative figure that was to reign over this world, but he turned his authority over to the devil.

The Bible says that Eve was deceived (1 Timothy 2:14), but Adam heeded her words (Genesis 3:17) and they both lost the leadership of the Holy Spirit. They quickly forgot they were spirit beings and replaced the voice of God with the voice of reason,[7] and this is where mankind has remained throughout history.

God was not caught off guard when Adam sinned—He always knew what was going to happen. When He created Lucifer, He knew that someday He would use him on the earth as a worthy opponent to prove mankind. When He created us, He designed us to aggressively engage in spiritual warfare to advance His kingdom for His glory, not to play defense. Through the life, death, and resurrection of Jesus Christ, He regained the original dominion Adam lost and now recreates our spirits so that we can rule over that same domain. In order to do that, we need to know who we really are in Him. We also need to know how to walk with the spiritual authority He gave us, as well as the parameters of our jurisdiction.

The Scriptures are true; God's Word is alive and powerful, and it changes lives when it is believed. As we learn more about our true spiritual identity and capability in the coming pages and then walk in that God-given spiritual authority, the impact will be so deep that it will affect us throughout eternity.

> *Even when we were dead in trespasses, [God] made us alive together with Christ (by grace you have been saved), and raised us up together, and made us sit together in the heavenly places in Christ Jesus.*
>
> *Ephesians 2:5–6*

The next step is to answer the question, "Who am I?"

Related Materials at LMCI.org

- Be a Proactive Warrior—Swing First (CD or MP3)
- New Creation Realities (CD- or MP3-set)
- Spiritual Boot Camp (CD- or MP3-set)
- True Confessions of Spiritual Warriors (Booklet)

Relevant Points

1. What scriptures tell us that Jesus has given us authority on earth?

2. In what areas of your life do you believe you need to start exercising your spiritual authority?

3. Explain the proper interpretation of the word "angels" in Psalm 8:5.

Chapter Two

Who Am I?

Why is it important to know who (or what) we are? To answer that question, let's look again at the theme verse for Exercising Spiritual Authority.

> *To open their eyes and to turn them from darkness to light, and from the* ***power [exousia, authority]*** *of Satan to God, that they may receive forgiveness of sins and an inheritance among those who are sanctified by faith in Me.* *Acts 26:18*

The Greek word *exousia* used in this verse for the word "power" is also found in Luke 9:1 NLT when Jesus gave power and "authority" (*exousia*) to His disciples so they could cast out demons and heal all diseases. If we are going to walk in His power as well, then it will help us to understand this word.

The prefix of *exousia* is *ek*, meaning "out of," and the root word is *esti*, which means "I am."[1] It could be literally translated, "out of [who] I am;" but a more practical translation would be, "that which comes out of me when I know who I am." This shows the significance of knowing who we are so that we can operate from our true identity.

- Authority is *exousia* (Greek)
    - *ek* out of
    - *esti* I am
    - Strong's usage #1849
    - Luke 9:1
- Authority is what comes out of you when you know who you are

Science has its own definition of who or what we are as humans; however, God is the One who made us, so it's significant that we find out what He says about who we are. In Proverbs 25:2 it says, "It is the glory of God to conceal a matter, but the glory of kings is to search out a matter."

As we search out the matter of mankind's makeup through the Scriptures, we will focus on the first usage of the word "man" in Genesis 1:26, as well as other aspects of that verse.

> *Then God said, "Let Us make* ***man*** *in Our image, according to Our likeness; let them have dominion over the fish of the sea, over the birds of the air, and over the cattle, over all the earth and over every creeping thing that creeps on the earth.*
>
> *Genesis 1:26*

The Hebrew word for "man" is *'adam*, which means "ruddy," or literally, "red."[2] Some believe this is referring to blood, while others believe it is referring to the red color of the earth ("dust of the ground") that God made him from according to Genesis 2:7. So, the first man was named for the container he was placed in rather than the image he was made in.

Made in His Image

The fact that God was speaking in a plural form in Genesis 1:26 ("let us") indicates that at least one other being was present and involved in putting man together "in Our image." If we can discover who He was talking to, it will clarify the image that man was made in.

The only two logical possibilities are the members of the Godhead or angels. Job 38:7 tells of the "sons of God" who witnessed the earth's beginnings.

> *Where were you when I laid the foundations of the earth? Tell Me, if you have understanding. Who determined its measurements? Surely you know! Or who stretched the line upon it? To what were its foundations fastened? Or who laid its cornerstone, when the morning stars sang together, and all the* ***sons of God*** *shouted for joy?*
>
> *Job 38:4–7*

The phrase "sons of God" refers to angels, according to other places where this phrase is used in Old Testament Scriptures. This verse in Job shows us that they were present when God put the foundations of the earth together, possibly even aiding in the process.

However, the more probable explanation for "us" in Genesis 1:26 is the first choice—the other members of the Godhead—the Son of God and the Holy Spirit. Along with God the Father, this triune entity makes up the supreme hierarchy (chain of command) of the spirit realm,[3] and there are various places in the Bible where all three are noted in the context (e.g., 1 Corinthians 12:4–6 that speaks of the Spirit giving the gifts, the Lord Jesus administering them, and God the Father energizing them).

Regardless of who God was talking to in Genesis 1:26, the main point is that they were spirit beings. John 4:24 tells us that God is spirit, and it is obvious that whoever He was talking with was also spirit. Therefore, the image that mankind was made in was spirit. *The essence of our makeup is spirit—we were created as spirit beings, first and foremost.*

You Are a Created Spirit

- First usage of "man" (mankind)
- Genesis 1:26—made in the likeness and image of God (the Godhead)
- You are a ***spirit*** being with a free will.

Made in His Likeness

Those who were present at the brainstorming conference in Genesis 1:26 were spirit beings living in a spirit realm, whether they were angels or Jesus or the Holy Spirit or all of the above. However, God went on to include His likeness within that image when He said, "Let Us make man in Our image, **according to Our likeness**." The *image* of God is spirit (John 4:24), and His *likeness* is included within it. I believe this is referring to His *will* since the will determines what someone will be *like*. The will, from which we make our choices, is wrapped up within the spirit part of our makeup. As we choose to be in relationship with Him, we will reflect His likeness.

The word for "will" predominately means a resolute determination, and our ability to make decisions is contained within our spirit and not our soul. This differs somewhat from the respected perspective of a past patriarch of the faith, Watchman Nee, who wrote that the will is in the soul. The Greek word for "will" (*boulemai*) means "desire,"[4] and I believe it resides within our spirit rather than our soul.

The following verse shows this word in reference to God's will, or desire, or determination.

> *But one and the same Spirit works all these things, distributing to each one individually as He wills.* 1 Corinthians 12:11

He made us in His likeness to have desire or determination just as He does. By our will we decide to either follow or turn away from Him, so not only does it determine our likeness but also our final judgment. Jesus is going to judge what we did with the ability He gave us to make decisions in our lives—to either obey or disobey Him.

> *For we must all appear before the judgment seat of Christ, that each one may receive the things done in the body, according to what he has done, whether good or bad.* 2 Corinthians 5:10

All spirit beings have a will. It was by God's will that He made man in His image and likeness. Hebrews 2:16 KJV notes that Jesus "took on the seed of Abraham," indicating a decision of His will. It also tells us in Hebrews that God wills by the Holy Spirit to distribute the gifts (Hebrews 2:4). Some of the angels sinned through the freedom of their will, and "kept not their first estate" (Jude 1:6 KJV). All spirit beings have a will. The following verses show that Lucifer possessed his own will apart from God's.

> *For you have said in your heart: "**I will** ascend into heaven, **I will** exalt my throne above the stars of God; **I will** also sit on the mount*

> *of the congregation on the farthest sides of the north;* ***I will*** *ascend above the heights of the clouds,* ***I will*** *be like the Most High."*
>
> *Isaiah 14:13–14*

Lucifer's will determined his likeness, just as our will determines ours. The next verses from Matthew show us that even demons possess a will of their own.

> *Now a good way off from them there was a herd of many swine feeding. So the demons begged Him, saying, "If You cast us out, permit us to go away into the herd of swine."*
>
> *Matthew 8:30–31*

The will originates from and resides within the spirit. We are spirit beings (the *image* of God) with a will (the *likeness* of God). The spirit is essentially what we are, and intrinsic within our spirit is the will to choose whether or not to live out of it instead of our soul and/or body. To the degree that we decide to live out of our regenerated spirit, we will have the likeness of Christ. However, if we decide to live mainly out of our soul instead, then we will have the likeness of an emotional man or woman who is up or down depending upon the circumstances; or if we decide to live out of our body, we will have the likeness of a carnal human concerned only with fulfilling his or her fleshly desires—much like an animal.

We are Not Animals

If we do not grasp that we are spirit beings, we will have difficulty exercising spiritual authority. The alternative is to view ourselves as smart animals, and this kind of thinking will eliminate any relational contact with our Creator and any blessings (including walking in His authority) that He has given us.

The first casualty in any war is truth; in fact, the way many wars start is by somebody believing a lie. Thinking that we are merely animals contradicts the truth of how God made us. Jesus warned us that the devil is the father of lies (John 8:44 NIV); and this was evident in the Garden when the serpent twisted God's words to lure Eve (quickly followed by Adam) into his lie. Thus began man's war with God, and it continues to this day in the lives of those who reject His truth.

> *Now the serpent was more cunning than any beast of the field which the LORD God had made. And he said to the woman, "Has God indeed said, 'You shall not eat of every tree of the garden?'"*
> *Genesis 3:1*

Satan's lies have continued throughout history and will do so all the way to his demise as seen in Revelation 20:10 where he is referred to as "the devil, who deceived them," leaving his epitaph as a liar.

> *And the devil, who deceived them, was cast into the lake of fire and brimstone where the beast and the false prophet are. And they will be tormented day and night forever and ever.*
> *Revelation 20:10*

One of the things Satan has lied about is our spirit nature. He has gone to great lengths throughout history, using science, philosophy, and literature to cloak the truth that we are spirit beings. He has also invested a lot of time and effort to promote and engrain the theory of evolution within the minds and hearts of our children so they will believe that man is just another rung on the animal ladder.

If we do not realize who we really are as spirit beings, we will continually wrestle with our souls and bodies. We will remain oblivious to the spiritual side of life and perpetually surrender to our emotions and fleshly urges. This victim mentality is not how

God designed us—He designed us as spiritual creatures who could rule over our bodies and souls and help to establish His kingdom on earth. He never intended us to be passive beings that would be molded by circumstances. *He designed us to be His sons and daughters who would bring His will to the earth.*

Spirit, Soul, and Body—Our Three-Part Makeup

Some Christians believe that man is only made up of body and soul, yet the Scriptures clearly teach that mankind is a tri-part being: spirit, soul, and body.

> *Now may the God of peace Himself sanctify you completely; and may your whole* ***spirit, soul, and body*** *be preserved blameless at the coming of our Lord Jesus Christ.*
>
> *1 Thessalonians 5:23*

NOTE: I used to think that the word "spirit" in 1 Thessalonians 5:23 referred to the Spirit of God. However, if that were true, then there would be no need for it to be "preserved blameless unto the coming of the Lord Jesus Christ." The context of this usage of "spirit" indicates that it can be blamed; therefore, it must be the spirit of man.

If we compare the makeup of man to a three-story house, the bottom floor would be the body, the second floor would be the soul, and the top floor (hopefully, the main floor) would be the spirit. All three parts are vital; but our spirits are who we really are and they are tapped into a higher plane, so to speak. Most Christians in the US are either ignorant of this truth or have received wrong teaching on it. One of the first times I presented this truth was in India in front of 1,500 very religious ministers. To my surprise, they already understood that man is essentially a spirit being, because Hinduism teaches this.

Satan is not threatened when non-Christians or those who practice witchcraft recognize that they are spirit beings—it only accelerates their worship of him (either indirectly or directly). However, he will do all he can to keep Christians from this knowledge, because he knows they could then start aggressively attacking his evil spirit realm.

Living in the earthly realm, we are constantly inundated with physical concerns and influences that make it challenging to hold on to the concept that we are primarily spirit beings. It's easy for our physical needs and desires to take priority over the spiritual. God's dominant focus for man is the spirit, and it is up to us to align our thinking to His order in 1 Thessalonians 5:23: spirit, soul, and body. As significant as our bodies are, they are merely the dwelling places where the *real* us—our spirit man—lives.

> *For the things which are seen are temporary, but the things which are not seen are eternal. For we know that if our earthly house, this tent, is destroyed, we have a building from God, a house not made with hands, eternal in the heavens. For in this we groan, earnestly desiring to be clothed with our habitation which is from heaven, if indeed, having been clothed, we shall not be found naked. For we who are in this tent groan, being burdened, not because we want to be unclothed, but further clothed, that mortality may be swallowed up by life. Now He who has prepared us for this very thing is God, who also has given us the Spirit as a guarantee.*
>
> *2 Corinthians 4:18b–5:5*

It's amazing to see how God designed man in three parts so that we could co-habit both the physical and spirit realms. Our physical bodies allow us interaction within the physical realm, and our souls enable us to learn and reason; but our spirits are in contact with the spirit realm—even when we are unaware of it. Everyone is exposed to spiritual impulses and spiritual information; but once the spirit is regenerated with the Holy Spirit, we are given direct access to hearing from Him. The Holy Spirit then becomes our "voice of the conscience," giving us heavenly wisdom and counsel.

The concept of "spirit, soul, and body" that we saw in 1 Thessalonians 5:23 also appears in Deuteronomy 6, although in different terminology.

> *You shall love the LORD your God with all your* ***heart****, with all your* ***soul****, and with all your* ***might****.*
>
> *Deuteronomy 6:5*

Here in Deuteronomy the word "heart" is equivalent to spirit; the word "soul" is the soul; and the word "might" represents the body. This verse lines up the spirit with the heart, from which we make our decisions and choices. Simply stated, y*our spirit is the heart of who you are.* It is who you are—it is you and your will. Basically, the heart is considered the innermost part of anything, e.g., "the heart of an artichoke" or "the heart of a matter." If we could peel the outer man from a person down to his core invisible component, to the ultimate center of what/who he is, we would discover the spirit or heart of that man—*the real person.*

Mankind as a whole, although individually composed of three parts (spirit, soul, and body), is essentially a race of spirit beings.

There is a consciousness in all three parts of man. There is a consciousness in your body; there is a consciousness in your soul; and there is a consciousness in your spirit. It's important to make these distinctions because the goal in *Exercising Spiritual Authority* is to grow in our spirit to the end of making it the dominant part of our three-part being. Since our spirit is our will, we can learn to exercise authority over ourselves—over our souls and bodies.

Our regenerated spirits should rule over our bodies and souls—even more so than those whose spirits have not been regenerated with the Holy Spirit through the new birth.[5] The key is submission or obedience; to the end that we submit to/obey Christ's reign in our lives, our regenerated spirit will have dominion over our bodies and souls.

Spirit, Soul, and Body

• Mankind is a spirit.
    • Genesis 1:26
• He lives in a body.
    • 1 Corinthians 9:27
• He (should) possess his soul.
    • Luke 21:19

Some Differences between the Spirit and the Soul

> *For the word of God is living and powerful, and sharper than any two-edged sword, piercing even to the division of soul and spirit, and of joints and marrow, and is a discerner of the thoughts and intents of the heart.* *Hebrews 4:12*

Hebrews 4:12 makes a clear distinction between the soul and the spirit, as does the following verse.

> *And the LORD God formed man of the dust of the ground, and breathed into his nostrils the breath of life [spirit]; and man became a living soul.* Genesis 2:7 KJV

The life that God breathed into Adam was spirit, and when it entered his body, which was formed from the dust of the ground, he became a living soul. The next verse (Luke 21:19) drives this point home even further.

> *In your patience possess your souls.* Luke 21:19

To possess something indicates you are greater than the thing you possess. If you can possess your soul, then you cannot *be* your soul. So we are not our bodies or our souls—*we are spirit beings who live in physical bodies and possess souls.*

> *For if I pray in a tongue, my spirit prays, but my understanding is unfruitful. What is the result then? I will pray with the spirit, and I will also pray with the understanding. I will sing with the spirit, and I will also sing with the understanding.*
> 1 Corinthians 14:14–15

This verse tells me that if I pray in a tongue, my *spirit* prays, again clarifying the difference between our spirit and our mind (understanding).[6] The next verse shows us that the spirit is what leaves the body at death.

> *No one has power over the spirit to retain the spirit, and no one has power in the day of death.* Ecclesiastes 8:8a

We do not have authority over our spirits in the day of death because that is God's jurisdiction. Psalm 31:15 says, "My times are in Your hand; deliver me from the hand of my enemies, and from those who persecute me."

This says, in essence, the same thing as Proverbs 20:27, "The spirit of a man is the lamp of the LORD, searching all the inner depths of his heart." The reason you know what is in you is because you are a spirit being, and it's the spirit that searches the heart. This is your consciousness in the spirit realm, which holds a greater reality and higher life form than your body or your soul.

> *But there is a* ***spirit in man****, and the* ***breath*** *of the Almighty gives him understanding.* *Job 32:8*

The "spirit" in this verse is man's spirit, whereas the "breath of the Almighty" is the Holy Spirit. When our spirits are regenerated through the new birth, revelation can then be transmitted from the breath of the Almighty—the Holy Spirit—to our regenerated spirits.

The Judgment Seat of Christ

There's a phrase from an old song that says, "You got to walk that lonesome valley." When it comes to the judgment seat of Christ, those lyrics ring loud and true. We will go alone, with no one holding our hand, before the Lord at the judgment seat of Christ. *You alone* will be held accountable for the things that you, by your will, have done in this life.

> *For we must all appear before the judgment seat of Christ; that every one may receive the things done in his body, according to that he hath done, whether it be good or bad.* *2 Corinthians 5:10 KJV*

If we do not divide our souls from our spirits, then we will have a hard time not being dominated by our souls. We are to possess our souls and *make* them obey our spirits, because our souls, which contain our minds with their imaginations and emotions, will not want to obey. Therefore, we must begin to confess that our souls have not been given the authority to control us. For example, if I'm praying and worshiping and my mind becomes distracted, I (as a spirit being) can command my mind, "Okay, if you don't behave yourself we are going to keep doing this for thirty more minutes."

The mind is not our enemy; but we have to discipline it and *make* it behave. Our emotions will run us around and wear us out if we do not rein them in to the truth. This is why we must discipline our minds to track after the Word of God. We cannot trust our feelings; we cannot trust our imaginations; and we cannot trust our intellect. If our minds are not lined up with the truth, they will be limited to receiving their information from our flesh; *and they will deceive us.*

There are concepts and beliefs that we've held onto for years and, in a sense, built altars to. Let's humble ourselves and admit when we are wrong about a belief. There have been a number of times that the Lord has taken great pleasure in plowing up my "hallowed" doctrines. We only have one Lord and His name is Jesus Christ; so if we turn our doctrines into our lords, then we are committing idolatry. **Jesus is more interested in our humility and love for others than He is in preserving our sanctified doctrines of exclusion.**

When we realize who we really are as spirit beings, we will begin to see how possible it is to walk in the spirit realm—to hear the voice of the Holy Spirit and obey Him. We are more than our body and soul. If we do not understand this and do not divide our spirit from our soul, we will have a hard time overcoming our human limitations and walking in the supernatural realm.

Related Materials at LMCI.org

- Christological Astronomy (Workbook, E-workbook, DVD-, CD-, or MP3-set)
- Mending Cracks in the Soul (Book, Audiobook, CD- or MP3-set)
- Spirit, Soul, and Body: Saving the Whole Man (CD- or MP3-set)

Relevant Points

1. What are you, essentially?

2. What part of your three-part being do you usually identify with?

3. Write a paragraph on how your perspective would change if you identified yourself more as a spirit being.

Chapter Three

The Spirit Nature of Man

We just saw that Man was originally designed to be a spirit being. Because of Adam and Eve's transgression, however, mankind was tainted with sin and that original design was perverted. Man's nature from that point on was twisted into children of wrath who would fulfill the lusts of the flesh and mind as Ephesians 2:2 and 3 states.

> *In which you once walked according to the course of this world, according to the prince of the power of the air, the spirit who now works in the sons of disobedience, among whom also we all once conducted ourselves in the lusts of our flesh, fulfilling the desires of the flesh and of the mind, and were by nature children of wrath, just as the others.* *Ephesians 2:2–3*

"Nature" comes from the Greek word *phusis.* The root word is *phuo*, which means "to beget," or "to be born."[1] Therefore, the birth, or beginning, state of something would be its true nature. Once it has been tampered with, it is no longer in its natural state. For instance, when a wilderness location has not been changed by man, we call it a natural setting. Hence, when we speak of the nature of man, we are considering his *original pure* state, before any outside forces altered it. Since man was originally created in the image of God, which is spirit, then the essence and true nature of man is spirit.

When Adam and Eve transgressed against God, their untainted spirit was contaminated. They lost their original, or natural, state and were literally changed into degenerated spirits. According to the *American Heritage Dictionary*, "degenerate" means "having declined, as in function or nature, from a former or original state." Their degenerated spirit was then genetically passed down to their children.

> *And Adam lived one hundred and thirty years, and begot a son in **his** own likeness, after **his** image, and named him Seth.*
> *Genesis 5:3*

Had Adam and Eve made the decision to obey the Lord, their children would have been born with the Lord's image and likeness, because that would have still been intact within them. Instead, their children were born in their corrupt image and likeness, and that altered state has been passed down to every subsequent generation. This means that even before a baby is born, seemingly unaffected by the world, his or her spirit is already degenerated—contaminated by the fallen state of mankind.

The decision Adam and Eve made to disobey the Lord's commandment and to eat of the tree of knowledge of good and evil was made by the freedom of their will. The will of man is in his spirit, and this was the devil's primary target when he tempted them.

One of the consequences of Adam and Eve's corrupted spirit was that they lost their connection with the Lord. Genesis 3:8 tells us that "they **heard** the sound of the LORD God walking in the garden in the cool of the day." At this point, they had to *hear* or *see* a physical manifestation to know that God's presence was close by them. Those who have received the new birth and have had their spirits regenerated back to their natural condition, have an inner awareness of His presence. This refers to the constant abiding assurance of His presence rather than feeling or sensing His presence, which happens when His anointing is upon us.

> *He Himself has said, "I will never leave you nor forsake you."*
> *Hebrews 13:5b*

Ephesians 2:1 shows the condition of our spirits when we were unsaved as "dead in trespasses and sin." When we accepted Christ, our dead spirit was regenerated.

> *Not by works of righteousness which we have done, but according to His mercy He saved us, through the washing of regeneration and renewing of the Holy Spirit.* *Titus 3:5*

We were made alive to God through Christ Jesus.

> *Likewise you also, reckon yourselves to be dead indeed to sin, but alive to God in Christ Jesus our Lord.*
> *Romans 6:11*

When His spirit was born in us, He regenerated our human spirits. He made us alive in Him and connected us to Him in the same way Adam and Eve were before they sinned. He rewired us so that we can receive spiritual information from Him anytime He chooses, and we can sharpen our spiritual senses to receive and utilize it.

We do not receive revelation from God in our soul but in our spirit, because it's our spirit that comes alive to God. For years I struggled with recognizing revelation, but then the Holy Spirit opened my eyes to this verse and showed me that revelation does not come to my soul or to my body—*it comes to my spirit.*

Before Jesus' sacrifice and the availability of the new birth, physical manifestations from God were necessary for anyone to know that He had spoken to them. That's why we see so many physical evidences in the Old Testament—the burning bush of Exodus 3:2, the pillar of cloud by day and pillar of fire by night of Exodus 13:21, the fire of God consuming the altar of 1 Kings 18:38, and the many appearances of the "angel of the Lord," to name a few. Something tangible was required in the earthly realm to demonstrate His presence, because Adam and Eve had lost that connection with Him through their fall.

Another lost aspect was man's ability to subdue the earth. Adam's original mandate was to "be fruitful and multiply; fill the earth and subdue it" (Genesis 1:28). It's interesting to see how this original mandate was revised by the time Noah stepped off the ark.

> *And as for you, be fruitful and multiply; bring forth abundantly in the earth and multiply in it.* *Genesis 9:7*

The mandate to subdue the earth was missing because the necessary power of the Holy Spirit to do this was no longer within man's spirit. Without the Holy Spirit's power, the best they could do was "be fruitful and multiply." As wonderful as the Abrahamic covenant of Genesis 17 and the blessings of Deuteronomy 28:1–14 were, in order for mankind to regain the Adamic covenant of dominion, the abiding presence of the Holy Spirit had to return.[2] This would only happen when God sent the perfect sacrifice to purify the spirit of man and return it to its natural state.

What Part of Man is Born Again?

When Nicodemus came to Jesus by night to inquire of Him, Jesus said the following.

> *Jesus answered and said to him, "Most assuredly, I say to you, unless one is born again, he cannot see the kingdom of God." Nicodemus said to Him, "How can a man be born when he is old? Can he enter a second time into his mother's womb and be born?" Jesus answered, "Most assuredly, I say to you, unless one is born of water and the Spirit, he cannot enter the kingdom of God. That which is born of the flesh is flesh, and* ***that which is born of the Spirit is spirit.*** *Do not marvel that I said to you, 'You must be born again.'"*
>
> *John 3:3–7*

Within the context of explaining the new birth, Jesus taught that what is born of the Spirit is spirit. The part of man that is regenerated, or born again, is the spirit. Christianity has assumed and taught over the years that it is the soul that is saved, but Jesus clearly stated, "that which is born of the Spirit is spirit." Our souls are comprised of our minds, which must be renewed according to the Word of God; whereas, our regenerated spirits are perfect because Christ is in us (Colossians 1:27).

The soul can be changed depending upon what it is exposed to. For nearly a century, doctors of psychology have practiced what they called behavior modification. This is nothing more than educating the mind (soul) to think differently; however, it does not change the essence (spirit) of the person. The only thing that can change the essence of a person is the new birth, which comes exclusively by confessing Jesus as Lord and believing that God raised Him from the dead.

> *That if you confess with your mouth the Lord Jesus and believe in your heart that God has raised Him from the dead, you will be saved. For with the heart one believes to righteousness, and with the mouth confession is made to salvation.* *Romans 10:9–10*

There are numerous testimonies of hardened criminals who have been transformed into loving, caring individuals when they received salvation through Jesus. Many of us could share similar personal accounts as a result of turning our lives over to Jesus and making Him our Lord and Savior.

Throughout my travels, I have met people of various religious beliefs. Some of the Hindus, Muslims, and even secular people I have encountered, seem to be genuinely good people. Only through the discerning eyes of the Spirit of God was I able to see the uncertainty behind their peaceful demeanors. There will always be an instability underlying the human spirit because it is dominated by its sin nature, regardless of how peaceful the soul is. Our human spirits must be created in righteousness and true holiness in order to be truly stable.

> *And that you put on the new man which was created according to God, in righteousness and true holiness.*
>
> *Ephesians 4:24*

> *But when the kindness and the love of God our Savior toward man appeared, not by works of righteousness which we have done, but according to His mercy* ***He saved us, through the washing of regeneration*** *and renewing of the Holy Spirit.*
>
> *Titus 3:4–5*

The Greek word for "regeneration" is *paliggenesia*, which means "a rebirth" or "spiritual renovation." Our *de*generated spirits were *re*generated, or born again, through God's plan of the ages—the blood shed by the holy Lamb of God. *Paliggenesia* comes from the words *palin*, meaning "anew, once more, or again"[3] and *genesis*, "to begin (beginning)" or "start." The Lord *saved* us according to His mercy, by the washing of regeneration, and renewing of the Holy Spirit. This is why we equate "saved" with "born again."

Literally, *we get to start all over or begin again.* This is what the new creation is all about. We should not be living in old habit patterns of defeat; we should be living as the new creations the Lord has regenerated us to be.

We are born again, not of corruptible seed, but of incorruptible seed (1 Peter 1:23). Our spirits were regenerated because of our obedience to God's Word to confess Jesus as Lord and believe that God raised Him from the dead. At that moment, our spirits were renewed by the Holy Spirit and we were born again. The two conditions we complied with were (1) confessing with our mouths the Lord Jesus, and (2) believing in our hearts that God raised Him from the dead.

After your spirit is regenerated, you are holy and godly in the innermost core of your being. This has nothing to do with your mind. In the innermost part of a believer, a true "good guy" has been born. His name is Jesus, and He now lives in us. We have been reborn into the image of God, just as Adam and Eve were made in His image. Our new holy nature is to think, act, and be like our Creator and Heavenly Father (Ephesians 5:1).

The deeper our comprehension of this, the more it will grieve us to hear remarks like, "I am a sanctified sinner." This is a contradiction. If we are sanctified, then we are literally set apart from the world for God. Our true nature is no longer that of a sinner; we are now set-apart Holy Spirit beings who truly desire to walk for God. This does not mean that we do not sin, but it does not define who we are. We have a new nature recreated, or born again, within us. It is the nature of Christ. This is our true identity.

Made Alive

And you He made alive, who were dead in trespasses and sins.
Ephesians 2:1

God warned Adam and Eve in Genesis 2:17, "in the day that you eat of it [the tree of the knowledge of good and evil] you shall surely die." The alteration of their spirits actually resulted in death. God's spirit did not die, but it did depart from them, leaving degenerated spirits behind. Of course, as theologians have espoused through the centuries, it is true that the "seeds" of death were planted in all of us from that day; but there was also an immediate death that took place within Adam and Eve's spiritual life as well. In their degenerated spiritual state, the potential for life was still there, but there was only one way for it to be made alive again—it had to be regenerated, or reborn.

In John 1:4 we read, "In Him was life; and the life was the light of men." This is very revealing when we remember that God created man in His image. Whatever properties are contained within God are also in us; they make up the essence of man from the time God spoke him into being.

> *The spirit of a man is the lamp of the LORD, searching all the inner depths of his heart.* *Proverbs 20:27*

The spirit is what examines your mind; the spirit is what probes your soul; the spirit is what reveals things to you even about your body. The spirit of man is the lamp of the Lord.

> *For what man knows the things of a man except the **spirit of the man** which is in him? Even so no one knows the things of God except the Spirit of God.* *1 Corinthians 2:11*

The good news is that Jesus' sacrifice on the cross made it possible for a resurrection of that lifeless spirit through the new birth. God literally changes us from a degenerate to a regenerated holy spirit being!

> *In which you once walked according to the course of this world, according to the prince of the power of the air, the spirit who now works in the* ***sons of disobedience****, among whom also we all once conducted ourselves in the lusts of our flesh, fulfilling the desires of the flesh [body] and of the mind [soul], and were* ***by nature [phusis] children of wrath****, just as the others.*
>
> *Ephesians 2:2–3*

We were by our very nature the children of wrath, even as those who have yet to confess Christ as their savior are. The context is clear that "children of wrath" are also "sons of disobedience." The Greek word for "wrath" is *orge*, which has as one of its definitions, "unbridled indulgence of passions."[4] In other words, "anything goes" or as the slogan from the 1960s went: "if it feels good, do it." The first commandment of the satanic bible is: "Do what thou wilt," so it's pretty clear where this line of thinking originated. Because of our contaminated nature, we were children of wrath or children of unbridled passions. If we did something and liked it (and did not get caught), we would most likely do it again.

This is what we *were* when we were dead in trespasses and sins, in our degenerated spiritual state while we were out of covenant with God. We were still without the abiding presence of the Holy Spirit and dead in trespasses and sins.

> *But God, who is rich in mercy, because of His great love with which He loved us, Even when we were dead in trespasses, made us alive together with Christ (by grace you have been saved).*
>
> *Ephesians 2:4–5*

Because of God's great love, when we received Jesus as our Lord, He made us alive together with Christ. We have a *new* nature through His grace. He saved us and regenerated our spirits back into the pure state that Adam and Eve originally had.

It is your spirit that is saved by the grace of God through the Lord Jesus Christ (Ephesians 2:8); therefore, the dominant desire of your regenerated spirit is to stand righteous before the Creator. *The sole desire of your new nature is to obey God.*

In essence, you are a holy spirit created by *the* Holy Spirit. You have more right to say, "I am a holy spirit," than to confess that you are a sinner. Yes, we will sin, because we are still in our fleshly body with its fleshly desires, but we are not sinners.

> *If we say that we have no sin, we deceive ourselves, and the truth is not in us.* *1 John 1:8*

We are partakers of God's divine nature. What an amazing reality for us to grasp.

> *By which have been given to us exceedingly great and precious promises, that through these* ***you may be partakers of the divine nature****, having escaped the corruption that is in the world through lust.* *2 Peter 1:4*

> *Therefore, if anyone is in Christ, he is a new creation;* ***old things have passed away****; behold, all things have become new.*
> *2 Corinthians 5:17*

The old nature was actually crucified according to Romans 6:6.

> *Knowing this, that our old man was crucified with Him, that the body of sin might be done away with, that we should no longer be slaves of sin.* Romans 6:6

Our new nature yields the spiritual fruit of righteous restraint or self-control (Galatians 5:22–23). We are now children of obedience with a new nature that desires to submit to God.

The Conscience

Our conscience is an integral part of our human spirit nature, which, although pure in its essence, can become corrupted when overridden by an undisciplined soul.

> *For when Gentiles [unbelievers], who do not have the law, by nature do the things contained in the law, these, although not having the law, are a law to themselves, who show the work of the law written in their hearts, their conscience also bearing witness, and between themselves their thoughts accusing or else excusing them.*
> Romans 2:14–15

Even before a person's spirit is changed in the new birth, he has the thumbprint of God on his spirit. Although he is dead in sin and trespasses, there remains an inner conscience engrained within his contaminated spirit that can distinguish between what's right and wrong. When a believer or unbeliever chooses to ignore that conscience, it can become seared or hardened.

> *Now the Spirit expressly says that in latter times some will depart from the faith, giving heed to deceiving spirits and doctrines of demons, speaking lies in hypocrisy, having their own conscience seared with a hot iron.* 1 Timothy 4:1–2

As Christians, the Holy Spirit is our Helper and Teacher and leads us into the "all truth," helping us to guard against hardening our hearts or consciences; and Jesus is our High Priest, ever living to make intercession for us according to Hebrews 7:25–26. The Holy Spirit is constantly working within us to conform us into the image of Christ (Romans 8:29). He has created us in righteousness and true holiness, which heightens our spiritual sensitivity.

> *And that you put on the new man which was created according to God, in righteousness and true holiness.*
>
> *Ephesians 4:24*

However, it is still available for believers to listen to the deceiving spirits and doctrines of demons above the voice of the Spirit, and this is what can cause even Christians to harden their consciences.

At the judgment seat of Christ, as well as at the great white throne judgment of Revelation 20:11–12, we will be judged according to our works whether good or bad. In other words, how did we respond to that heightened sensitivity? How well did we obey the voice of the Lord?

> *For we must all appear before the judgment seat of Christ, that each one may receive the things done in the body, according to what he has done, whether good or bad.* *2 Corinthians 5:10*

The Gift of Eternal Life

If we compare the spirit of man to a car battery before the new birth, we would say it was dead. But the potential of that battery or spirit is that it can be recharged or regenerated. When we confessed with our mouths Jesus as Lord and believed in our hearts that God raised Him from the dead, God recharged our spirits with His eternal spirit that does not die.

Within that recharged "battery" lies the gift of the Holy Spirit, which gives us eternal life.

> *Then Peter said to them, "Repent, and let every one of you be baptized in the name of Jesus Christ for the remission of sins; and you shall receive the gift of [from] the Holy Spirit."*
> *Acts 2:38*

> *For the wages of sin is death, but* ***the gift of God is eternal life*** *in Christ Jesus our Lord.* *Romans 6:23*

We have the gift of eternal life! It doesn't get any better than that. When we met the conditions laid out by God in Romans 10:9 and 10, we were born again of incorruptible seed—*it can never die.* Not only did the Lord implant an incorruptible, eternal seed of life within us, but at the same time He also "electrocuted" our old man nature. The old man died and the new man was made alive. In the truest sense, we have one nature (and one nature only), and it longs to be like God. When anything contrary to our new nature enters our thoughts, it's like sandpaper running across the grain of our new spirit. That is because we have been recreated in our spirit according to true holiness. We are alive to God and dead to sin.

> *Likewise you also, reckon yourselves to be dead indeed to sin, but alive to God in Christ Jesus our Lord.*
> *Romans 6:11*

> *Therefore we were buried with Him through baptism into death, that just as Christ was raised from the dead by the glory of the Father, even so we also should walk in newness of life.*
> *Romans 6:4*

Unlike Adam and Eve, we have been given the ability (the power) to live by the regenerated spirit that dwells within us rather than by our physical senses.

> *But you are not in the flesh but in the Spirit, if indeed the Spirit of God dwells in you. Now if anyone does not have the Spirit of Christ, he is not His. And if Christ is in you, the body is dead because of sin, but the Spirit is life because of righteousness.* ***Therefore, brethren, we are debtors—not to the flesh, to live according to the flesh.*** *Romans 8:9–10, 12*

This regeneration of your spirit is life and light.

> *For you were once darkness, but now you are light in the Lord. Walk as children of light.* *Ephesians 5:8*

> *You are all sons of light and sons of the day. We are not of the night nor of darkness.* *1 Thessalonians 5:5*

We are now able to spiritually feel, hear, see, smell, taste, and touch—to understand spiritual things. We are spirit beings who are alive to the spirit realm, and our spiritual perception is highly activated. That is why we can walk into a room and immediately tell when something is spiritually off. We can sense unrighteousness as well as righteousness. We can perceive confusion as well as peace. This spiritual perception is vital for exercising our spiritual authority.

> *And immediately,* ***when Jesus perceived in His spirit*** *that they reasoned thus within themselves, He said to them, "Why do you reason about these things in your hearts?"* *Mark 2:8*

Spiritual sensitivity can be developed to guard your conscience against corruption. You choose the programming of your conscience—*what you feed it determines its sensitivity to the Holy Spirit.*

In order to look and act like Jesus, we need to behold His face every day—we must stay connected to Him.

> *But we all, with unveiled face, beholding as in a mirror the glory of the Lord, are being transformed into the same image from glory to glory, just as by the Spirit of the Lord.*
> *2 Corinthians 3:18*

Fasting

Fasting is a spiritual principle, rather than a physical or even a mental one. As you, by your will (spirit), tell your body and your mind (soul) "NO" repeatedly, it releases the control of your body and mind to you and teaches your spirit man to dominate over these other two parts of your being. Fasting is generally done by a believer to become more spiritually minded.

> *Moreover, **when** you fast, do not be like the hypocrites, with a sad countenance. For they disfigure their faces that they may appear to men to be fasting. Assuredly, I say to you, they have their reward. But you, **when** you fast, anoint your head and wash your face, so that you do not appear to men to be fasting, but to your Father who is in the secret place; and your Father who sees in secret will reward you openly.* *Matthew 6:16–18*

Jesus did not say *if* you fast; He said *when* you fast. In the context of Matthew 6, we see that Jesus includes it in the "big three" of praying, giving, and fasting; yet, fasting is often the one of these three spiritual actions that is left out of our lives. *Do not leave it out.*

Fasting has revolutionized my life. It has given me victory over alcohol, coffee, and sugar, as well as strengthening my self-control—not only over my body but also over my soul.

The spiritual benefits of fasting are huge (in addition to the health benefits). For one, it shuts demons right up—or makes them want to speak up, thus exposing them. Jesus indicates we can actually exercise authority over a demon through fasting. When the disciples came to Him because they could not cast the demon out of a boy, He explained that "this kind does not go out except by prayer and fasting" (Matthew 17:21).

Fasting is one of the greatest tools I have found in exercising authority over demons, as well as over my body and soul by strengthening my spirit man (the Holy Spirit within me) to reign over them both. By strengthening the spirit man through fasting, we build up our true nature, which enables us to more easily exercise our spiritual authority.

Related Materials at LMCI.org

- The Anointing In and On (Booklet)
- Developing Your Spiritual Sensitivity (CD- or MP3-set)
- The Law of Conscience (CD or MP3)
- New Creation Realities (CD- or MP3-set)
- The Old Man Is Dead (Free article in e-store)
- Re-GENE-erated (CD or MP3)
- Spiritual Boot Camp (CD- or MP3-set)

Relevant Points

1. What happened to your spirit when you made Jesus Lord of your life?

2. How does this differ from the spirit of man you had before receiving Christ?

3. Write down a behavior that could change if you subjected your soul and body to the spirit of Christ in that specific area of your life; then also write down some pertinent scripture references that can strengthen you to do this.

Chapter Four

Exercising Spiritual Authority over the Soul

The soul is the second floor of our three-story house. It is composed of our intellect, imaginations, and emotions. Simply put, the soul is the mind. It is not the soul of man that is saved at the time of the new birth—it is the spirit of man that receives salvation. Salvation of the soul is a process that requires time and obedience.

> *And do not be conformed to this world, but be transformed by the renewing of your mind [within the soul], that you may prove what is that good and acceptable and perfect will of God.*
>
> *Romans 12:2*

Some people ask the Holy Spirit to renew their minds. The Holy Spirit can give us new ideas and/or reveal truths, but we are ultimately responsible to change our thinking to conform to the Scriptures. Our minds (souls) belong to us and we are responsible to submit them to God on a daily basis *by feeding upon His Word.* You are not subservient to your soul; it is your servant and needs to obey you.

> *Casting down imaginations, and every high thing that exalteth itself against the knowledge of God, and bringing into captivity every thought to the obedience of Christ.*
>
> *2 Corinthians 10:5 KJV*

It is available to control our imaginations and thoughts because we are spirit beings. It is also our responsibility to do so, regardless of our present or past circumstances.

The mind (soul) is the source for our emotions. (There is an interesting book called, *Emotions: Sometimes I Have Them/Sometimes They Have Me*[1] that teaches about this.) As wonderful as emotions can be, we absolutely do not want them to "have" us. As spirit beings, we can control our emotions; and if we find that we cannot control them—if we are consumed by worry, anxiety, or fear, for instance—the cause could be either an evil spirit or an iniquity. Regardless, through the regeneration of our spirits by the Holy Spirit, we can exercise spiritual authority over any onslaught from the evil spirit kingdom upon our emotions.

Probably the most difficult and intricate person you will ever have to understand is you! And now that you know you are a spirit being, you can start learning how to exercise spiritual authority over your own soul and body.

One of the first places we need to exercise our spiritual authority is over our own lives. If we are not submitting our own souls and bodies to the Holy Spirit, then how can we expect to walk in authority in other areas? And how can we help others do the same if we are not already setting the example?

> *He restores my soul; He leads me in the paths of righteousness For His name's sake.* *Psalm 23:3*

God restores our souls as we discipline ourselves to implant His Word into our minds. He leads us, but we still are the ones who choose to either obey or disobey.

It is not the soul (or the body) that is changed by the new birth. This is why we still wrestle with our thoughts as Paul talked about in Romans 7. Our souls still need to be saved, and it is an ongoing process.

> *Therefore lay aside all filthiness and overflow of wickedness, and* ***receive with meekness the implanted word, which is able to save your souls.*** *James 1:21*

The implanted word received with meekness is what saves our souls. A cursory reading of the Scriptures is not sufficient to dig up the old soil of our souls and allow those seeds of truth to be sowed into them; it requires an intentional discipline of reading and meditating upon the Scriptures daily. When we receive those words of spirit and life with meekness, then our souls become progressively whole and holy. As we hunger for truth and ask the Holy Spirit to teach us, He will reveal and engraft those truth seeds deep within our souls.

> *Now the just shall live by faith; but if anyone draws back, my soul has no pleasure in him. But we are not of those who draw back to perdition, but of those who believe to [unto]* ***the saving of the soul.***
>
> *Hebrews 10:38–39*

Jesus saves the spirit; but the soul is saved as we surrender it to the Holy Spirit's revelation—whether it is direct or through the written Word of God.

This is basic to understanding exercising spiritual authority: as spirit beings, we can be the masters of our souls. With the amount of wrong doctrine taught in the church concerning the separation of spirit and soul, it is evident that the enemy of our souls does not want us to believe or apply this powerful truth.

When we are trying to help someone who is throwing a pity party and they make statements like, "You don't understand how hard my life has been" or "You don't understand why I can't control my mind," we need to remember this truth: *we are spirit beings who have the ability to make our minds obey.* Even natural man has this ability; however, with the new birth we have a Helper—the Holy Spirit—who makes it much easier. When we couple His help with exercising the spiritual authority Christ has given us, the combination is unbeatable. We have the potential to be more than conquerors in every situation.

Our regenerated spirit is designed to be the master over our souls and our bodies; however, we are required to surrender them to His leadership. The body can be a wonderful servant but a lousy master; yet when it is under the direction of the soul that is subservient to the regenerated spirit in us, it will glorify God. The soul was not designed to be the master either, and this is why it must be subservient to our regenerated spirits—especially since it is the soul that will be judged at the judgment seat of Christ! There is a heavenly record being kept of the works of our souls, while the spirit is already saved by the grace of God (Ephesians 2:8).

> *For we must all stand before Christ to be judged. We will each receive whatever we deserve for the good or evil we have done in this earthly body.* *2 Corinthians 5:10 NLT*

The Battlefield of the Mind

Since our souls are what will be judged at the judgment seat of Christ, we need to focus on reining them in to the obedience of the Spirit of Christ within us. Our souls are subjected to the world around us and Satan is the god of this world; so it should come as no surprise that our minds (souls) will fight against the will of our spirits. It has been estimated that approximately 75% of people in mental institutions in the US are Christians. Even though they experienced the new birth and their spirits have been regenerated, they either were not taught about their new nature or they decided to rebel against it. Their new nature is one of "righteousness and true holiness," but they continued to live in sin.

The Holy Spirit within us is faithful to convict us when we rebel, and this is why those who continue in their rebellion suffer from an internal relentless battle. Their rebellion could be demonic, but it could also result from not being taught how to overcome the pull that the world has upon their flesh. Regardless of the reason, rebellious "believers" are those who still feed upon the worldly things they used to feed upon before God regenerated them through the new birth.

We are new creations in Christ Jesus. The regenerated spirit inside us yearns for the holy bread of life. If we will eat that bread of life (the Word of God) and live by the spirit, then we will not be confused and disoriented in this life. We will produce the fruit that comes from subjecting our bodies and souls to the spirit of God inside us.

> *For God has not given us a spirit of fear, but of power and of love and of a sound mind.* *2 Timothy 1:7*

> *But the fruit of the Spirit is love, joy, peace, longsuffering, kindness, goodness, faithfulness, gentleness, self-control. Against such there is no law. And those who are Christ's have crucified the flesh with its passions and desires. If we live in the Spirit, let us also walk in the Spirit.* *Galatians 5:22–25*

Even though we know that our old man was crucified with Christ (Romans 6:6), we still need to exercise our spiritual authority in order to crucify our flesh with its "passions and desires." We are to cast down our imaginations and every high thing that exalts itself against the knowledge of God and bring into captivity every thought to the obedience of Christ, according to 2 Corinthians 10:5 KJV. This is something *we* must do, and it will line us up with God's nature of holiness, which is our new and true nature. This is where we will experience the most joy and peace.

> *Likewise you also, reckon yourselves to be dead indeed to sin, but alive to God in Christ Jesus our Lord.*
>
> *Romans 6:11*

True freedom is found by exercising our spiritual authority over our bodies and souls. God's nature within us matures as we make the conscious effort to be led by the Spirit instead of by our flesh (Galatians 5:16–17, 25).

God has equipped us for this battle by regenerating us into His own image, giving us the Holy Spirit as our Helper, constantly making intercession for us, and giving us His words of life to nourish us. But it is our decision to rise to the challenge of disciplining ourselves to partake of these great and precious promises (2 Peter 1:4). The things that He has prepared for those who decide to cross that line of commitment are far greater and more wonderful than anything we could ever imagine. Ephesians 1:17 and 18 says that He opens our eyes so we can understand such spiritual matters.

> *But as it is written: "Eye has not seen, nor ear heard, nor have entered into the heart of man the things which God has prepared for those who love Him." But God has revealed them to us through His Spirit. For the Spirit searches all things, yes, the deep things of God. For what man knows the things of a man except the spirit of*

the man which is in him? Even so no one knows the things of God except the Spirit of God. Now we have received, not the spirit of the world, but the Spirit who is from God, that we might know the things that have been freely given to us by God. These things we also speak, not in words which man's wisdom teaches but which the Holy Spirit teaches, comparing spiritual things with spiritual. But the natural [psuchikos—soulish] man does not receive the things of the Spirit of God, for they are foolishness to him; nor can he know them, because they [the things of the Spirit of God] are spiritually discerned.
1 Corinthians 2:9–14

Exercising Spiritual Authority over Our Souls

God designed our spirit to be the dominant part of our tri-part beings, and our regenerated spirits give us an increased ability to possess, or dominate, our bodies and souls. There is no reason for us as Christians to lose control emotionally when He has given us the ability to submit our souls to His truth.

The regenerated spirit we have received is "Christ in us" (Colossians 1:27). Just as Christ is the exact image of the Father, so is our spirit man the exact image of Christ. A myriad of Godly characteristics have been infused into our regenerated spirits from Him, e.g., goodness, gentleness, self-control, etc. (any of the fruit of the Spirit listed in Galatians 5:22). I have chosen one of these Godly characteristics to show an example of how our spirits should rule over our bodies and souls instead of the other way around. The one I have chosen is **patience.**

In your patience possess your souls. Luke 21:19

As a divine characteristic, patience (or long-suffering) was regenerated in our spirits when we received Jesus as our Lord.

*Im*patience is the enemy of peace, and when we lose our patience we also lose our peace. As Christians, when we walk in the spirit, we are full of peace; and that peace helps us to maintain a true spiritual awareness.

> *For to be carnally minded is death; but to be spiritually minded is life and peace.* *Romans 8:6*

God is the God of patience (Romans 15:5), so impatience is against His character, which is now our character. Hebrews 6:12 says that we inherit the promises through faith and patience; and Hebrews 10:36 KJV teaches us that patience is a significant factor to receiving from the Lord.

> *For ye have need of patience, that, after ye have done the will of God, ye might receive the promise.* *Hebrews 10:36 KJV*

James 1:4 says that when we allow patience to have its perfect work, we will be perfect and complete, lacking nothing.

> *But let patience have its perfect work, that you may be perfect and complete, lacking nothing.* *James 1:4*

Impatience is motivated by selfishness and the desire to have our own way rather than to obey our regenerated spirit, namely, the Holy Spirit within us. It is a willful determination to go against peace; and, as such, it puts us out of sync or spiritually out of tune in our walk with Him. When we start saying things like, "I cannot wait any longer," or "I have no more patience," it's an indication that impatience has impaired our spiritual vision.

Societies and cultures that recognize they are spirit beings tend to be more patient than us; but much of western culture does not recognize that man is a spirit being who can control his body and mind—even with an un-regenerated spirit. In our fast-paced society, we often allow our minds and/or bodies to rule over our spirits instead of the other way around, and this results in the tendency to hurry or rush.

As I mentioned earlier, all of the fruit of the Spirit are within us once we are born again. If we think of the opposites of all of them and throw in the works of the flesh from Galatians 5:19–21, we will have a pretty good idea of what happens when we exercise no control over our souls and/or bodies.

God designed our spirit to be the dominant part of our tri-part beings and even more so when it is regenerated through the new birth. Even though it has been perfected by the indwelling Holy Spirit, we still need to surrender our souls and bodies to its leadership. Our minds (souls) belong to us and we are responsible to submit them to God on a daily basis *by receiving His Word with meekness and obeying it.*

Related Materials at LMCI.org

- The Gospel of the Kingdom (DVD-, CD-, or MP3-set)
- Overcoming Depression (CD or MP3)
- Patience: Bearing Up (CD or MP3)
- Second Peter 1:1–15 Character after Salvation (CD or MP3)
- Temperance: the Fruit of the Spirit (CD or MP3)
- To Rejoice Is a Choice (CD or MP3)
- Why Should We Forgive? (CD or MP3)

Relevant Points

1. What part does the soul play in our three-part makeup?

2. What are some practical steps you can take to subject your soul to your spirit?

3. Pick one of these practical ways to subject your soul to your spirit (from question #2) and discipline yourself to do it.

Chapter Five

Exercising Spiritual Authority over the Body

The order of the words "spirit, soul, and body" in 1 Thessalonians 5:23 helps us to understand the most important part of the three parts of man—the spirit. The spirit is the will, the soul is the mind, *and the body is simply the flesh.*

The body is remarkably made as Psalm 139:14 notes, "I will praise You, for **I am fearfully and wonderfully made**; marvelous are Your works, and that my soul knows very well." As wonderful as the body is, it is the least important part of our three-part makeup. It is composed of the elements that are found in the earth, as Genesis 2:7 clearly states, "The Lord God formed man of the dust of the ground." Ecclesiastes 12:7 notes, "Then the dust will return to the earth as it was, and the spirit will return to God who gave it." The body houses the spirit and soul of man and is our vehicle for perceiving the physical realm through seeing, hearing, smelling, touching, and tasting—none of which changed at the time we were born again.

What is the Flesh?

> *Knowing this, that our old man was crucified with Him, that the body of sin might be done away with, that we should no longer be slaves of sin. For he who has died has been freed from sin.*
>
> *Romans 6:6–7*

Our flesh is *not* our sinful nature, as some teach (e.g., the New International Version of the Bible indicates this in its translation of Romans 8:1–9). The old man died at the moment of our new birth, setting us free from its sinful nature. God actually implanted His holy nature permanently within us, providing a constant inner awareness of what's right and what's wrong. But we can easily miss the Holy Spirit's guidance if we allow our flesh (our bodily desires) to dominate us. When we feed more on earthly things than heavenly things, we end up producing the works of the flesh, as follows.

> *Now the works of the flesh are evident, which are:* ***adultery, fornication, uncleanness, licentiousness, idolatry, sorcery, hatred, contentions, jealousies, outbursts of wrath, selfish ambitions, dissensions, heresies, envy, murders, drunkenness, revelries, and the like;*** *of which I tell you beforehand, just as I also told you in time past, that those who practice such things will not inherit the kingdom of God.*
>
> *Galatians 5:19–21*

If we walk in the patterns of our old (now dead) sinful nature, it's as if we are trying to resurrect our old man that was crucified with Christ.

> *For you died, and your life is hidden with Christ in God. When Christ who is our life appears, then you also will appear with Him in glory.* *Colossians 3:3–4*

The practical way to prevent this is to become alive to the spirit realm; for the more alive we are to the spirit realm, the less excited we will be with sin. It will, in fact, become distasteful; and we will have no desire to dig up that old putrid dead man and "party" with him.

Sin is most definitely *not* our friend. If we allow ourselves to get caught up in it again, we will not only have to repent, but we will also have to deal with the memories that leave their impressions upon our souls. Honestly, it is too much work to let ourselves get entangled in the web of sin.

> *Stand fast therefore in the liberty by which Christ has made us free, and do not be entangled again with a yoke of bondage.*
> Galatians 5:1

If we focus upon the life and light of God's Word, we will find it much easier to walk by the Spirit. This will protect us from fulfilling the lusts of the flesh.

> *I say then: Walk in the Spirit, and you shall not fulfill the lust of the flesh.* Galatians 5:16

As we behold Him and become spirit minded through feeding upon His spiritual words of life, we will glow with His presence. We will also be sharper to perceive things in our spirits the same way Jesus did.

Exercising Spiritual Authority over Our Bodies

Exercising spiritual authority over our flesh can be a real challenge for many of us; but God knows our bodies are weak and He has compassion on us.

> *As a father has compassion on his children, so the LORD has compassion on those who fear him; for he knows how we are formed, he remembers that we are dust.* Psalm 103:13–14 NIV

Our bodies' natural instincts like self-preservation and pro-creation make it necessary to maintain control over them, just as we must control our souls. Overeating and laziness are common areas to deal with; and even if we don't struggle with those, there are other physical weaknesses that may hinder us. Recent statistics reveal that 85% of Americans are overweight and 35% are obese,[1] yet these problems are controllable by exercising spiritual authority over our bodies.

Proverbs 23:2 states, "And put a knife to your throat if you are a man given to appetite." Gluttony will kill you. It's amazing to me that there are those who teach that drinking a glass of wine will send you to hell, yet they have no problem with gorging themselves on pie and ice cream. *Please get control of your mouth—not only in what you say, but also what you put into it.*

> *Do you not know that those who run in a race all run, but one receives the prize? Run in such a way that you may obtain it. And everyone who competes for the prize is temperate in all things. Now they do it to obtain a perishable crown, but we for an imperishable crown. Therefore I run thus: not with uncertainty. Thus I fight: not as one who beats the air. But I discipline my body and bring it into subjection, lest, when I have preached to others, I myself should become disqualified.*
>
> *1 Corinthians 9:24–27*

Verse 25 tells us that even unbelievers who compete for a prize realize that they are to be "temperate in all things," which literally means to "exercise self-restraint." They exercise self-restraint so they can win a crown that's going to perish. We should do it for a far greater prize—a crown that will *never* perish. If we don't discipline our bodies ("keep under my body" in the KJV) by subduing our physical desires, we are more likely to die before our time, which means we will not be able to finish our course.

In 1 Corinthians 9:27, "disqualified" literally means "unapproved" or "rejected." This is significant when it comes to obtaining an incorruptible crown, as well as an entrance to the millennial kingdom. The gospel of the kingdom is a gospel of commitment. I'm excited about living for 1,000 years in a devil-free world!

We all will find ourselves before the judgment seat of Christ someday, and our judge will not be fooled by the fleshly successes we garnered while on the earth. He will not care what we looked like, or how much money we acquired in this life, or how high up we climbed the corporate ladder. He will be concerned with whether or not we were diligent to steward what He designated to us, as in the parable of the good and faithful servant.

> *His lord said to him, "Well done, good and faithful servant; you were faithful over a few things, I will make you ruler over many things. Enter into the joy of your lord."* *Matthew 25:21*

Luke 16:10 says, "He who is faithful in what is least is faithful also in much." *We must be accountable for our bodies.* The least in your three-story house of spirit, soul, and body is your body; yet it is also the vehicle that carries you around during your time here on earth. We must be faithful in maintaining healthy habits with our bodies; otherwise, we will make it easy for the devil to take us out of the race—in spite of all our efforts to walk in the spirit and save our souls.

It's very difficult to accomplish anything in the spirit if we don't first exercise spiritual authority over our souls and bodies. We can exercise spiritual authority to conquer worry, fear, anger, and lust, for instance. We can overcome our habits of overeating and laziness. God will even give us the energy we need regardless of a lack of sleep if we stay in the spirit realm of our third floor. We have a race to run, and we cannot afford to let our bodies dictate where that race ends. It is imperative that we finish it where God wants us to, and that we finish it well.

If we will do our best to become and stay healthy through exercise and diet, we will reap the benefits of a longer and happier earthly life. This will increase our chances of finishing the race and glorifying Him in the process.

The body is the least of man's three-part being, yet it is the physical vehicle that allows us to run the race that is set before us. When we exercise spiritual authority over our flesh, His spirit empowers us to bring it into subjection to Him. If we do not surrender our minds and bodies to the Holy Spirit, we take the risk of allowing a back door to open in the spirit realm.

It's time to rise to our believing privileges and exercise spiritual authority over our minds and bodies as living, holy sacrifices to Him.

> *I beseech you therefore, brethren, by the mercies of God, that you present your bodies a living sacrifice, holy, acceptable to God, which is your reasonable service. And do not be conformed to this world, but be transformed by the renewing of your mind, that you may prove what is that good and acceptable and perfect will of God.*
>
> *Romans 12:1–2*

Related Materials at LMCI.org

- The Cancer Answer (Booklet or E-book)
- Fit for the Kingdom (DVD-set)
- Healthy Living (CD or MP3)
- I Ain't Takin' Acid Anymore (Booklet, CD, or MP3)
- The 1,000 Year Reign of Jesus Christ on the Earth (Book)
- Overcoming Addictions (CD or MP3)
- The Satanic Deception of Knife & Fork (Booklet)

Relevant Points

1. What part does the body play in our three-part makeup?

2. What are some practical ways you can subject your body to the spirit of Christ in you?

3. Write a goal that will help you to focus upon God's Word to a greater degree than you do now. Make sure it is one that you know you can keep long-term. To develop it as a lifestyle, discipline yourself to do it for one month and then record your results below.

PART TWO

DILIGENT DISCIPLESHIP

Chapter Six

The Authority of a Disciple

Exercising spiritual authority is for disciples—those believers who are hungry enough for the things of God that they are willing to discipline themselves to follow Jesus. Any born-again believer has the authority within them but they may lack the maturity to use it. You can be a believer without being a disciple, but you cannot be a disciple without being a believer.

> *And when He had called His twelve* ***disciples*** *to Him, He gave them power [exousia—authority] over unclean spirits, to cast them out, and to heal all kinds of sickness and all kinds of disease.*
>
> *Matthew 10:1*

Those who have confessed Jesus as Lord in their lives and *believed* that God raised Him from the dead (Romans 10:9 and 10) are believers in Christ. However, if they stay at that level and never really move forward to maturity and commitment, they could still be considered believers but not mature followers or disciples. Becoming a disciple requires an intimate relationship with the Lord, and this is the fountainhead of our authority. Intimacy is vital to our spiritual walk and ability to hear His voice and follow Him, and it is within this proximity that the Lord can reveal truths that will help us exercise His authority.

For instance, in an intimate moment with the Lord, He revealed to me that His Hebrew name (Yeshua) was also His warrior name and when I used it, demons would tremble in fear. Since receiving and obeying this revelation, I have witnessed demons flee, principalities bow down and melt, and spiritual darkness flee—all as a result of calling upon the name of Yeshua! And ultimately, as a result of seeking intimacy with Him.

> *And you will seek Me and find Me, when you search for Me with all your heart.* *Jeremiah 29:13*

As we grow nearer to the Lord, our desire to follow Him will also deepen. In this sense, there are varying levels of commitment even within discipleship. To cross over the threshold between an immature believer and a disciple by seeking intimacy with the Lord is only the first step. The Holy Spirit will help to pattern us into disciples—those who discipline themselves to follow the Master to become good and faithful servants.

What Does Authority Mean?

The Scriptures show that there is a marked difference between the authority of a disciple and that of a believer. There is also a difference between the power we have and the authority to walk in it. *The Holy Spirit is our source of power, but Jesus is the source of our authority.*

> *Then Jesus came and spoke to them, saying, "All authority has been given to Me in heaven and on earth."*
>
> *Matthew 28:18*

The Greek word for "authority" in this verse is *exousia.* The King James Version translated this word as "power," but it is more accurately translated "authority" (as the NKJV has it). In the following verse, the word "power" is the Greek word *dunamis.*

> *But you shall receive power [dunamis] when the Holy Spirit has come upon you; and you shall be witnesses to Me in Jerusalem, and in all Judea and Samaria, and to the end of the earth.*
> *Acts 1:8*

The difference between these two words is that power (*dunamis*) is the *ability* to do,[1] whereas authority (*exousia*) is the *right* to do. Authority is the granted jurisdiction, or the permission, to do something. It would be very frustrating to be given a task if we were not also given the authority to do it. God is not a micromanager—when He commands us to do something, He also gives us the ability and authority to do it.

Jesus allocated certain authority to His disciples. I believe all Christians have the authority to cast out demons, but the only ones who will actually do it are the ones who take their responsibility seriously enough to discipline themselves to follow Him. The following passage shows this difference between believers and disciples.

> *And great multitudes followed Him—from Galilee, and from Decapolis, Jerusalem, Judea, and beyond the Jordan. And seeing the multitudes, He went up on a mountain, and when He was seated His disciples came to Him.* *Matthew 4:25 and 5:1*

Great multitudes followed Jesus after they saw Him deliver and heal the sick in their region; but when He went up on the mountain, it mentions only His disciples being with Him. They were the ones who were not content to wait below even though it was easier. This is where the "cut" is made for the team, so to speak. We have to determine whether or not we are willing to climb up the mountain—to discipline ourselves—to follow our Master. *A disciple is a follower—one who will take the hard path when necessary to follow the Master.*

If we want to exercise spiritual authority, we must be willing to pay the price of becoming a disciple.

Spiritual Maturity

In Matthew 10:1, we see that the authority to cast out evil spirits was given to disciples. In contrast, John 1:12 shows us the authority that is given to believers (children of God).

> *But as many as received Him,* ***to them He gave the right [exousia—authority] to become children of God,*** *even to those who believe in His name.* *John 1:12*

There is also a distinction in the Bible between "children" and "sons and daughters" of God. When the word "child" or "children" is used, the reference is to one who is less mature. When "son" or "daughter" is used, the reference is to a disciplined or mature believer—a disciple. Anyone who has received Jesus as Lord and Savior is a child; but not every child grows up to become a son or daughter, spiritually speaking. The contrast between a child and a son or daughter of God is not determined by their age, but by their spiritual maturity. Jesus proved this early in life when His parents found Him in the temple already pursuing the things of His Father at the age of 12.

> *And He said to them, "Why is it that you sought Me? Did you not know that I must be about My Father's business?"*
> *Luke 2:49*

At that young age, Jesus spoke one of His greatest revelations, showing that He was no longer a child but a son *and* a 12-year-old disciple. He already knew His purpose and was intentionally focused on fulfilling what He was sent to do. Regardless of earthly or spiritual age, when we get serious about doing our God-given purpose (the Father's business), Jesus will increase our authority to match the difficulty of the task.

We see this in the prayer of Jabez.

> *Now Jabez was more honorable than his brothers, and his mother called his name Jabez, saying, "Because I bore him in pain." And Jabez called on the God of Israel saying, "Oh, that You would bless me indeed, and* ***enlarge my territory,*** *that Your hand would be with me, and that You would keep me from evil, that I may not cause pain!" So God granted him what he requested.*
>
> *1 Chronicles 4:9–10*

Even though he was birthed in much pain, as we see reflected in his name (which means "sorrow" or "pain"), Jabez was more honorable than his brothers because he hungered to fulfill God's purpose for his life. He knew that his name did not reflect that purpose and so he cried out to the Lord, "Oh that You would bless me indeed." Not only did he ask the Lord to bless him, but he also prayed that He would enlarge his territory. He was literally crying out to God to increase his authority. He used the phrase, "that Your hand would be with me," which is indicative not only of a blessing, but also of authority. He was beseeching the Lord for more grace and a bigger job. It would be like an athlete asking the coach to let him off the bench so he can play in the game.

Crossing the Threshold

When our specific purpose is defined, we are then able to cross the threshold of commitment. Practically speaking, this is our "jurisdiction" or area of authority. Once we determine to pursue that purpose, God will correspondingly give us the necessary authority and grace (empowerment) to carry it out.

There is freedom in knowing what our God-given purpose is and then walking in it. God has commissioned me to help people liberate their ministries, and He has given me the corresponding authority to carry it out. Once we know what He has called us to do, we can seek Him for the authority to fulfill it.

NOTE: If you do not already know what your God-given purpose is, I encourage you to download my free e-book, *Realizing & Fulfilling Your Personal Ministry* at http://lmci.org/RFYPMebook.pdf.

Logically, we cannot discipline ourselves to carry out our specific calling if we do not know what it is. It is also possible that we may discipline ourselves to work hard at something He did *not* designate to us. None of us desires to stand before the judgment seat of Christ and hear Him say, "Well, I see that you did a good job; but you did not do what I asked you to do."

Seek the Lord to know your unique calling, and move out of the murkiness of ignorance. Ignorance can be simply defined as living anywhere outside of your calling from God. For instance, what if you were trying to live out your life as an evangelist when the Lord had actually called you to be a prophet?

The devil has worked hard to keep you from knowing what your purpose is, just as he has worked hard at perverting the concept of authority. But He who is in us is greater than he who is in the world (1 John 4:4). The Lord is faithful to reveal Himself and His ways to us as we truly seek Him (Jeremiah 29:13).

The Scriptures reveal what true godly authority is, and the Holy Spirit is faithful to do His job as our Helper. When we know who we are according to what God says about us, and we have matured through our intimacy with Him, and we know our individual calling and purpose as the Holy Spirit reveals it to us, then we can move out in the authority that belongs to a disciple.

As you discipline yourself to search for Him and to study the Scriptures, you will mature into a son or daughter who is ready to walk in that authority. Not only will you have reached the level of maturity that is necessary, but somewhere in the process, the Holy Spirit will have revealed to you your specific purpose. The authority that a disciple has is given to him because he is focused; he knows where he's going—he knows because the Lord has revealed His specific will to him for his life.

The Spiritual Battle

The reason you need a higher level of authority (which is what you receive when you make the decision to cross that threshold of commitment to be a disciple) is because you are about to become a threat to the evil kingdom. I believe there is some truth to the saying, "a higher level, a higher devil." For this reason, it behooves every true disciple of Christ to have some knowledge of the spiritual battle he or she will inevitably face. We need to understand the enemy's devices as 2 Corinthians 2:11 encourages us to.

The three basic categories of wicked spirits in Satan's kingdom are as follows.

- **Principalities** (from the Greek word *arche,* meaning "first in order or rank") are higher-ranking evil spirits that dwell in the heavenlies. They cannot be cast out but can be bound.
- **Powers** (from the Greek word *exousia*, meaning "exercised strength" or "authority") are lower-ranking heavenly beings

that work to enforce the mandates of their superiors. These also cannot be cast out but can be bound.

- **Demons** are terrestrial spirits who walk the face of the earth and can live in people as well as whisper in their ear to commit offences against God. These can be cast out.

As we become serious about fulfilling our part in the body of Christ, the devil will assign his subordinates to hinder us. When we were aimlessly wandering as children of God with no real focus, the devil was not threatened. Once we become focused and disciplined to carry out the Father's will in our lives, we will become a verifiable force. The enemy will counter by assigning his forces (such as the three just listed) to distract and defeat our heavenly callings. The battle we wage against him is not against flesh and blood; it's a spiritual battle, and the superior spiritual power we have is *Christ in us—the Holy Spirit.*

Disciples choose to intentionally seek the Lord and abide in His presence. He will protect us (Psalm 91) and He will increase our ability to target and defeat the enemy (Psalm 144:1). The Lord turns the situation around so that the devil becomes the target instead of us.

We cannot afford to slack off or fall asleep, even when it seems the attack has lessened. We may have defended our territory, but are we making any advancements for the kingdom of God? If we are going to be overcomers in this life and walk out our destinies, we need to know how to be aggressive against the enemy's attacks so that we gain ground, rather than simply play defense.

As the lights of the world (Philippians 2:15), we move out in the power, love, and sound thinking that our Father has given us.

> *For God has not given us a spirit of fear, but of power and of love and of a sound mind.* 2 Timothy 1:7

He that is in us is greater than he who is in the world (1 John 4:4), and He is on our side.

> *What then shall we say to these things?* ***If God is for us, who can be against us?*** Romans 8:31

Jesus is the head of all principalities and powers, according to Colossians 2:10, which also states that we are complete in Him. He is the head of His body, and He has all authority in heaven and earth (Matthew 28:18); so do not allow the enemy to talk you out of stepping across the threshold. You absolutely *can* fulfill what God has called you to do, because not only did He give you the authority, He also gave you the *power* through the gifts of the Spirit. This is especially true for disciples because of their renewed level of faith, commitment, and favor (grace) from the Lord.

If you have been a child of God up until now and have not yet stepped over that line of commitment to become a disciple, it's not too late! You can begin by confessing, "I want to be about my Father's business." The more determined you are, the more your desires will cease from being selfish ones to being His desires. Please do not wait to become a disciple—*step over that line of commitment now.*

The decision to move from believer to disciple or from child to son or daughter will not last if it is an emotional one that can be affected by circumstances. In order for this transformation to be eternal, it must be based upon a spiritual understanding from the Word of God (Ephesians 4:14–16; 1 Peter 1:23–25).

If we want to truly walk in the authority He has given us, we need to be in closer proximity to Him. This will require us to climb the mountain of discipleship—to come up higher to where He is. Now is the time to make up our minds to cross that line of commitment and come up higher.

Related Materials at LMCI.org

- Exercising Spiritual Authority for Yourself and Your Ministry (DVD- or CD-set)
- Exercising Spiritual Authority over Principalities and Powers (CD- or MP3-set)
- Spiritual Boot Camp (CD- or MP3-set)
- The 1,000 Year Reign of Jesus Christ on the Earth (Book)

Relevant Points

1. What is the difference between a disciple of Christ and a believer in Christ?

2. Do you know what your specific God-given calling is? If yes, write it clearly as Habakkuk 2:2 exhorts. If not, read *Realizing & Fulfilling Your Personal Ministry* (available as a free e-book at http://lmci.org/RFYPMebook.pdf) and write down any insights you gained in regards to your calling after finishing it.

3. Once you know your calling, you are ready to cross the threshold of commitment to become a _______________. At this point, God will give you a higher _____________ of

________________ to overcome the spiritual warfare that will come your way.

Chapter Seven

The Authority to Re-Present Jesus

Everyone has a calling that God foreordained before the beginning of the world (Ephesians 1:4). He assigned a personal divine purpose to each of us—a specific sphere in which we can operate to our fullest potential. If we desire to exercise spiritual authority, we should know what that calling is, because it will greatly determine our jurisdiction.

Our jurisdiction draws the boundaries around what we are authorized to reign over in life. We see examples of this every day in the world around us in the physical limits given to various governmental authorities. A good scriptural example of this is found in Luke 23:6 and 7.

> *When Pilate heard of Galilee, he asked if the Man [Jesus] were a Galilean. And as soon as he knew that He belonged to Herod's jurisdiction [exousia], he sent Him to Herod, who was also in Jerusalem at that time.* *Luke 23:6–7*

Pilate used the boundaries of his authority as an excuse to pass a difficult responsibility on to another. There were obvious limits to his jurisdiction that were determined by Roman law.

The same holds true within the laws of God. He has given us spiritual authority with certain limitations. In the area where He has delegated us to operate, we have authority. It's like the cowboy movies when the sheriff and his deputies are desperately pursuing the outlaws who are headed for the border. If the bad guys make it past the border, the law officials cannot continue their chase because that's where their authority ends.

God is not the author of confusion (1 Corinthians 14:33), so there is an order to everything He does. This is the opposite of Satan, who would have us "run wild with recklessness" to do whatever we want. If football players ran wherever they wanted during a game, they would not accomplish a thing. But when they focus on the strategies drawn up by their coach and play by the rules, they can purposely execute the plays that will move them down the field to their goal.

We do not have authority over areas where God has not assigned us. This is why we must understand where our personal spiritual sphere of jurisdiction is. Within that place, God will grant us amazing spiritual authority and grace.

Defining Your Purpose

God does not dangle our divine purpose like a carrot in front of our nose, just out of reach to tease us. That would be contrary to His nature as seen in Romans 8:31 and 32.

> *What then shall we say to these things? If God is for us, who can be against us? He who did not spare His own Son, but delivered Him up for us all,* ***how shall He not with Him also freely give us all things?*** *Romans 8:31–32*

The Lord is on our side (Psalm 118:6a), and He does not withhold good things from His children (Psalm 84:11). If you do not know what your calling is, it's not because He is hiding it from you. His will is that we would know and understand our calling.

> *The eyes of your understanding being enlightened; that you may know what is the hope of His calling, what are the riches of the glory of His inheritance in the saints.* *Ephesians 1:18*

Jesus said, "And all things, whatever you ask in prayer, believing, you will receive" (Matthew 21:22).

Our divine purpose is not meant to be a nebulous mystery or an elusive thing off in the distance. The Holy Spirit will define it for us if we will ask Him to. The devil will do his best to distract us from it by keeping us busy, doing anything and everything else but fulfilling our main purpose. Or he may attack our confidence, leaving us feeling weak and deficient. He knows the fruit that our gifts can yield and how it will help bring the Father's heavenly will down to earth.

> *Now there are diversities of gifts, but the same Spirit. And there are differences of administrations, but the same Lord.*
> *1 Corinthians 12:4–5*

In verse 4, the gifts represent the power or ability to accomplish, but in verse 5 the administrations represent the distribution of responsibility. When our ministries are clearly defined, the authority *and* the corresponding gifts of the Spirit to accomplish them are given to us. Remember that the power comes from the Holy Spirit, and the authority comes from Jesus.

Where God has authorized us and given us jurisdiction in this life, we are dynamically equipped to succeed. That's why the devil is determined to stop us from discovering our spheres and reigning over them. He fears the potential authority we carry within those assigned spheres—authority to destroy his works. No wonder he does everything in his power to keep us from them.

For this reason, the greatest spiritual battles we will deal with will typically lie within the boundaries of our God-given callings. The first thing we must overcome is the lie that our enemy is more powerful than we are. The truth is that we have the living God within us and He is on our side.

> *You are of God, little children, and have overcome them, because He who is in you is greater than he who is in the world.*
> *1 John 4:4*

The Bible also reveals that the time of his deception is soon coming to an end.

> *And the God of peace will crush [suntribo—to shatter, completely crush][1] Satan under your feet shortly.*
> *Romans 16:20a*

The truth is that the Lord has created us as powerful spirit beings designed and assigned to reign in this life. He has given us the spiritual authority necessary to walk in our God-given callings. When we walk in authority, we will walk in peace; and peace is a powerful weapon that crushes Satan.

Once we realize the specific divine purpose He has given us, we can cross over the threshold of commitment and become seriously focused. Our time, energy, ability, and resources will be directed to that end. We will stop running around in circles, because our purpose and direction will be defined.

To Each a Portion

> *But to each one of us grace was given according to the* ***measure*** *of Christ's gift.* *Ephesians 4:7*

The Greek word for "measure" is *metron*, and it simply means a determined measure or portion.[2] This indicates that we each have a specific portion meant just for us.

> *For I say, through the grace given to me, to everyone who is among you, not to think of himself more highly than he ought to think, but to think soberly, as* ***God has dealt to each one a measure of faith.*** *For as we have many members in one body, but all the members do not have the same function, so we, being many, are one body in Christ, and individually members of one another.* ***Having then gifts differing according to the grace that is given to us, let us use them:*** *if prophecy, let us prophesy in proportion to our faith; or ministry, let us use it in our ministering; he who teaches, in teaching; he who exhorts, in exhortation; he who gives, with liberality; he who leads, with diligence; he who shows mercy, with cheerfulness. Let love be without hypocrisy. Abhor what is evil. Cling to what is good.*
>
> *Romans 12:3–9*

These verses in Romans 12 unfold the truth that our gifts are unique and that we need to use them. God has given us the specific necessities to succeed in our individual callings—a "measure" of faith sufficient to do the job. This measure of faith supplies the spiritual ability to do certain things well, which is why we enjoy doing what He has called us to do. Our allotted portion will be the area that we passionately desire to minister within.

There are boundaries that surround our jurisdictions, which is in contrast to Jesus' earthly ministry. Jesus was not given a limited portion—He had it all. His only limitation was to do the Father's will (John 5:30; 8:28–29).

> *For He whom God has sent speaks the words of God, for God does not give the Spirit by measure [metron].*
> *John 3:34*

We may be called as evangelists, prophets, intercessors, ministers of mercy, or teachers, etc.; but Jesus was all of these. He set the standard for each and every ministry and calling. No one can fulfill any of these as perfectly as He did, yet we are each given the opportunity to fulfill that specific portion He has given us. To the degree that each individual member of the body of Christ carries out his own portion, Jesus will be represented on the earth. We can corporately walk in the same overall authority that He did, but across an even wider terrain since the body of Christ is spread out over the globe.

One member of the body of Christ alone will not exert the same overall authority as He did. But as we work together—each member functioning within their specific calling—we will begin to see the fullness of who He is on the earth.

> *Now you are the body of Christ, and members individually [meros, a portion, an allotted share].* *1 Corinthians 12:27*

We all have a measure of the gift of Christ—not the full measure, but a portion. That portion gives us what we need in order to replicate a particular aspect of Jesus. Although we should discipline ourselves to be like Him in every way, there will be that one part of

Him into which we will more naturally fit because of the spiritual DNA (**D**ivine **N**ature **A**ttributes) we were given. As the body of Christ rises up to this collectively, a complete picture of who Jesus really is will begin to emerge around the world.

When we understand the significance of what we have been called to do, we will not be competitive with or jealous of each other. Instead, we will desire to work with one another to see the ultimate representation of Jesus on earth fulfilled.

Staying in Our Individual Lanes

> *For in fact the body is not one member but many. If the foot should say, "Because I am not a hand, I am not of the body," is it therefore not of the body? And if the ear should say, "Because I am not an eye, I am not of the body," is it therefore not of the body? If the whole body were an eye, where would be the hearing? If the whole were hearing, where would be the smelling? But now God has set the members, each one of them, in the body just as He pleased. And if they were all one member, where would the body be? But now indeed there are many members, yet one body. And the eye cannot say to the hand, "I have no need of you;" nor again the head to the feet, "I have no need of you."*
>
> *1 Corinthians 12:14–21*

Just as an arm does not do the job of a leg in our physical bodies, so is it within His body. For instance, if an evangelist tries to operate as a pastor, the potential for competition with a true pastor could arise—not to mention the travesty of the lost people who will remain unreached by the evangelist who is outside his jurisdiction. There are accounts in 2 Corinthians of believers stepping beyond the limits of their individual portions and causing confusion. They moved out of their own lane, so to speak. Some of them even claimed to be the apostolic fathers of the work in Corinth in an effort to usurp Paul's rightful authority.

> *We, however, will not boast beyond measure, but within the limits of the sphere which God appointed us—a sphere which especially includes you.* *2 Corinthians 10:13*

Paul's response shows his determination to stay within his God-appointed sphere. He knew that he had a limited portion allotted to him and that the church at Corinth was within his assigned boundaries.

> *For we are not extending ourselves beyond our sphere (thus not reaching you), for it was to you that we came with the gospel of Christ; not boasting of things beyond measure, that is, in other men's labors, but having hope, that as your faith is increased, we shall be greatly enlarged by you in our sphere, to preach the gospel in the regions beyond you, and not to boast in another man's sphere of accomplishment. But "He who glories, let him glory in the Lord." For not he who commends himself is approved, but whom the Lord commends.*
>
> *2 Corinthians 10:14–18*

In addition to staying within our own spheres, Paul also made clear that our ultimate goal should be to bring glory to the Lord. If we feel a need to boast of our own callings or accomplishments, then perhaps it's time to step back and realign ourselves with the truth that it is about the Lord, and not us. It is He who commends us; it is not our job to commend ourselves. As we operate within our true jurisdictions (spheres), the Holy Spirit will anoint and empower us to fulfill our specific callings. It should be obvious that a believer walking within his or her divine jurisdiction has been commended by the Lord and not by men.

Predestined before Time Began

> *Remember the former things of old, for I am God, and there is no other; I am God, and there is none like Me, Declaring the end from the beginning, and from ancient times things that are not yet done, saying, "My counsel shall stand, and I will do all My pleasure."*
>
> *Isaiah 46:9–10*

You could say that before our omniscient (all-knowing) Father started this whole thing, He "took a walk through it" to see how it would play out. This means that no sudden circumstance can catch Him off guard, because He already previewed the event and knows how it will play out to bring His ultimate purposes to pass. His counsel will stand, and He will do all His pleasure, no matter how it looks to us at the time.

Regardless of our ineptness, God clearly states that He predestined us to become His children through the new birth of our spirits. He also foreordained us unto good works.

> *For we are His workmanship, created in Christ Jesus for good works, which God prepared beforehand that we should walk in them.*
>
> *Ephesians 2:10*

Not only did He know you before time began, but He also pre-programmed within you a purpose uniquely yours.

> *Who has saved us and called us with a holy calling, not according to our works, but according to His own* ***purpose*** *and grace which was given to us in Christ Jesus before time began.*
>
> *2 Timothy 1:9*

The Greek word for "purpose" is the word *prothesis.* This word literally means, "a setting forth of a thing, placing of it in view."[3]

It is to put an item in a specific place before it is needed, with the knowledge that at a future point in time, it will serve its purpose. For instance, an electrician would install the wiring into a home before its completion, knowing that someday whoever lives there will need it. He will place the outlets in areas that the architect strategically pinpointed for the most efficient usefulness. According to 2 Timothy 1:9, that which God, the master architect, strategically placed in us before time began is our "holy calling." This means He established within us the ability to produce fruit well within a specific area, and He predetermined the time at which your calling would serve His purpose on the earth. In other words, you are not a random person born into a random time and place.

NOTE: In the last few years, I have discovered how one's purpose and spiritual identity are also encoded in their celestial birth announcement. I believe the specific revelation gleaned from these "Christological Astronomy profiles" more clearly defines our spirit man with its unique gifts and potential messianic likenesses.[4] This information provides yet another piece of the puzzle—along with our spiritual gift evaluations (http://lmci.org/personal_ministry.cfm), other keys discussed further in this chapter of *ESA*, and the Holy Spirit's leading—to help us discern our God-given purpose.

Your Purpose

- Purpose is the Greek word ***prothesis*** from ***protithemai***, meaning "placed ahead of time."
- Pre-placed, knowing it will be needed
- You have been called and purposed for "such a time as this."

Psalm 31:15a verifies this in David's proclamation: "My times are in Your hand." When we gain an understanding of this, we will not be anxious over seemingly difficult circumstances surrounding us. We will be at peace, knowing that He knows the end from the beginning and will cause everything to work together for good for us—because we have been called to this time and place according to His purpose.

> *And we know that all things work together for good to those who love God, to those who are the called according to His purpose.*
> *Romans 8:28*

Although the enemy is presently wreaking havoc in the world, we have the victory through Christ. God uses even the bad circumstances to bring His will to pass in our lives. The next verse indicates that all of these things will help us to be conformed to the image of His Son.

> *For whom He foreknew, He also predestined to be conformed to the image of His Son, that He might be the firstborn among many brethren.* *Romans 8:29*

The Greek word for "conformed" is *symmorphos,* which is composed of two words: *syn* (with) and *morphē* (the form by which a person or thing strikes the vision).[5] According to *Vine's Expository Dictionary of New Testament Words*, this implies "having the same form as another."[6] In other words, God has predestined you to fit into a certain form of Christ designed just for you. As an example, when pouring concrete for a pillar or a specific architectural design, a form (or mold) would first have to be built. The same holds true when pouring plastic or metal into a mold. Not only does the mold first have to be designed and built, but the substance that will be poured into it must also be pliable. The more flexible we are to God's purposes, the easier we can be poured into the mold

He has already designed for us. Many times, heat must be applied to a substance to soften it; and in a spiritual sense, this can occur through difficult situations we encounter—*if we respond to them correctly.*

The correct response would be an attitude of humility before the Lord, because that is what will allow the heat of the battle to soften us. If we are rigid and resistant to what He wants to do within us as we go through hard times, then our consciences will become brittle through pride. Pride caused Lucifer to fall from heaven and can embitter us so that we cannot be poured into the specific image of Christ that was designed for us. However, if we choose to humble ourselves under the mighty hand of God, He will fashion us and shape us to fit into His form. In this way, He will exalt us.

> *Likewise you younger people, submit yourselves to your elders. Yes, all of you be submissive to one another, and be clothed with humility, for "God resists the proud, but gives grace to the humble."* ***Therefore humble yourselves under the mighty hand of God, that He may exalt you in due time.*** *1 Peter 5:5–6*

There is a preparation process that must occur in order for us to be poured into His mold. If we compare it to raising a child, we can see that from the moment children are born the parents are preparing them to leave home. There is a balance as to how this should be done, and we can see it played out in the differing ways a typical father and mother work with their children. Fathers tend to prepare them for independence, while mothers tend to generate within them a perpetual dependence. Both of these are important—we need to be independent (or brave) enough to venture out into what God has planned for us; but at the same time, we must be constantly aware of our dependence upon Him.

Perhaps you have read the following short story called "The Teacup" that wonderfully depicts these truths.

The Teacup

> There was a couple who used to go to England to shop in the beautiful stores. They both liked antiques and pottery and especially teacups. This was their 25th wedding anniversary.
>
> One day in this beautiful shop they saw a beautiful teacup. They said, "May we see that? We've never seen one quite so beautiful." As the lady handed it to them, suddenly the teacup spoke.
>
> "You don't understand," it said. "I haven't always been a teacup. There was a time when I was red and I was clay. My master took me and rolled me and patted me over and over and I yelled out, 'let me alone,' but he only smiled, 'Not yet.'"
>
> "Then I was placed on a spinning wheel," the teacup said, "and suddenly I was spun around and around and around. 'Stop it! I'm getting dizzy!' I screamed. But the master only nodded and said, 'Not yet.'"
>
> "Then he put me in the oven. I never felt such heat. I wondered why he wanted to burn me, and I yelled and knocked at the door. I could see him through the opening and I could read his lips as He shook His head, 'Not yet.'"
>
> "Finally the door opened, he put me on the shelf, and I began to cool. 'There, that's better,' I said. And he brushed

and painted me all over. The fumes were horrible. I thought I would gag. 'Stop it, stop it!' I cried. He only nodded, 'Not yet.'"

"Then suddenly he put me back into the oven, not like the first one. This was twice as hot and I knew I would suffocate. I begged. I pleaded. I screamed. I cried. All the time I could see him through the opening, nodding his head saying, 'Not yet.'"

"Then I knew there wasn't any hope. I would never make it. I was ready to give up. But the door opened and he took me out and placed me on the shelf. One hour later he handed me a mirror and said, 'Look at yourself.' And I did. I said, 'That's not me; that couldn't be me. It's beautiful. I'm beautiful.'"

"I want you to remember, then," he said, "I know it hurts to be rolled and patted, but if I had left you alone, you'd have dried up. I know it made you dizzy to spin around on the wheel, but if I had stopped, you would have crumbled. I knew it hurt and was hot and disagreeable in the oven, but if I hadn't put you there, you would have cracked. I know the fumes were bad when I brushed and painted you all over, but if I hadn't done that, you never would have hardened; you would not have had any color in your life. And if I hadn't put you back in that second oven, you wouldn't survive for very long because the hardness would not have held. Now you are a finished product. You are what I had in mind when I first began with you."[6]

God is the Potter and we are the clay. We may not like everything that we go through, but if we will surrender to His working in our lives, we will like what we see when we come out of the oven.

> *But now, O LORD, You are our Father; we are the clay, and You our potter; and all we are the work of Your hand.*
> *Isaiah 64:8*

All Christians could wear a T-shirt that reads: "Work in Progress!" No matter where we come from or what we've been through, the last chapter in our lives has not yet been written. However, we do have the opportunity to determine how our story will end. If we decide to harden ourselves against the Potter's hand, we will never realize the magnificent mold that He could have poured us into. On the other hand, if we choose to humble ourselves, He can have His way with us and exalt us in due time. The teacup did not have a choice, but we do. When we recognize that He is a loving God and only has our best interests at heart, we will let go and allow Him to mold us. Only then will we be able to fulfill all that He has called us to do as individual members in the body of Christ.

> *I, therefore, the prisoner of the Lord, beseech you to have a walk worthy of the calling with which you were called, **with all lowliness** and gentleness, with longsuffering, bearing with one another in love.*
> *Ephesians 4:1–2*

Although many qualities are mentioned following Paul's exhortation in verse 1, the first one listed is "lowliness." This again drives home the truth that humility is a major key. When you find a believer who desires to do "the victory dance" for God alone, rather than to bring attention to his or her own life, then you have found someone with the kind of humility necessary for the Potter's mold. That man or woman realizes the only One worth pleasing in life is God. He or she wants nothing more than to have the Lord proudly proclaim, "That's My boy!" or "That's My girl!" In other words, "Well done, good and faithful servant" (Matthew 25:21 and 23).

This is why faithfulness is so vital. When we stand before the judgment seat, Jesus is not going to ask us how much money we made, what kind of car we drove, what kind of house we lived in, or how popular we were. He is going to judge us on how faithful we were to do His will.

> *His lord said to him, "Well done, good and faithful servant; you were faithful over a few things, I will make you ruler over many things. Enter into the joy of your lord."* *Matthew 25:21*

Faithfulness is possible because, along with our unique callings, God gives us the specific grace to fulfill them. It is within the area of your individual calling that you are able to do the most good for God's kingdom and the most destruction to the enemy's kingdom. That is why it's so important for you to understand that the Lord has a unique form of Christ to pour you into. None of us will be like anyone else—and that is all part of His design. He predestined you not just to be born again but to be conformed to the image of His Son. He specifically designed you to walk out the unique destiny He chose for you before the foundations of the world.

God has called us with a holy calling that will mature us if we step out and respond to it. This is God's will, and we should accept nothing less than His will for our lives. In truth, He holds us accountable to that. Once we see what that calling is (by revelation), we will seek after the necessary maturity to fulfill it. The Holy Spirit builds an anticipation and excitement in us to step out into the great adventure that awaits us. The Lord has birthed His purpose within our spirit, and with it, He has also placed the passion to please Him by fulfilling it.

Age doesn't matter and neither does your past. Joseph was only 17 years old when he began having visions from God (Genesis 37:2–5), yet Anna the prophetess was 84 years old when she prophesied in the temple concerning Jesus being the Messiah (Luke 2:36–38). We don't need to wait until we reach a certain age, nor do we need to think we are "over the hill" when it comes to fulfilling the Lord's will for our lives. Today is the day He wants you to walk in your ministry. If you will take the leap of faith now, you can avoid (or leave) "No-Purposeville" (that empty place outside of where God has called you).

As you begin walking out your calling, God will be faithful to do His part by pouring out the grace you need to fulfill it. That grace has always been there for you; He has just been waiting for you to step up to the plate to activate it. Once you know what your divine purpose is, you will need to discipline yourself to stick to the revelation that He gave you—and His grace will empower you to do this. He has given you spiritual authority that you can exercise over the purpose He gave you—authority to reign over that specific sphere in which He has placed you. This enables you to clear out the hindrances that the enemy has, up until now, put in your way.

Pressing Toward the Goal

> *I press toward the goal for the prize of the upward call of God in Christ Jesus. Therefore let us, as many as are mature, have this mind; and if in anything you think otherwise,* ***God will reveal even this to you.***
>
> *Philippians 3:14–15*

When our individual purpose is defined, we will have a clearer perspective of the goal we should be pressing toward. We also have a safeguard through the Father who will reveal to us when we are getting off course.

Each of us will stand before His judgment seat someday, accountable for what He called us to do.

> *So then each of us shall give account of himself to God.*
> *Romans 14:12*

As we humble ourselves before Him and remain pliable in His hands, we cannot lose. He is faithful to do His part as we do ours. He will ensure that we finish our race victoriously. Our primary responsibility is to make sure our will lines up with the Lord's. If you are still not sure what your part is, keep reading for more helpful keys in your journey of discovery. The Lord is faithful. He will reveal it to you.

Saved and Called

We have been saved and called with a holy calling, according to 2 Timothy 1:9.

> *Therefore do not be ashamed of the testimony of our Lord, nor of me His prisoner, but share with me in the sufferings for the gospel according to the power of God, who has saved us and called us with a holy calling,* ***not according to our works****, but according to His own purpose and grace which was given to us in Christ Jesus before time began.* *2 Timothy 1:8–9*

These verses define two major aspects of our lives:

- We were saved—not according to our works.
- We were called—and our calling is a holy one.

These two aspects of our lives were in the plan of God "before the world began," and they define who we really are. We were saved by grace and are children of God who will mature by responding to our holy callings.

Remember that the book of 2 Timothy was addressed to born-again Christians whose spirits were saved by His grace; and it applies to us today as well. Our abilities do not determine our callings, because they do not necessarily define who He has made us to be. It has everything to do with His purpose and grace, which was given in Christ Jesus before the world began. Anything other than His purpose being fulfilled in our lives will be meaningless. If we try to figure it out on our own according to our talents and abilities, it may seem logical but if it is outside of His will and purpose we will be trying to force a square peg into a circular hole—it just won't work.

A Personal Epiphany of Christ

One of the ways the Lord can show us our callings is through a revelation picture (epiphany) of them through the life of Christ.

> *Who has saved us and called us with a holy calling, not according to our works, but according to His own purpose and grace which was given to us in Christ Jesus before time began, but has now been revealed by the* ***appearing*** *of our Savior Jesus Christ, who has abolished death and brought life and immortality to light through the gospel.*
> *2 Timothy 1:9–10*

The word "appearing" is the key word in verse 10. The Greek word is *epiphaneia, from which we get the word "epiphany." Epiphaneia* is composed of *epi*, which basically implies "a distribution upon," and *phaino,* "to lighten."[7]

In theology, the word "epiphany" is often used regarding the return of Christ. But it is not confined to His return alone, and the context of it in this verse does not indicate that meaning because it says, "but has **now** been revealed." I believe it applies here to the way the Holy Spirit reveals Jesus to us as individuals.

The phrase "but has now been revealed by the appearing of our Savior Jesus Christ," is set in contrast with "before time began." In other words, this is not speaking of an appearance before time began; it is speaking of a "now" revelation. So what is it that has now been revealed by the appearing of our Savior Jesus Christ? The immediate context of verse 9 is speaking of our salvation *and* our holy calling. *This indicates that the appearance of Jesus Christ not only reveals our salvation, but also our calling.* When our spiritual ("real") eyes behold Him, we will receive a unique enlightenment that is relevant to our calling.

How You See Jesus Is the Image You Will Fit

- It is your "special" revelation of Him.
  - 2 Timothy 1:9–10
- It is what the Holy Spirit reveals to you.
  - Ephesians 1:17
- It is the spiritually discerned predestined image of God's Son that you conform to.
  - 1 Corinthians 2:14

For instance, when you think about Jesus, do you envision Him in His prophetic role? Or do you see Him teaching? Perhaps the main picture you hold of Him is one in which He is healing someone. Or maybe you see Him forgiving people. This could indicate a calling of mercy. The main picture you carry of Him will reflect your own calling. For instance, if you picture Him laughing with a group of His disciples, you could have a ministry of cheer. Jesus encompasses all the callings and ministries, and we are His body. As such, we are each to demonstrate a certain aspect of Him.

Each of us has been called to replicate the ministry of Jesus Christ in a specific way. I call it re-presenting Him. The portion that you have been given is the image into which you are to conform. Ask the Lord to give you a revelation, an epiphany, of who He is—to show you what part of Him He designed you to replicate. (We can also see this in the celestial word of God when we interpret the Christological Astronomy profiles of our birth skies.)

> *That the God of our Lord Jesus Christ, the Father of glory, may give to you the spirit of wisdom and revelation in the knowledge of Him, the eyes of your* ***understanding*** *being enlightened; that you may know what is the hope of His calling, what are the riches of the glory of His inheritance in the saints.*
> *Ephesians 1:17–18*

The word "understanding" in Ephesians 1:18 is the Greek word *kardia*, which means "heart."[8] This goes deeper than the soul—it is a spiritual understanding. For example, in your soul, you may want to be a professional baseball player when, in reality, the Lord has called you to be an intercessor. Even if you succeeded in the field that your soul desired, it would pale in comparison to what God had in store for you. The point here is that the aspiration of your soul may or may not line up with the aspiration of your spirit. The thing your soul desires could actually be what the Lord is calling you to—but it just as easily may not be what He is calling you to. *You will not know which it is until you have a Holy Spirit revelation that leads you to your true calling and purpose.* God can, and will, tell you the form He wants you to fit into—if you are willing to seek Him and then listen to what He says.

This is not to say that someone could not fulfill his spiritual calling while still fulfilling a secular career. Someone could have the spiritual calling of an intercessor but at the same time also love to play baseball—and God has a plan for both to be fulfilled. It would be ideal to have a profession in which that calling could be utilized; however, if all of our energies are consumed by the career and we leave our main purpose undone, then we would have lived our lives in vain. Our God-given purpose should be our first priority; the secular career we choose should take a back seat to this.

A friend of mine has done this for years. His secular job has provided adequate care for his family, but his main priority has been to travel to India and cast out demons because that is what he is called to do. He has become a spiritual "terrorist" in the demon community and has trained many other believers in spiritual warfare as well. Jesus can make any of us a superhuman like my friend if we keep our main calling from Him our priority.

This is why we should seek Him for that divine revelation picture of our calling. The Scriptures already tell us that the Holy Spirit desires to manifest Jesus to us, as seen in John 14:21.

> *He who has My commandments and keeps them, it is he who loves Me. And he who loves Me will be loved by My Father, and* ***I will love him and manifest Myself to him.***
> *John 14:21*

There is no right or wrong answer to how we see Him; the main thing is that we do receive an epiphany of Him by using the real eyes of our spirit. In other words, we can only realize our ministry when we use our real eyes.

How Reading the Scriptures Can Help Us

Another way we can seek Him for that epiphany is by reading the Scriptures.

> *These things we also speak, not in words which man's wisdom teaches but which the Holy Spirit teaches,* ***comparing spiritual things with spiritual.*** *1 Corinthians 2:13*

The Scriptures are spiritual, and as we ask the Holy Spirit to direct our reading of them, we will be looking at spiritual words with spiritual (real) eyes—"comparing spiritual things with spiritual." The Holy Spirit can cause certain sections of the Bible to affect us deeply. When we sense this, take notice—the Lord is endeavoring to show us something. He may cause the words on the page to appear larger or highlighted; He may bring a picture to mind; or it could simply be an inner knowing. He works with us in individual ways, but as we are sensitive to Him, He can give us the epiphany we need. One way or the other, there will be certain words of life that will arrest us and hold our attention depending on what He wants to show us at that time in our lives.

Pay attention to what He is revealing and seek to understand it more. Look for more scriptures to deepen the revelation and ask the Holy Spirit to guide you. At some point He will reveal that particular truth about Jesus that He wants you to see.

Those who have already been doing this can probably attest to the reality that the Holy Spirit has been "running a movie in the background" for them, allowing them to visualize Jesus doing particular things. For years I envisioned Jesus teaching in the boat by the seaside, or confronting the Pharisees of their hypocrisy, or miraculously healing people. Perhaps you have seen Him showing mercy or winning the lost. Whatever picture (or pictures) the Holy Spirit gives us as we read the Scriptures will indicate the direction He wants us to go. Remember that this guidance will come from the spirit—not from the soul. It is only through our real eyes that we will realize our callings.

> *But the natural [psychikos—soulish] man does not receive the things of the Spirit of God, for they are foolishness to him; nor can he know them, because they are spiritually discerned.*
>
> *1 Corinthians 2:14*

Even Jesus in His earthly existence had to come to that realization of who He was. The book of Hebrews shows a declaration of His personal epiphany from the Scriptures.

> *Then I said, "Behold, I have come—in the volume of the book it is written of Me—to do Your will, O God."*
>
> *Hebrews 10:7*

Purpose of Heart

If we do not understand what the Lord has specifically called us to do within the body of Christ, we will lack focus or purpose. How significant is it for us to have purpose in our lives? Look at the exhortation Barnabas gave the believers when he visited them in Antioch.

> *Then news of these things came to the ears of the church in Jerusalem, and they sent out Barnabas to go as far as Antioch. When he came*

> *and had seen the grace of God, he was glad, and encouraged them all that with* ***purpose of heart*** *they should continue with the Lord.*
>
> *Acts 11:22–23*

When we have that focus or purpose of heart, it helps us to faithfully follow the Lord. The King James Version reads, "[He] exhorted them all, that **with purpose of heart they would cleave unto the Lord**." It is so much easier to cleave to Him when we know what He wants us to do. With our purpose clearly defined, we will more readily hold tightly to the One who pours His grace on us to accomplish it. When each individual in a group of believers (a church) knows his or her specific calling and rises up to fulfill it, the result will be a purposeful team effort to bring the Father's will to their geographical location. I believe this contributed to the rapid growth of the church in Antioch, as we see in the next verse.

> *And a great many people were added to the Lord.*
>
> *Acts 11:24b*

If you are a leader in the body of Christ, then you need to realize the same thing Barnabas did: *people need purpose of heart.* They must understand their callings and take the necessary steps to fulfill them. Leaders cannot dictate to them what their purpose is, because they belong to the Lord and He is the One who ultimately must reveal it to them. But we can certainly direct people to Him to receive that revelation.

> *Therefore take heed to yourselves and to all the flock, among which the Holy Spirit has made you overseers, to shepherd the church of God which He purchased with His own blood.*
>
> *Acts 20:28*

Overseers are responsible to steer God's people toward Him, so that He can fashion them into the image of His Son. An overseer can also set an example for them by walking in his or her own specific ministry or calling.

Each of us within the body of Christ has been given a specific purpose or calling, and it is within that individual sphere that we will have the spiritual authority and grace to walk. It is imperative that we seek the Lord to find out what that calling is so that we do not lose ourselves in No-Purposeville, outside of where God has designed us to be.

Related Materials at LMCI.org

- Christological Astronomy (Workbook, E-workbook, DVD-, CD-, or MP3-set)
- Realizing & Fulfilling Your Personal Ministry (E-book, CD- or MP3-set)
- True Confessions of Spiritual Warriors (E-book)
- Utilizing Gift Ministries (Book)

Relevant Points

1. What defines our spiritual jurisdiction for exercising our spiritual authority?

2. Write down the specific part of Jesus that you believe you are to replicate.

3. If you have not already done so, go to http://www.lmci.org/ca.cfm?Start=Yes and see what God wrote in your birth sky. Write a brief synopsis of your Christological Astronomy profile.

PART THREE

SPIRITUAL WARFARE

Chapter Eight

Overcoming the Power of the Enemy

> *Behold, I give you the authority to trample on serpents and scorpions, and over all the power of the enemy, and nothing shall by any means hurt you.* — *Luke 10:19*

Jesus gave His disciples authority to overcome the power of evil spirits, as we saw in chapter 6. When it comes to the broader subject of spiritual authority, the truth of exercising it in this specific area is vital because it is so prevalent in the Scriptures. For this reason, much of my teaching ministry is focused upon this aspect.

This is where a true disciple will show up. We can all sing hymns, but who will swing swords for the King? Exercising our rights and privileges to overcome demonic powers will be part of the entrance requirement into the millennial reign where the chosen have the honor of ruling with Yeshua.

Once we have crossed over the threshold of commitment into discipleship and have received the epiphany of our God-given destiny, we become a verifiable force to be dealt with in the spirit realm. With the higher level of spiritual authority we have as disciples, it is crucial that we understand our enemy and his strategies in order to more effectively overcome his devices. He will do everything he can to get us off track from worshiping and obeying the true God. If he cannot get us to openly worship him, then he will try to distract us from our true purpose. This is what he tried to do to Job.

> *My days are past,* ***my purposes are broken off****, even the thoughts of my heart.* *Job 17:11*

Because of the great tragedy and physical devastation Satan brought into his life, Job declared that his days were past and his purposes were broken off. Just as we discussed in the last chapter, without focus and purpose, we will wander aimlessly and eventually find ourselves in No-Purposeville. Job reached this point when he made this sad declaration. He could no longer focus on the main point of his life—to love, fear, serve, glorify, and worship God.

> *Let us hear the conclusion of the whole matter: Fear God and keep His commandments, for this is the whole duty of man.*
> *Ecclesiastes 12:13*

> *Jesus said to him, "You shall love the Lord your God with all your heart, with all your soul, and with all your mind."*
> *Matthew 22:37*

We should be free in our hearts and minds to keep our focus where it belongs; but when we are victims of the devil's attacks, it is very difficult to do this. God never put us on this planet to be victimized by His archenemy. He put us here to rule over the works of His hands and to establish His heavenly dominion on the earth.

> *What is man that You are mindful of him, And the son of man that You visit him? For You have made him a little lower than the angels [elohim—the Creator God], And You have crowned him with glory and honor. You have made him to have dominion over the works of Your hands; You have put all things under his feet.*
> *Psalm 8:4–6*

This honor was not intended for God-rejecters and mockers, but for those who love Him and desire to obey Him. There is a constant spiritual battle going on in the heavens as Satan and his cohorts fight for control over earth and its inhabitants. As Christ followers, we cannot afford to be complacent or ignorant of this truth, because neither complacency nor ignorance will eradicate evil. If we choose to look the other way instead of stepping up to the responsibility the Lord has given us, we open ourselves up to an attack. Our armor will be down, making us vulnerable. This not only affects our personal lives, but it can also distract us from walking in the power and authority necessary to help others.

Peace through Superior Power

The only way to overcome Satan's attacks and have peace in our lives is through superior firepower. We will never gain victory through negotiation or reasoning, because he is a liar and a deceiver. Only as we exercise our spiritual authority to attack his evil works within our spiritual jurisdiction will we gain the victory and allow the peace of God to reign.

One of the definitions for *shalom*, the Hebrew word for "peace," is "the absence of agitation or discord."[1] The enemy is an expert at bringing agitation and discord into our lives, but we have the superior firepower to overcome him through the Holy Spirit.

> *You are of God, little children, and have overcome them because He who is in you is greater than he who is in the world.*
> *1 John 4:4*

The Lord lives within us, and He has already defeated the enemy and all his cohorts.

> *Having disarmed principalities and powers, He made a public spectacle of them, triumphing over them in it.*
> *Colossians 2:15*

Even though Satan has ultimately been defeated, he still maintains his position as the god of this world because he has successfully deceived people into paying him credence and allowing him to rule over their lives. Sadly, some of these people are Christians. Even seasoned disciples can be tempted through carnal pleasures and entrapments that are sometimes so subtle that those who seem the strongest have fallen for them. We cannot be lights in this dark world if we completely sequester ourselves from it; therefore, we need to be constantly vigilant and alert to tend, maintain, and police our own gardens, so to speak. If we were as diligent to keep our spiritual eyes open to Satan's devices as we are in the physical realm to protecting our homes and property, we would have far less distraction and stress in our lives.

> *Keep [guard] your heart with all diligence, for out of it spring the issues of life.* *Proverbs 4:23*

If we came home and discovered the back door open, we would probably arm ourselves with a weapon and go through every room, including the attic and/or basement, checking behind and under the furniture, and investigating every possible hiding place to ensure that there was no intruder. We have to maintain that same kind of awareness and keenness in our spiritual walk to guard our spiritual homes (our hearts), and this is done by exercising spiritual authority over our lives.

> *Be sober, be vigilant; because your adversary the devil walks about like a roaring lion, seeking whom he may devour.*
> *1 Peter 5:8*

The sword of the spirit is the most powerful weapon we can use in any spiritual battle to defend our perimeters and establish territory for the King and His kingdom. We must diligently feed ourselves on His words of life to keep it sharpened and ready for use. The evil spirit realm, though invisible to our physical eyes, is very real. Evil-spirit beings did not exist only in Bible times, nor are they imaginary mythical characters from fairytale land. Demons, as well as principalities and powers, are very real. They have methods and strategies given them by their commander in chief, Satan; and his main purpose is "to steal, kill, and destroy" (John 10:10).

Contrary to the thief, Jesus came to give life more abundantly. He authorized us to have dominion over the evil spirit kingdom and empowered us to overcome the intents and purposes of Satan. When we wield the sword of the Spirit with authority and proclaim the truth of the Scriptures with bold faith, we can overcome any and every attack that could come against us. However, we must approach the battle aggressively, so we are not constantly playing defense.

War Rules

When we understand the methods the enemy uses, we will see how manageable demons really are—and this is *only* because Jesus has given us authority over them.

> *Behold, I give the authority to trample on serpents and scorpions, and over all the power of the enemy, and nothing shall by any means hurt you.* *Luke 10:19*

One of the reasons Jesus came was to open our eyes to turn us away from the darkness and power of Satan and bring us to the light and glory of our God (Acts 26:18). He is the Father of lights in whom there is no shadow of turning (James 1:17). He has delivered us from the power of darkness and placed us in His kingdom with the spiritual authority and abilities to help others experience the same freedom.

> *He has delivered us from the power of darkness and translated us into the kingdom of the Son of His love, in whom we have redemption through His blood, the forgiveness of sins.*
>
> *Colossians 1:13–14*

If we have already been legally delivered from the authority of darkness, why do we so often still experience bondage? (The answer lies in either the ignorance of our legal rights or our inconsistency in claiming them.) Jesus defeated the devil at Calvary, but Satan remains a deceiver. By continually guarding our hearts and minds with the Scriptures, we proactively guard against the evil one's deception and we push the fight in an aggressive way rather than waiting for the fight to come to us.

> *Put on the whole armor of God, that you may be able to stand against the wiles of the devil. For we do not wrestle against flesh and blood, but against principalities, against powers, against the rulers of the darkness of this age, against spiritual hosts of wickedness in the heavenly places. Therefore take up the whole armor of God, that you may be able to withstand in the evil day, and having done all, to stand. Stand therefore, having girded your waist with truth, having put on the breastplate of righteousness, and having shod your feet with the preparation of the gospel of peace; above all, taking the shield of faith with which you will be able to quench all the fiery darts of the wicked one. And take the helmet of salvation, and the* ***sword of the Spirit, which is the word of God****.*
>
> *Ephesians 6:11–17*

The enemy cannot put us back into bondage if we keep our armor on and remain vigilant. This is the way to experience and maintain the freedom we have in Christ.

Expelling Demons

I truly believe there is nothing that demonstrates God's superiority and establishes His dominion over the devil like expelling demons.

> *And when He had called His twelve disciples to Him, He gave them power [exousia—authority] over unclean spirits, to cast them out, and to heal all kinds of sickness and all kinds of disease.*
> *Matthew 10:1*

There are many within the US church who say Christians cannot have a demon. I suggest that those who speak this way need to get out more—namely, to parts of the world that are not tainted with westernized Christianity's religious doctrine. After spending substantial time in India, I can speak from some real-life experience about casting out demons; and believe me, Christians can most certainly be demonized. Even if the "rules" say that they cannot, since when have demons obeyed the rules?

Regardless of who the enemy chooses to demonize, we have the dominion as Christ followers. Most Christians know that Jesus cast out evil spirits during His earthly ministry, but the commonly dismissed companion truth is that He gave us authority over them as well.

> *Most assuredly, I say to you, he who believes in Me, **the works that I do he will do also; and greater works than these he will do,** because I go to My Father.* *John 14:12*

As those who believe in Him, we have His permission and authority to do the works He did and greater. This means we also can expell demons and set the captives free—and the spirit inside us yearns to do so. Just as Jesus' nature and purpose was to this end, so is ours. Wrapped up within our individual DNA (divine nature attributes) is the desire and ability to set others free. However, if we choose to look the other way and ignore the enemy's attacks on our own lives, we will become so consumed with our personal struggles that we will not reach out to help others.

This is why we cannot passively sit by while the spiritual battle rages all around us. We must take up our heavenly armor and get involved now—before the attack comes. This requires a warrior's mentality and a certain amount of spiritual aggression.

> *And from the days of John the Baptist until now the kingdom of heaven suffers violence, and the violent take it by force.*
> *Matthew 11:12*

The spirit realm is a kingdom of warfare which demands spiritual violence and faithful diligence. There will be specific times when we will have to go into intense battle; but the war is always raging, which means our armor must be on at all times. Passivity has no place in the Christian life. If we follow the lives of Jesus' 12 apostles after His ascension, we discover that they did not sit around meditating all day long. They actively followed Jesus' example of setting the captives free—which is why 11 of them ended up martyred, and the 12th one (John) survived being boiled in oil. I'm not saying this to scare or deter you but simply to make the point that they were aggressively moving God's kingdom on the earth.

> *Yes, and all who desire to live godly in Christ Jesus will suffer persecution.* *2 Timothy 3:12*

If we are not suffering persecution, we are probably not really pushing the fight to live godly in Christ Jesus. This is a violent kingdom and we must commit not only to the fight but also to the victory.

I believe "They will take up serpents," (Mark 16:18) carries a deeper meaning than accidentally picking up a physical snake. It spiritually implies the need for an aggressive attitude in engaging the evil spirit realm; and this kind of attitude acknowledges that there are times when demons must be cast out of people.

The first record of demons being expelled in the New Testament occurred when Jesus entered a synagogue after His 40 days of temptation in the wilderness.

> *Then they went into Capernaum, and immediately on the Sabbath He entered the synagogue and taught. And they were astonished at His teaching, for He taught them as one having authority, and not as the scribes. Now there was a man in their synagogue with an unclean spirit. And he cried out, saying, "Let us alone! What have we to do with You, Jesus of Nazareth? Did You come to destroy us? I know who You are—the Holy One of God!" But Jesus rebuked him, saying, "**Be quiet**, and come out of him!" And when the unclean spirit had convulsed him and cried out with a loud voice, he came out of him. Then they were all amazed, so that they questioned among themselves, saying, "What is this? What new doctrine is this? For with authority He commands even the unclean spirits, and they obey Him."* *Mark 1:23–25*

When the evil spirits in the man saw Jesus, they immediately recognized Him and called Him, "Jesus of Nazareth." The "spokesman" of the group declared, "I know who You are—the Holy One of God!" The phrase "Be quiet" (or "Hold thy peace" in the King James Version) comes from the Greek word *phimoo*, which means, "to close the mouth with a muzzle."[2]

According to Matthew 28:18, God gave Jesus all authority that is in heaven and on earth, and that is why these demons had to obey Him. The Scriptures say that Jesus was the "firstborn among many brethren" (Romans 8:29). He had the anointing of the Holy Spirit here on earth and we now have that same anointing.

> *But the anointing which you have received from Him abides in you.*
> *1 John 2:27*

> *Now He who establishes us with you in Christ and has anointed us is God, who also has sealed us and given us the Spirit in our hearts as a deposit.* *2 Corinthians 1:21–22*

When we received the gift from the Holy Spirit, we became God's kingdom enforcers. Kingdom enforcers do not allow demons to dominate. The Holy Spirit gives us the power to cast out demons; but to do this, we must understand the rules they play by.

Unclean Spirits

> *When an unclean spirit goes out of a man, he [the unclean spirit] goes through dry places, seeking rest, and finds none. Then he says, "I will return to my house from which I came." And when he comes, he finds it empty, swept, and put in order. Then he goes and takes with him seven other spirits more wicked than himself, and they enter and dwell there; and the last state of that man is worse than the first.*
> *Matthew 12:43–45a*

When an "unclean spirit" dwells within a person, it is typically a demon; however, there are larger, more powerful unclean (evil) spirits that can inhabit the atmosphere and rule over geographical regions. The categories of evil spirits are basically the three that were listed earlier: principalities, powers, and demons.

> *To the intent that now the manifold wisdom of God might be made known by the church to the principalities and powers in the heavenly places.* *Ephesians 3:10*

Some believe that principalities and powers are the fallen angels that were cast down from the third heaven with Lucifer after his rebellion (Revelation 12:4); and that is a probable explanation since these evil spirit beings had to originate from somewhere. Regardless of what they are or where they originated, we know that they are powerful spirit beings that now inhabit the second heaven—the spiritual atmosphere of earth.

Demons (our main focus of the three) must be handled differently than principalities and powers. Just as a good hunter studies his prey in order to gain the advantage, we need to understand our prey so that we are the hunter and not the hunted. The unclean spirits that are able to inhabit people's bodies and minds are demons, not principalities or powers.

NOTE: Some people argue that principalities can inhabit bodies as well; however, I cannot back this up scripturally.

There are flesh-and-blood "princes" (people) in high-ranking positions in the world, who should not be confused with the high-level spirits called principalities, even though they often work together. The Bible sometimes refers to these wicked human princes who are dedicated to Satan's agendas as "sons of Belial."

The phrase in Matthew 12:43 about an unclean spirit who "goes through dry places, seeking rest," not only implies that demons are earthbound but that, when they are cast out, they immediately start searching for a new (or the same) habitat. Once a demon gets evicted from one person, it will seek another. This is why it is so important that the delivered person is taught how to maintain their deliverance by keeping the "entry door" locked and sealed.

Demons also have a different origin than principalities and powers. An understanding of where they originally came from will help us to distinguish them from principalities and powers and also to have the proper perspective of their size. This will increase our faith in dealing with them, because if we think they are "big and bad," we will be afraid to attack them.

Nephilim

There is much debate and misinformation on who or what the nephilim are, but they were (and still are) a significant aspect of Satan's kingdom. I will endeavor to explain what I understand of them in this section. I also recommend an article I wrote a few years ago called, "Principalities, Powers, and Demons," which is available at LMCI.org.

The following passage in Genesis 6 gives us an initial look at this misunderstood breed of spirit beings.

> *Now it came to pass, when men began to multiply on the face of the earth, and daughters were born to them, that the* ***sons of God*** *saw the daughters of men, that they were beautiful; and they took wives for themselves of all whom they chose. There were giants on the earth in those days, and also afterward, when the sons of God came in to the daughters of men and they bore children to them. Those were the mighty men who were of old, men of renown.*
>
> *Genesis 6:1–2, 4*

"Sons of God" is a phrase used in other scripture references to describe angels (Job 1:6, 2:1). The apocryphal books of Jubilees and Enoch call these angels who cohabited with women, "watchers." They differ from the typical angel in that they were given physical bodies so they could walk upon the earth. Because of their disobedience when they "came in unto the daughters of men," they were chained in a place called Tartarus (rendered "hell" in most translations) where they await the judgment of God (2 Peter 2:4). In other words, they broke the law and are now in jail awaiting judgment.

> *For if God didn't spare angels when they sinned, but cast them down to Tartarus, and committed them to pits of darkness, to be reserved for judgment.* *2 Peter 2:4 WEB*

The word "giants" in Genesis 6:4 was translated from the Hebrew word *nephilim.* The implication here is that the giants, or *nephilim*, were the offspring of the watchers and women—meaning they were half angel and half human. They had physical bodies that looked human; but because they were also half angel they had the ability to become men of renown. When the flood wiped them out, their spirits left their bodies; but because they were not wholly human, their spirits were left without a destination. Thus, they wandered the earth constantly seeking a habitat, a warm body to live in—preferably human. These are known as demons.

The following chart shows some of the differences between principalities and powers and demons.

Principalities & Powers	Demons
Fallen Angels	Disembodied spirits of the nephilim
Live in the heavenlies	Live on the earth
Are displaced	Are cast out

The angels (watchers) who impregnated the women were bound in a pit and are still there to this day. These higher-ranking spirits are scheduled for release in the end times, according to Revelation 9 and the apocryphal books of Enoch and Jubilees. The infamous "beast" that will come out of the pit (Revelation 11:7) is of this supposed superior breed and he will lead the rest to wreak havoc on the earth. The fact that there is little information or inclusion of this category of spirit beings in eschatology or theology is why I stated earlier that there seems to be general ignorance and/or misunderstanding of them.

In this chapter, "Overcoming the Power of the Enemy," it is significant to know about these disobedient angels (watchers) that will one day be released. They are a much higher level than demons (the disembodied spirits of their offspring) and must not be treated the same (when that day comes).

When that day does come, the already rapidly falling moral decline we see now will drop to an even lower level, similar to that of Genesis 6:5–7.

> *Then the LORD saw that* ***the wickedness of man was great in the earth****, and that* ***every intent of the thoughts of his heart was only evil continually****. And the LORD was sorry that He had made man on the earth, and He was grieved in His heart. So the LORD said, "I will destroy man whom I have created from the face of the earth, both man and beast, creeping thing and birds of the air, for I am sorry that I have made them."*
>
> *Genesis 6:5–7*

The sons of God from Genesis 6 are referred to in Jude 1:6 KJV as the angels who "kept not their first estate," which is not talking only about their heavenly status but also their holiness status. They disobeyed the Lord when they cohabited with women and the fruit of their unholy union was a perverse hybrid offspring. The already contaminated human race degenerated to an even lower state of depravity, causing great sorrow in the Lord's heart.

However, as He looked upon mankind, there was one man and his family who stood out.

> *But Noah found grace in the eyes of the LORD. This is the genealogy of Noah. Noah was a just man, perfect in his* ***generations****. Noah walked with God.* *Genesis 6:8–9*

The word "generations" means "descendants."[3] Noah and his family were apparently the only humans on the face of the earth whose lineage had not been corrupted by the angels that left their first estate.

The serpent (devil) was, in part, fulfilling the prophecy the Lord had spoken in Genesis 3:15 when He spoke of the devil's seed and the woman's seed. I believe Satan tempted the watchers into this sin in order to pervert the seed of the woman—endeavoring to circumvent the coming of Christ. Throughout the Old Testament we can see him time and time again trying to obstruct the Godly lineage that would eventually bring about the Christ; and this is why we see God stepping in every time to defend His people and preserve the Christ line.

God was, and still is, far greater than the deceiver and had set apart a Godly man, Noah—even in the midst of the Genesis 6 degradation. Noah walked with God and followed His instructions to build an ark that saved himself and his family (Genesis 7:1). The remainder of the earth's populace drowned—including the nephilim, and this posed a problem. Human spirits are designed to go to God and await the judgment day; however, the nephilimic spirits are not this way. As already mentioned, these spirits were bound to the earth and destined to seek a habitation—namely humans, although they sometimes settle for animals.

These wandering spirits were the ones who dwelt within the hybrids (giants) of whom God said, "every intent of the thoughts of his heart was only evil continually." Apocryphal writings reveal just how evil these creatures were—including not just murder but cannibalism as well. They were horribly wicked creatures, and their spirits wander the earth to this day, craving the habitation of warm physical bodies.

Even though the watchers and their offspring (the giants) were very powerful, their spirits (demons) are not of the magnitude or power of a principality or power that rules over whole cities or even nations. Demons are simply unclean spirits who can only rule over one human at a time; and as such, they can be overcome by the superior spirit of Christ that lives in us: that is, the Holy Spirit.

Functions of Demons

There is a difference between a demon and a devil that can be seen within their definitions. When the term "devil spirit" or "devil" is used, it sensationalizes the subject and intimidates Christians into believing that demons are as powerful as angels. The Greek word for "demon" is *daimonion* (plural) or *daimon* (singular), whereas the Greek word for devils is *diabolos* and is reserved for *the* devil—Satan (Revelation 12:9). If we call demons "devils," it elevates them to a higher level or power, which can cause us to be intimidated by them. They have a rank in Satan's kingdom similar to chess pawns or perhaps privates in the army.[4] Some have higher ranks than others, but they are all manageable because of the highest ranking spirit in the universe—the Holy Spirit—that lives in us.

Note: *Diabolos* is a compound word: *dia*, meaning "through," connoting a penetration, invasion, infiltration, or entrance; and *ballo*, meaning "to throw," as in throwing a ball or rock.[5]

Can a Christian be Possessed?

One of the first truths we must acknowledge concerning demons is that they cannot actually "possess" a Christian; however, they can demonize Christians. Even though the King James Version uses the phrase "possessed with devils" 25 times, it is not an accurate translation. The phrase comes from one Greek word, *daimonizomai*, which should be translated "demonized."[6]

Possess means to own, depicting total and complete ownership, rather than a partial habitation. It would be like owning a house rather than renting it. The Holy Spirit dwells in us and already owns us, thereby making it impossible for any other being to own us. However, the soul and/or the body might not be purified through the Holy Spirit because of disobedience. The process of holiness is a continual one, and if we are not daily submitting ourselves to His rule in our lives, then our souls and bodies can be open to demonic invasion.

> *Or do you not know that your body is the temple of the Holy Spirit who is in you, whom you have from God, and you are not your own?* ***For you were bought at a price;*** *therefore glorify God in your body and in your spirit, which are God's.*
>
> *1 Corinthians 6:19–20*

We have already been purchased by God with the blood of Jesus, and we are now legally His possession. This means that a Christian cannot be possessed by any other entity. We literally belong to Christ and to our heavenly Father.

> *Therefore let no one glory in men. For all things are yours: whether Paul or Apollos or Cephas, or the world or life or death, or things present or things to come—all are yours. And you are Christ's, and Christ is God's.* *1 Corinthians 3:21–23*

> *Knowing that you were not redeemed with corruptible things, like silver or gold, from your aimless conduct received by tradition from your fathers, but with the precious blood of Christ, as of a lamb without blemish and without spot.* *1 Peter 1:18–19*

Those who believe Christians cannot be demonized fail to realize that demonization is not the same as ownership. A person who is demonized is not owned, they are inhabited. Since man is a three-fold being and a Christian's spirit is regenerated into a holy spirit, the only parts of a Christian that can be demonized or inhabited by a demon are the body and soul.

Possessed vs. Demonized

- To possess means to totally own.
  - Demons do not totally control a person.
  - They control a ***portion*** of the person.
- A Christian can be demonized in their soul and/or body, but not in their spirit.
  - Greek noun is ***daimon*** = demon
  - Greek verb is ***daimonizomai***

When anyone unwittingly allows, or knowingly invites, evil into their life, they legally open a door for a demon(s) to inhabit either a part of their mind/soul or a part of their body. So, although it is true that Christians cannot be possessed, they certainly may be inhabited in their souls and/or bodies.

In physical warfare, an enemy will attack at the weakest point; and so it is with demons in spiritual warfare. They will work on the weakest area of a Christian's life to further wear it down until a portal opens for them. If we do not strengthen our weak areas with truth (through Scripture reading and application of biblical principles for mental and physical health), eventually a portal will be opened for demonic entry—whether in the soul or the body.

The god of this world uses various temptations, devices, and/or doctrines to debilitate people's souls and bodies. Generational iniquity (in the form of genetic weaknesses) causes us all to "come from the factory," so to speak, with "broken parts" or infirmities already in our minds and/or bodies. If an easy entrance is not found within these pre-existing conditions, demons will endeavor to work on them until a portal eventually opens.

This may be what happened in Acts 5:1–11 where Ananias and Sapphira had the bad idea of agreeing to tempt the Holy Spirit. That opened them up to an attack from the evil spirit realm and the end result was their deaths. A few years ago while in India, I saw firsthand a similar situation. The Lord revealed to me that a particular pastor there was still praying to the gods of his village, even though he was born again and spirit filled. By God's grace, I was given the opportunity to confront him, and he repented and was spared the consequences.

Any act of disobedience against the Holy Spirit, any act of idol worship or consulting the evil spirit realm for knowledge, power, and/or authority can open a portal for a Christian to be demonized. This includes reading horoscopes or dialing psychic hotlines or seeking help on their websites. If you have done this, now is the time to repent and ask God's forgiveness. He is our help and source of strength and knowledge, and we must entrust our lives only to Him.

An open invitation is extended to the evil-spirit realm anytime someone asks Satan to do something for them that only God has the power to do. If we are tapping into any spiritual devices to find answers that can only be found in the Lord, then we could be in danger of this deception.

Demonization happens in the soul and body realm through deception. No one wakes up in the morning with the idea, "Okay, today I'm going to go out and get deceived. I can hardly wait to get tricked by the devil." It usually happens subtly and slowly.

> *Now the Spirit expressly says that in latter times some will depart from the faith, giving heed to deceiving [seducing] spirits and doctrines of demons, speaking lies in hypocrisy, having their own conscience seared with a hot iron.* *1 Timothy 4:1–2*

Demonic doctrines are contrary to Scripture but promoted by the world; e.g., alternative sexual lifestyles, drug and/or alcohol addictions, hurting or stealing from others to "get ahead," etc. Television sitcoms or movies that promote adultery or premarital sex fall into this category. Phrases like: "Be enlightened," "Be open-minded," "Think progressively," "Get with the times," "Everybody's doing it," or "If it feels good, do it," are all deceptive and seductive words that pressure people to indulge in sinful activities.

These ideas prey upon people's iniquity and/or ignorance. Even Christians can fall for these devices when their defenses are down through lack of scriptural nourishment, prayer, and fellowship with the Lord and the community of believers. Plus, the majority of Christians do not understand that they are spirit beings with spiritual power to fight off these spiritual attacks.

Doctrines of demons may also be taught via the examples set by those who are admired and respected. This is not exclusive to the secular realm; many Christians have also at some time succumbed to the wrongful influence of various church leaders and ended up either deceived and/or disillusioned as a consequence.

Whether we choose to fall into one of these traps or are naïvely deceived into it, a portal can open in either the mind or body to allow in one of those demons who has been looking for a new home. We do not need to fear them, but we do need to be on guard by keeping the truth in our hearts and in our walks.

Seducing Spirits

Seducing spirits are the ones that whisper to us, like the ones we see depicted in cartoons as a "devil" sitting on someone's shoulder.

The seduction lies in their ability to make us think that their words are actually coming from our minds—in other words, they sound like our thoughts. As spirit beings, we are in constant contact with the spirit realm, and we all have thought patterns that consistently run through our minds. As we begin to sharpen our spiritual senses through engrafting truth into those thought patterns, we will be able to discern between what comes from our spirit and what comes from our soul (mind). Once we ascertain that it is coming from our soul, we need to ask ourselves if it lines up with scriptural truth.

Not everything in our souls will be worldly; the more we nourish ourselves with the truth, the more our souls will produce truth-filled thoughts. If our thoughts disagree with Scripture, then we must lead them captive to the obedience of Christ.

> *For the weapons of our warfare are not carnal but mighty in God for pulling down strongholds, casting down arguments and every high thing that exalts itself against the knowledge of God, bringing every thought into captivity to the obedience of Christ.*
>
> *2 Corinthians 10:4–5a*

There is a difference between thinking and listening. Demons will often speak in the first person, causing their victim to believe that the words are coming from their minds. For instance, thoughts like "I am angry," or "I am depressed," or "I hate myself (or 'him' or 'her')," are probably demonically generated. This does not necessarily mean we are demonized; it could mean we are simply being influenced by worldly sources that have infiltrated our thinking.

Thoughts that are contrary to those of our loving, heavenly Father are coming from the opposite source; so when these kinds of thoughts start running through our minds, it is time to recognize that we are under a spiritual attack. If we do not discern what is really happening and we continue to allow those thoughts to dominate our thinking, then eventually a door (a portal) will be opened for that harassing demon to come into us rather than to just whisper in our ears. This is one way people can become demonized.

It is not unusual for Christians to be tempted this way, just as non-Christians are. Even Jesus had to fight off these kinds of attacks as seen in His 40 days in the wilderness, so why would we be exempt? The Scriptures also say that He was tempted in every way *we* are (Hebrews 4:15).

> *Now when the devil had ended every temptation [upon Jesus in the wilderness], he departed from Him* ***until an opportune time****.*
>
> *Luke 4:13*

The devil departed from Jesus "until an opportune time," meaning these 40 days in the wilderness was not the only time He was under spiritual attack. The most obvious future opportune time was in the Garden of Gethsemane right before He went to the cross, when He wrestled with the will of the Father to drink from the cup of suffering.

Demons have two immediate goals to gain entrance into our hearts or bodies: (1) to get our thoughts to agree with their words, and (2) to get us to vocalize those thoughts. Once they achieve these two goals, they are well on their way to entering our mind or body. From my own experience of expelling demons, I can attest that about 90% of them were expelled from the victims' mouths. I believe this is because that was also their entry point.

Typically, the same place demons gain entrance is where they will exit. If they entered through the eyes because the victim witnessed a traumatic event, they will then exit through that person's eyes. If they entered someone's ears when abusive words were shouted at them, then they will exit from their ears.

The main truth that we must cling to is that the One who is within us is far greater than these small and manageable evil spirits called demons. It is not that difficult to pull out the roots that initially allowed them entrance because we have the superior spirit of Christ in us, coupled with the authority He gave us to cast out demons.

Not only do we house the Holy Spirit (the great I Am) within us, but He has also supplied us with the resources of His angelic army. God's mighty angels battle in the spirit realm for us; and they obey His Word when it is spoken with faith.

> *Praise the LORD, you his angels, you mighty ones who do his bidding, who obey his word.* *Psalm 103:20 NIV*

This is why it is imperative that we learn the Word of God and speak it aloud. Even without a revelation word direct from the Lord, we can speak forth commandments of the Lord simply by speaking the written scriptures that pertain to our situation; and the angels will obey and carry out those words. This is not just for us but it is for those who come to us for help—we can help direct them to the verses that best apply to their weakness.

All of God's children are wonderful and beautiful in His sight. We are accepted in the Beloved, according to Ephesians 1:6. This could be literally translated as "endued with special honor" or "highly favored" in Christ. We are precious in God's sight and we are the apple of His eye (Deuteronomy 32:10; Psalm 17:8; Zechariah 2:8).

> *Yet in all these things we are more than conquerors through Him who loved us. For I am persuaded that neither death nor life, nor angels nor principalities nor powers, nor things present nor things to come, nor height nor depth, nor any other created thing, shall be able to separate us from the love of God which is in Christ Jesus our Lord.*
>
> *Romans 8:37–39*

In the spiritual battle, we can choose to be either the target of the enemy or one of the Lord's weapons. The Lord has given us dominion over the evil spirit realm, and once we understand how the enemy works and who his minions are, we will recognize how much greater our power is than theirs. The problems we face are not beyond our control because we have Christ in us, the hope of glory, and He is greater than anything in this life we could ever face.

Related Materials at LMCI.org

- Angels in the Army (Book)
- Closing Gates of Hell (Booklet)
- Exercising Spiritual Authority over Principalities & Powers (CD- or MP3-set)
- Exposing Sons of Belial (Booklet)
- God Damn Satan (Book)
- Mending Cracks in the Soul (Book, Audiobook, CD- or MP3-set)
- Perfect Redemption (Book, DVD- or CD-set)
- Principalities, Powers, and Demons (Free article in e-store)
- Understanding & Breaking the Schemes of the Devil (Book, E-book, CD- or MP3-set)

Relevant Points

1. What are some scriptures that declare our authority over evil spirits?

2. What did Jesus use to defeat Satan's temptations in the wilderness?

3. Write down three scripture references that can help you overcome a specific temptation in your life. Commit yourself to memorize at least one a week and check off each of the three references as you do so.

Chapter Nine

Closing Portals of Demonic Entry

As the Lord's kingdom enforcers, we need to understand how demons gain access into people's lives so that we can help them be set free. This chapter deals with seven common portals (open doors) through which demons are able to enter their victims' souls; and although there are probably more than these seven, I believe these are the major ones.

Once we begin to see how these doors are opened and closed, we will be able to more efficiently minister deliverance to those who desire it. The Lord has supplied the necessary knowledge and power to rescue those who have been victimized by demons and restore what was stolen from them. However, they must desire it enough to supply the repentance and obedience.

When demons attack and/or inhabit their victims, their main objective is to steal from and destroy them (John 10:10 and 1 Peter 5:8); but the Lord is the mighty deliverer who renews the vitality and life that is stolen and destroyed. My wife and I have witnessed this firsthand. Shortly after casting four demons out of a woman, my wife saw her at church and said she looked ten years younger. How humbled we were that the Lord used us to bring His deliverance to this woman—not only was she set free but her youth was restored in the process! The ministry of deliverance is exciting and rewarding, and every Christ follower has an opportunity to take part in it; however, it definitely helps to have some knowledge of how people get demonized in the first place.

There are definite spiritual rules that allow demonic portals to open in a person's life. If the earth is the Lord's and "all its fullness" (Psalm 24:1), then what allows a demon the right, or authority, to harass the earth's people? It has been done, and continues to be done, through deception—just as the serpent deceived Eve to start us all down the wrong road. However, there are also ancestral iniquities that must be considered, because these have weakened us all in different areas of our lives, allowing us to more readily be deceived in those places.

The original sin of Adam and Eve was the first act of disobedience that opened the door for Satan and his cohorts to have any rights at all on the earth. In like manner, the bottom line of authority for a demon to gain entry into any individual is the same today as it was then—*sin*.

A great example of this is an account I heard awhile back about a minister who was endeavoring to cast a demon out of a woman. In the midst of the situation, the demon exclaimed, "I don't have to come out of her—she *invited* me in!" The minister asked, "When was that?" and the demon replied, "When she watched that pornographic movie." Of course, in this case, the demon displayed his stupidity by actually revealing his entry point; but in most cases, we have to do a little more homework (unless the Holy Spirit reveals it to us).

Sinful actions can open a doorway for an evil spirit. Once the individual recognizes their sin and applies the blood of Jesus through repentance, the demon will come out. The Lord Almighty is never short on power, so if a demon refuses to leave, it might still have a legal right to be in that person. As we look at these seven major portals that allow demons to enter, we will see how they gained a legal right and how to take it back from them.

TRUCOPS

Since acronyms are helpful in recalling important truths, I like to use the acronym TRUCOPS to remember the seven basic portals of demonic entry. These seven are not the only portals demons use to gain access to an individual, but they offer a starting place for those who want to be free and set others free too. The understanding of it is as follows:

Portals of Entry into the Mind (Soul)
• T Trauma • R Rejection • U Unforgiveness • C Curses • O Occult practices • P Physical objects • S Sin

Not only does TRUCOPS help us to remember these seven portals, but it also reminds us who we are. When we act as God's representatives in setting the captives free, we are "true cops" (TRUCOPS), or kingdom enforcers, utilizing the power and authority Jesus has given us to subdue the evil spirit realm—to deliver ourselves and others from its deceptions and entanglements.

Demons will either work on people from the outside or from the inside. Outward demonic influences do not require expulsion; however, if they are not dealt with initially, they will eventually find their way in. At that point, they will need to be expelled.

Any one of these seven areas that have not been covered by the blood of Jesus Christ can be an open door to the enemy. Once these doors are closed, you can cast the evil spirit out and prohibit any future access.

Since the last letter in the acronym (S) represents Sin, which is the most common entry, we will start with that one and work backwards through the rest.

S—Sin

The Greek word for "sin" is *hamartia*, and it means "to miss the mark."[1] According to the Scriptures, there are three kinds of sins: sin, transgression, and iniquity.

A *sin* is an unintentional error—one of which the offender may later say, "I did not mean to do that," whereas a *transgression* is an intentional error—i.e., "I knew better, but I did it anyway." An *iniquity* is an inner weakness that makes us susceptible to repeating a particular transgression relative to the weakness. People usually justify this repetitive sin by considering it to be a part of their personality or identity. They may explain it away by saying, "It's just who I am." The only thing that eradicates all three of these (sin, transgression, and iniquity) is the blood of Jesus Christ; and this is why demons fear His blood so much.

NOTE: *Perfect Redemption* is a book I wrote a few years ago that deals with what Jesus did to set us free from sin, transgression, and iniquity. It will give a more indepth understanding of why and how we are able to walk in freedom from the power of sin over our lives.

Sin. One of the functions of the Holy Spirit is to convict us of sin. He obviously knows what is going on in our lives—even in the depths of our heart.

> *Nevertheless I tell you the truth. It is to your advantage that I go away; for if I do not go away, the Helper will not come to you; but if I depart, I will send Him to you. And when He has come, He will convict the world of sin, and of righteousness, and of judgment.*
> *John 16:7–8*

Not only will He convict us of sin, but He will also bring to our remembrance all things that He said to us (John 14:26). This means if we ignore Him when He convicts us the first time, He will bring it up again. However, we should humble ourselves to obey His guidance the first time, because our resistance to His conviction can allow more evil to come upon us. Continued resistance can also cause an unintentional sin to turn into a transgression. When we recognize His love for us, we will see that He convicts us of our sins for our own good—not to take away something we like to do or think that we need.

Some sins are blatant and some are hidden in our souls through our rationalization and human reasoning. We need the Lord's guidance to recognize those sins in our lives. (This was handled in chapter 3 under the subheading "The Conscience.")

The Holy Spirit is our best Helper. Although we can confess our sins to each other in the body of Christ and hold each other accountable, He is ultimately the One who perfectly reveals our sins to us. We can fool each other, and even ourselves, all day long; but we cannot fool Him. He will continue to peel back the layers and reveal what we need to repent of—if we will honestly respond to Him. However, if we don't respond, then He may choose to use a brother or sister to confront us. An example of this is found in the Old Testament when Nathan the prophet confronted David about his sins of adultery and murder (2 Samuel 12:1–12). When it comes to sins, transgressions, and iniquities in our lives, we should desire to cut the work short by humbling ourselves and asking God what we need to confess and repent of.

> *Nevertheless the solid foundation of God stands, having this seal: "The Lord knows those who are His," and, "Let everyone who names the name of Christ depart from iniquity."*
> *2 Timothy 2:19*

Once we confess our sin, we are responsible to truly repent by departing from it. Then we need to diligently guard our hearts from that point on in that area of weakness. Deliverance cannot be maintained without a strong desire to stay free. In order to walk away from our area of weakness and never return to it, we must view that particular sin as an enemy. We would not hang out around the campfire with our enemies—we would walk away from them. This is true repentance and true freedom.

The word "repentance" is the Greek word *metanoeo*, which literally means "to change the habit of your thinking." [2] It's more than saying, "I'm sorry"—*it is to never go back to that sin again.*

Transgression. If we begin nurturing fond thoughts of that enemy, we will devise ways to justify hanging out with it again, leading us into slavery once more. When we reach the point where we intentionally commit the sin and refuse to acknowledge it as such, we cross over the line from a sin to a transgression. However, if we call that sin what God calls it and declare war on it, He will rise up and attack it with you. *Sin is not our friend—it is our enemy.*

I sometimes think the reason believers struggle with sin is because our pictures are on the wall in the "devil's post office." When we were living in agreement with the world's ways, he had no reason to attack us so consistently. However, once we were delivered out of his kingdom and into the Lord's, he stepped up his efforts to destroy us because God's purposes have now become our desire. Ultimately, Satan is about destroying God's kingdom, and one way he can do that is by hindering us from fulfilling our spiritual destinies.

We must be diligent to keep the Scriptures first and foremost in our thinking so that we remain humble before the Lord and recognize His conviction in our hearts and acknowledge our sin.

> *How can a young man cleanse his way? By taking heed according to Your word. With my whole heart I have sought You; Oh, let me not wander from Your commandments! Your word I have hidden in my heart, That I might not sin against You.*
> *Psalm 119:9–11*

Iniquity. The transgressions that stem from iniquity are much more stubborn to deal with. This could be because the iniquity is so engrained within our physical genetics that it seems impossible to be rid of it. The four basic iniquities are fear, lust, anger, and pride; and each is a destroyer in a person's life.

The iniquity that we carried genetically into this life could have been from transgressions that were committed by our parents or grandparents, or even further back in our lineage. Exodus 34:6–7 says it can go back three or four generations.

> *And the LORD passed before him and proclaimed, "The LORD, the LORD God, merciful and gracious, longsuffering, and abounding in goodness and truth, keeping mercy for thousands, forgiving iniquity*

and transgression and sin, by no means clearing the guilty, visiting the iniquity of the fathers upon the children and the children's children to the third and the fourth generation."

Exodus 34:6–7

God is merciful and longsuffering, so He actually "pro-rates" the death penalty (Romans 6:23—"the wages of sin is death") that our ancestors deserved. Human life is corruptible and we will all die some day; but technically, we should all die at the moment of our first sin. Because of God's mercy that endures forever (Psalm 136), He rationed it through our future generational lines and allowed all of us to live out our earthly lives.

For all have sinned and fall short of the glory of God.

Romans 3:23

Iniquity is the recurrent place of sin. We should have been taught about this aspect of our lives in our first Sunday school class as children; but alas, it is rarely ever taught—even to adults. The door of iniquity is a slippery portal because it is one that demons are convinced is theirs. We must exercise spiritual authority to overcome this area of our lives and keep it closed.

The portion (iniquity) that each of us received through the transgressions of our ancestors is in the form of a genetic weakness that makes us especially susceptible to sinning in that area of our life. For example, you may find yourself to be an especially fearful person because you received an iniquity of fear. This could play out in an obvious way in your life, causing you to have anxiety attacks, for instance. However, it can also play out in a more subtle way, leading to sins of omission—like not paying your tithes for fear you won't have enough provision; or not being a witness for Christ or standing up for unpopular truths because of what others may think. It could also cause you to seek approval from others more than from God, making you a "man pleaser."

Someone else may have received an iniquity of lust, which can manifest itself as gluttony, alcoholism, gambling, adultery, masturbation, etc.

The iniquity of anger could lead to road rage, child abuse, a disagreeable or judgmental attitude, gossip, etc. If not tempered or nullified through the acceptance of what Jesus accomplished for us, it could even ultimately lead to murder.

Pride is probably the most deceptive iniquity that someone could have, because its very nature denies its existence. It declares, "There is nothing wrong with me." Pride refuses to consider any error, and the individual is convinced that he or she is just fine. The iniquity of pride can lead to apathy, egotism, narcissism, or a superiority complex, etc. It may manifest itself through elitism, such as gender or racial discrimination, because the individual is convinced that they are better than others.

If any of the attitudes or sins mentioned under these four major iniquities is perpetually present in your life and seems beyond your control, then it is likely due to a generational iniquity that has not been surrendered to the Lord. He has already conquered it at the cross; but if we do not believe and receive what He did for us, we will not rise up to overcome it in our lives. We will lack control over our spirits and be defenseless and weak as Proverbs 25:28 says.

> *Whoever has no rule over his own spirit is like a city broken down, without walls.* *Proverbs 25:28*

Jesus spoke of the increase of iniquity in the last days:

> *And because iniquity shall abound, the love of many shall wax cold.*
> *Matthew 24:12 KJV*

This verse shows the power of iniquity—it can actually cause love to wax cold. The devil is hard at work during these last days to cause people's iniquities to abound and come to the surface. Second Thessalonians 2:7 indicates that his ultimate agent—the antichrist—will bring the mystery of iniquity into full completion.

The good news for all mankind is that Jesus was bruised, which indicates internal bleeding, for our iniquity.

> *But He [Jesus] was wounded for our transgressions, He was bruised for our iniquities; the chastisement for our peace was upon Him, and by His stripes we are healed.* *Isaiah 53:5*

His bruising for our iniquity enables us to break free from its control. It's natural to identify ourselves by the iniquity that was handed down to us from our ancestors because of their sin. We might even justify our own sins by saying, "that's just the way I am—that's my personality," or even, "that's who I am because I was born that way." In other words, we find our identity within our iniquities; and this is one of the first lies we need to undo. Our iniquity does *not* define who we are. **The truth is that we are God's masterpiece, bought back from the devil's power and his deception.**

> *Therefore, if anyone is in Christ, he is a new creation; old things have passed away; behold, all things have become new.*
> *2 Corinthians 5:17*

We are new creations whose inner spiritual longing is to please the Lord. Jesus did not seek His own will, but the will of the Father (John 5:30); He always desired to do His Father's will, and it is His spirit that now dwells within us. Although He was "in all points tempted as we are," He never sinned (Hebrews 4:15). He is the "lamb without blemish and without spot" (1 Peter 1:19); and He became the perfect payment for all of the iniquity, sin, and transgression of the entire world.

Repent of your sins.

P—Physical Objects

As we continue backwards through the TRUCOPS acronym of demonic portals, we come to "P," which represents **P**hysical objects. The use, or ownership, of certain physical objects can give evil spirits entry rights into someone. I learned this while ministering deliverance and healing to women in India—if they kept certain pieces of jewelry on, the evil spirits would not leave. It's as if someone fastened a sign to them that read, "This is my property." Some of the jewelry these women wore was connected to the worship of false gods, which are abundant in India. They may not have been aware of the spiritual connotations of the jewelry, but they still opened a demonic portal by wearing it. The same holds true with certain body piercings and tattoos, which may also involve a spirit of rebellion.

Once during a deliverance service, a young girl began thrashing about because the demon within her was refusing to come out. When one of the ministers pulled her toe ring off, the evil spirit came right out of her. This particular ring was a cursed object that gave the demon a legal right to be in her.

A woman with self-inflicted wounds once came to me for prayer. Besides the obvious razor cuts and cigarette burns on her arms, I noticed that she was wearing a yin yang charm on a necklace. When I asked her about it, she told me it was a gift from a friend.

I said, "It may have been a gift, but your 'friend' could possibly be a witch, or perhaps she purchased it from one." At that point, the woman realized her problems began around the same time she received the necklace. Another possible portal that gave access to the demon was a crescent moon and star tattooed on her ankle. (The crescent moon and star is considered a sorcerers' sign.)

Receiving inappropriate gifts, as this woman did, can be the source of cutting off the blessings of God. We can find ourselves in a downward spiral because of physical objects on our bodies or in our homes that God does not want us to have anything to do with.

A scriptural example of cursed objects brought into a home is found in Judges 8:4–27 when Gideon took several things from the Midianites that brought "a snare to Gideon and to his house." Seemingly innocent artifacts, souvenirs, compact discs, paintings, photographs, tapestries, figurines of people or animals, clothing, and/or insignias (logos) that have been sewn onto articles of clothing, etc., could be open to demonic influence, depending upon their origin, symbolism, and/or curses spoken over them.

> *And you, by all means keep yourselves from the accursed things, lest you become accursed when you take of the accursed things, and make the camp of Israel a curse, and trouble it.*
>
> *Joshua 6:18*

> *You shall burn the carved images of their gods with fire; you shall not covet the silver or gold that is on them, nor take it for yourselves, lest you be snared by it; for it is an abomination to the LORD your God. Nor shall you bring an abomination into your house, lest you be doomed to destruction like it; but you shall utterly detest it and utterly abhor it, for it is an accursed thing.*
>
> *Deuteronomy 7:25–26*

Remember, the Spirit of God will convict us of sin. He will show us if there is anything in our homes that should not be there. If a close friend or relative gives us something that doesn't glorify God and we don't want to offend them by throwing it away—watch out! This can be a snare to keeping something that could ultimately bring destruction into our lives. For example, why would a Christian have an image of an African war god hanging in the entrance way of their home? This is the type of physical object that can invite evil spirits into their lives. I believe the same holds true for "dream" catchers; these innocent looking decorations do not catch dreams—they catch demons (seriously).

Get rid of spiritual junk, remove any body piercings that are questionable, and do not get a tattoo. If there are tattoos present now on your body, then anoint them with oil and pray over them.

In the book of Acts, the early Christians realized the significance of such trinkets and possessions and actually burnt any that fell into this category. We can free ourselves from physical objects that legally allow evil spirits to influence us and our families.

> *And many who had believed came confessing and telling their deeds. Also, many of those who had practiced magic brought their books together and burned them in the sight of all. And they counted up the value of them, and it totaled fifty thousand pieces of silver. So the word of the Lord grew mightily and prevailed.*
>
> *Acts 19:18–20*

O—Occult Practices

Occult practices are mentioned early in the Scriptures (Genesis 31:19) and deal with the worship of strange gods, idols, and/or false gods. Even if we have not participated in any occult activities within our own lives, there are curses that can be passed down to us from ancestors who have. For instance, a great-grandfather could have been a warlock or perhaps your grandmother was a medium. Either of these is sufficient to bring a curse on you even before you were born.

Some of us may have participated in occult practices without realizing it. For instance, Ouija boards are used by witches who call them "witch boards;" and playing with them even in innocence can have dangerous spiritual repercussions. Reading horoscopes and fortune cookies are other examples of apparently innocuous activities. Though they are regarded as harmless, they can produce negative consequences in our lives.

Some people find séances entertaining, while others conduct them to seriously explore the spirit realm. But Scripture verifies that God condemns those who try to contact the spirits of the dead (necromancy) and considers them an abomination to Him.

> *There shall not be found among you any one that maketh his son or his daughter to pass through the fire, or that useth divination, or an observer of times, or an enchanter, or a witch. Or a charmer, or a consulter with familiar spirits, or a wizard, or a necromancer.* ***For all that do these things are an abomination unto the LORD****: and because of these abominations the LORD thy God doth drive them out from before thee.* *Deuteronomy 18:10–12 KJV*

Regardless of whether it was our ancestors or ourselves that participated in the occult, the blood of Jesus is stronger than any demon and the solution is the same: emphatically renounce the invitation to the demon, rebuke it, and command that it leaves in the name of Jesus Christ. Aggressively and relentlessly claim your freedom in the name and blood of Jesus and go on the offense with the sword of the Spirit by memorizing, quoting, and fearlessly utilizing victorious Bible verses that are appropriate to your situation.

C—Curses

Curses open another major portal of demonic entry—in truth, they can open a huge lesion—that needs to be dealt with and closed. The "art" of cursing is little known and/or practiced in the US; but this does not mean that it is not done here, albeit in less obvious ways.

Curses are basically word tools or weapons that are used against people, generally invoking a demon and/or opening a door for one. They can cause great harm to a person's soul if spoken by someone he or she looks up to as an authoritative figure in their life. This is why parents, teachers, spouses, and/or religious leaders need to be wise and loving with the words they speak to those in their spheres of influence. These are just a few examples of those whose words are generally accepted and believed—whether they are positive or negative.

During a deliverance service, the Holy Spirit revealed to a man that he had been cursed by his third-grade teacher when she said, "You are retarded." When he accepted her words as truth, a portal was opened for a demon to enter him and cause him to be dyslexic. Once the Holy Spirit revealed this to him, he was able to forgive the teacher and receive deliverance. Praise God, this man went on to become a successful college graduate!

Curses spoken by parents against their children are extremely powerful. The words of a spouse can also deeply hurt the husband or wife to whom they are spoken. For example, a husband who is critical of his wife may say, "Honey, you can't cook—you burn everything!" Even when words like this are spoken as a joke, they can still have a negative effect upon a sensitive soul. As Christians, we have probably also witnessed spiritual leaders who have wrongfully cursed others—perhaps peers they were jealous of or people within their congregation. Many times, pride is the underlying cause that prompts them to speak like this. Ironically, that same pride often prevents them from repenting of their unrighteous words.

When Jesus is our first love, His words will take precedence over anyone else's. If we esteem the words of another above His words, then we are in danger of being spellbound.

> *Princes also sit and speak against me, But Your servant meditates on Your statutes.* *Psalm 119:23*

As we meditate on His words, it will not matter what anyone else says to us or about us. This takes time, but then so does deception. As informed Christians, we are not generally deceived quickly; it usually works its way into our thoughts through words spoken over a period of time. But we can overcome the deception of the accuser's words by meditating upon the words of the One who loves us.

It is critical also that we forgive those who have spoken curses against us, as we will see in the next part of the TRUCOPS acronym. Forgiveness takes away the power of these words and prevents the executioner from controlling us.

U—Unforgiveness

Unforgiveness is a poison that embitters and hardens the soul. Sadly, this element is so common in people's souls that it has become probably the most prevalent demonic portal.

> *Then his master, after he had called him, said to him, "You wicked servant! I forgave you all that debt because you begged me. Should you not also have had compassion on your fellow servant, just as I had pity on you?" And his master was angry, and delivered him to the torturers until he should pay all that was due to him. So My heavenly Father also will do to you if each of you, from his heart, does not forgive his brother his trespasses.* Matthew 18:32–35

In Matthew 6, Jesus speaks of forgiving those who have sinned against us, referring to the sin as a "debt."

> *And forgive us our debts, as we forgive our debtors.*
> Matthew 6:12

And in Luke 11, He speaks of those who have sinned against us as being "indebted to us."

> *And forgive us our sins, for we also forgive everyone who is indebted to us.* Luke 11:4a

When we feel we have been wronged in some way and do not take the high road of forgiveness toward the alleged offender, bitterness and resentment eventually take root within our souls. We believe the other person owes us—that they are indebted to us—and we write out a mental IOU against them.

A woman once shared with me how much she hated her ex-husband. Even though her feelings were justified, since he had slept with her mother and succeeded in legally gaining full custody of their children, I still knew that the hatred was poisoning her soul. When I found out the offense was 15 years old at the time, I asked her if she wanted to give him the next 15 years of her life as well. At first she didn't understand, but as I went on to explain that the bitterness in her soul was robbing her of life and would continue to do so if she did not forgive, she got it.

Forgiveness is a decision, not an emotion. If we wait until we feel like it, it may never happen. Forgiveness comes out of our spirits—not our souls. Our will is housed within our spirit, and we must will ourselves to forgive. Emotions come from the soul, but your spirit is superior to your soul. *We choose to forgive.*

Genuine forgiveness is the opposite of emotional blackmail. We do not continue to beat others up for how we think they have wronged us. We may think we are enslaving them by holding that IOU against them, but in reality, we are the ones who are enslaved to the bitterness in our souls. Let it go and be free! Someone once said that not forgiving is like drinking rat poison and then waiting for the rat to die. In other words, when we refuse to forgive, the resulting bitterness is like a poison within us. We think we're hurting the offenders by holding a grudge against them; but in reality, we are the ones who get hurt.

Give the IOU to Jesus and let Him be the collector. If the person does not repent, Jesus will take care of it in a just and righteous way because He is the righteous judge.

R—Rejection

We have all experienced rejection at one time or another and may think we deserve a pity party. But when we behold Jesus and His sufferings, we realize no one has ever been rejected as badly as He was—and He did nothing to deserve it. He was tempted in all points, yet never sinned; and He always did the Father's will. Yet the world rejected and crucified Him.

> *He is despised and rejected by men, a man of sorrows and acquainted with grief. And we hid, as it were, our faces from Him; He was despised, and we did not esteem Him. Surely He has borne our griefs and carried our sorrows; yet we esteemed Him stricken, smitten by God, and afflicted. But He was wounded for our transgressions, He was bruised for our iniquities; the chastisement for our peace was upon Him, and by His stripes we are healed. All we like sheep have gone astray; we have turned, every one, to his own way; and the LORD has laid on Him the iniquity of us all. He was oppressed and He was afflicted, yet He opened not His mouth; He was led as a lamb to the slaughter, and as a sheep before its shearers is silent, so He opened not his mouth.* *Isaiah 53:3–7*

> *For we do not have a High Priest who cannot sympathize with our weaknesses, but was in all points tempted as we are, yet without sin.*
> *Hebrews 4:15*

He took all the rejection anyone could ever face; but He has accepted you.

> *To the praise of the glory of His grace, by which He has made us accepted in the Beloved.* *Ephesians 1:6*

> *For both He who sanctifies and those who are being sanctified are all of one, for which reason He is not ashamed to call them brethren.*
> *Hebrews 2:11*

Jesus is the remedy for rejection. We need a spiritual revelation of His love for us. Our worth does not come from the acceptance or love of people, but from His love. His love is so deep for us that He paid the highest possible price to win us—His life. This makes us the most costly commodity in all creation. When someone rejects us, they are rejecting a treasure worth more than all the wealth of the world.

Knowing that you were not redeemed with corruptible things, like silver or gold, from your aimless conduct received by tradition from your fathers, but with the precious blood of Christ, as of a lamb without blemish and without spot. 1 Peter 1:18–19

You were bought at a price; do not become slaves of men. 1 Corinthians 7:23

For you were bought at a price; therefore glorify God in your body and in your spirit, which are God's. 1 Corinthians 6:20

Nothing we can do can keep people from rejecting us; but when we receive a revelation of God's love for us and become more focused on what He thinks of us than what people think of us, we will be free! This change in our thinking will close that portal (and keep it closed) faster than anything else.

T—Trauma

Trauma can cause fractures to develop within our souls (minds). A car accident, an act of violence (whether we were involved in it or witnessed it), physical or emotional abuse, or even something as seemingly insignificant as being embarrassed by a teacher in school can all cause trauma. A trauma leaves a dominant fearful memory in the mind, which can be triggered by a physical and/or emotional shock to open the door for demons to come in. Traumas are major portals of entry for evil spirits—especially for spirits of fear. Demons can enter these breaches and live in that area of injury.

A wholesome tongue is a tree of life: but perverseness therein is a breach in the spirit. Proverbs 15:4 KJV

Although the following verse in Ecclesiastes is in reference to unintentional sin or deliberate transgression, the same principle holds true. A trauma is like a broken hedge in the soul, and when there is a broken hedge, a serpent (demon) can enter.

> *He who diggeth a pit shall fall into it; and whoso breaketh an hedge, a serpent shall bite him.* *Ecclesiastes 10:8 KJV*

A major area of trauma for many people is rejection, which we just covered. A situation in which a person was (or even felt) betrayed or forsaken by someone they trusted causes a deep traumatic fissure in the soul. The "perpetrator" may have even done this innocently or inadvertently. For instance, a woman I was ministering to shared that when she got into heavy traffic, she would have serious panic attacks. As I was praying I asked the Holy Spirit to bring back to her mind what originally caused this situation. The Holy Spirit revealed to her that when she was a young girl, she was involved in a car accident with her mother. I then asked the Lord to reveal to her where He (Jesus) was when the accident happened. He faithfully showed this woman that He was sitting in the car with her. The horror of that situation became instead a memory of protection from the Lord, transforming it into a revelation of Jesus' presence in her life instead of a memory of betrayal (rejection) and/or fear.

Our minds are very complex; and no one really understands the depth of what has happened in our souls except the Lord. Extreme trauma can cause schizophrenia, which is multiple or fragmented personalities. Incidents of horror, shock, and trauma can crack the soul, allowing a demon (or demons) to take up residency within the distorted memories etched into your mind.

In these kinds of situations, the healing is usually not a one-time fix, but an ongoing process that the Holy Spirit will continue to do if we allow Him to. This could take years of Him bringing back past memories that have caused us to be dysfunctional in certain ways. The emotion behind the memory is the key to detecting the evil spirit that hides within it. Long time feelings of anger, abandonment, rejection, shame—all of these emotions can be followed to disclose the source. The Lord can reveal Himself in those places that just "won't let go." When we see the truth He shows us concerning the situation, the lies that were perpetrated in our souls will be dispelled.[3] The truths of His peace and comfort will take the place of those lies, for He has promised to not leave us comfortless.

> *I will not leave you comfortless: I will come to you.*
> *John 14:18*

Maintaining Deliverance

In order to minister deliverance correctly, we need to follow in the steps of our example—Jesus Christ, *the* deliverer. After He cast out the demons from the madman of Gadara, we see Him doing something very significant to maintaining this man's deliverance (Mark 5:1–20; Luke 8:26–39). In Luke 8:35, we find the man "sitting at the feet of Jesus," which indicates a master teaching a student in their culture. I believe that Jesus was teaching him how to keep the door closed to the enemy. A newly delivered person desperately needs to know how to do this, because if the demon is allowed to return, he will bring others with him.

> *Then he goes and takes with him seven other spirits more wicked than himself, and they enter and dwell there; and the last state of that man is worse than the first.* *Matthew 12:45a*

If the door through which the demon(s) originally entered is not locked shut, it (or they) could return in greater force, making the last state of that person worse than the first.

The Lord is on our side, and with His help we can be set free and help others to be free. No Christ follower should remain enslaved to any evil thing that has controlled them in the past. We all need to come to the feet of Jesus and allow Him to deal with each of us personally. Only He has the power to deliver us, and freedom is vital if we want to be able to follow Him.

> *And he said: "The LORD is my rock, my fortress and my deliverer."*
> *2 Samuel 22:2*

NOTE: In my live classes,[4] I make available a deliverance service to cast out demons and close the portals. This would be difficult to do through a book; however, I do also have a recorded class entitled "Discerning of Spirits and Casting Out Demons" that quite adequately handles this.

Demons gain entrance to people through portals, which are doorways that can be opened to the soul or body through a variety of ways. By learning what these major portals are and how they can be opened and closed, we can learn how to free ourselves and others through the power of the Holy Spirit.

Related Materials at LMCI.org

- Discerning of Spirits and Casting Out Demons (CD- or MP3-set)
- Exposing Sons of Belial (Booklet)
- God Damn Satan (Book)
- Mending Cracks in the Soul (Book, Audiobook, CD- or MP3-set)
- Perfect Redemption (Book, DVD- or CD-set)
- Quantum Physics, continued: Entanglement/Entrainment/Observation (CD or MP3)
- T.R.U.C.O.P.S. (E-book)
- Understanding & Breaking the Schemes of the Devil (Booklet, E-book, CD- or MP3-set)
- Victory over Iniquity (Free article in e-store)

Relevant Points

1. What are the seven portals represented by the acronym TRUCOPS?

2. ________________ actions can open a ________________ for an evil spirit.

3. What is indicated from Luke 8:35 that is essential to keeping the door(s) shut after expelling a demon or demons?

PART FOUR

OUR AUTHORITY TO RE-PRESENT JESUS IN CHARACTER

Chapter Ten

Developing the Character of Christ

Some Christians think that once they are born again, the rest of their lives will be a stroll through Grace Park. They don't believe they need to change anything about their lifestyles—they are going to heaven by grace and can therefore continue doing the same things they always did.

This kind of thinking needs some serious adjustment. If we're going to grow up in Christ as He desires us to, we have to be determined to do whatever it takes to be like Him. *This requires daily training and discipline.* The fictional character of Rocky Balboa serves as a great example of someone training to become a champion. Remember the original *Rocky* movie where he first makes that decision? Instead of slouching around like he did before, he begins a strict regimen.

A similar lifestyle change should be evident in our lives. When we first came to Christ, we made Him the new Lord of our lives. This means that we should have repented of our old ways. However, true repentance is more than confessing our sin and saying we're sorry; there should be a real change in our lives, just as evidenced in Rocky's. The proof of his commitment was seen in his daily regimen of waking up early, donning his grungy T-shirt, cracking those eggs into a glass and gulping them down. Even more convincing proof was his frozen-beef-carcass punching-bag workout in a meat locker and daily run up the 72 front steps of the

Philadelphia Museum of Art. After a while, however, he realized there was a limit to what he could do on his own; and that's when Mickey—his manager/personal trainer—became an integral part of his life.

Those who have tried to live righteously before making Christ their Lord and Savior know how unattainable it is. Once He resides in us through the Holy Spirit, however, the work becomes much easier. The Holy Spirit becomes our manager and personal trainer, giving us the grace—the empowerment—to discipline ourselves to live a holy life. As we submit to Christ, His Holy Spirit supernaturally changes us from the inside out. However, there is still a lot to do from our end as we follow His leading and instruction; and this is where discipline and diligence comes in. The Holy Spirit will train us, but it's still our responsibility to obey His instruction. While He is patient, He is also holy and expects us to be the same (1 Peter 1:15–16).

Growing Up

When the Holy Spirit indwells us, He becomes our leader, our manager, and our personal trainer. On the Day of Pentecost, Peter quoted this from the book of Joel to let everyone know that this prophecy was coming to pass in front of their eyes. God had poured out His Spirit that day.

> *And it shall come to pass in the last days, says God, That I will pour out of My Spirit [the Holy Spirit] on all flesh; your sons and your daughters shall prophesy, your young men shall see visions, your old men shall dream dreams. And on My menservants and on My maidservants I will pour out My Spirit in those days; and they shall prophesy.* *Acts 2:17–18*

Although the prophecy appears to address different age groups, I believe the deeper meaning is the potential spiritual growth process available to every child of God. When God poured His Spirit out on the Day of Pentecost, it gave all His sons and daughters the ability to prophesy; however, most of us did not start prophesying immediately because we needed time to mature.

It also says that "your young men shall see visions." Prophecy can be inspired from the spirit dwelling within us; however, visions must come from *the* Holy Spirit (the Father, not the gift) to the indwelling spirit. This moves us from inspiration to revelation.

The variations in maturity noted in these verses indicate points of spiritual growth in our lives and our ability to receive either inspiration or revelation in various forms based on where we are. The spiritual growth process takes us from the new birth to different levels of maturity. As we obey our personal trainer and discipline ourselves to His ways, we will go through the necessary training to overcome our sin and the world and run our race successfully to the end.

This growth process is also mentioned in 1 John 2:12–14.

> *I write to you, little children, because your sins are forgiven you for His name's sake. I write to you, fathers, because you have known Him who is from the beginning. I write to you, young men, because you have overcome the wicked one. I write to you, little children, because you have known the Father. I have written to you, fathers, because you have known Him who is from the beginning. I have written to you, young men, because you are strong, and the word of God abides in you, and you have overcome the wicked one.*
>
> *1 John 2:12–14*

Verse 13 tells us that the "little children" have "known the Father;" whereas, verse 14 tells us that the "fathers" have "known Him who is from the beginning." Even though both are speaking of an experiential knowledge (from the Greek word *ginosko*), they reveal two different levels that are determined by maturity. The children's knowledge of the Father is from a personal experience of their new birth and His love to save them. The fathers, on the other hand, have a deeper understanding and experiential knowledge of God that begins to comprehend His eternal being, as "Him who is from the beginning." This is an intimacy not yet developed by newborn babes in Christ.

Young men have disciplined themselves to not purposely sin. That doesn't mean they never sin, because 1 John clearly states that if we say we don't sin, we are deceiving ourselves and calling God a liar (1 John 1:8–10). However, young men are those who have "overcome the wicked one," indicating true repentance—an intentional turning away from sin. The word "overcome" comes from the Greek word *nikao*, which means "to conquer." The root word is *nike*, meaning "victory,"[1] and was apparently the inspiration for the athletic supply company of the same name. Nike's slogan is "just do it," which is basically what it takes for Christians to overcome the wicked one. If we are going to conquer sin in our lives, we must determine to *just do it* God's way, no matter what. That sounds simple, but with the Holy Spirit's help we can make those moment-by-moment decisions to become the super-conquerors spoken of in Romans 8:37. Without Him, we do not have the necessary strength to resist and flee from sin to be more than conquerors. Only through Him can we receive the wisdom and empowerment to train and run our race.

> *Yet in all these things we are more than conquerors* ***through Him*** *who loved us.* *Romans 8:37*

Putting on the Whole Armor of God

The armor of God (Ephesians 6:10–18) provides us with the training gear that we need to run the spiritual race from start to finish. Verse 10 tells us that we are strong in the power of the Lord's might. Verse 11 informs us that when we put on His whole armor, we are able "to stand against the wiles of the devil."

The armor of God keeps us holy in our souls. Each part we put on helps us to live a life of obedience to God. We can also submit ourselves to God and receive grace from Him to resist the devil.

> *But He gives more grace. Therefore He says: "God resists the proud, but gives grace to the humble." Therefore submit to God. Resist the devil and he will flee from you.* *James 4:6–7*

We have already seen that although it is our flesh that often wants to sin, our wrestling match is not against flesh-and-blood opponents, according to Ephesians 6:12. Instead, we war against evil spirits; and this is why we need God's spiritual armor as our gear—not just during our training, but within the competition (the race set before us) itself. It's important to know that the battle is ongoing, even if we think we are merely training. It's never one or the other, but rather both.

God's admonition of putting on His whole armor begins in Ephesians 6:13.

> *Therefore take up the whole armor of God, that you may be able to withstand in the evil day, and having done all, to stand. Stand therefore, having girded your waist with* ***truth****, having put on the breastplate of* ***righteousness****, and having shod your feet with the* ***preparation of the gospel of peace****; above all, taking the shield*

> *of* ***faith*** *with which you will be able to quench all the fiery darts of the wicked one. And take the helmet of* ***salvation****, and the sword of the Spirit, which is* ***the word of God****; praying always with all* ***prayer*** *and supplication in the Spirit, being watchful to this end with all perseverance and supplication for all the saints.*
>
> *Ephesians 6:13–18*

These are our armaments:

- **Truth**—to gird our loins (defensive)
- **Righteousness**—as our breastplate to guard our heart (defensive)
- **Preparation of the gospel of peace**—to cover our feet (offensive)
- **Faith**—as our shield to ward off the enemy's fiery darts (defensive)
- **Salvation**—as a helmet to cover our heads (defensive)
- **Word of God**—as our sword of the Spirit (offensive)
- **Prayer**—for the believers (offensive)

Prayer

Prayer is a part of the armor not usually mentioned and yet we are admonished to pray *always*. We can never overstate the significance of this spiritual weapon. The way we encroach upon and hold back the devil's kingdom is through prayer, and it is a vital part of our job description as we work at our Father's business. When we bring others before Him in intercession, we are growing up in Him. We are no longer children who are sitting at home being coddled—we are out there fighting and laboring in prayer to see His kingdom come, His will be done.

Prayer is where we begin to learn about the spirit realm by discerning the Holy Spirit's voice, as well as recognizing when it's not His voice. Prayer is also what invites God to enter into the fray.

There are those who believe that because God is sovereign and can do whatever He wants, there is no real need to pray; yet He tells us to pray. *By His sovereign will, He has made our prayers a part of His plan of action.*

It was His decision to put man in authority over this planet. We are citizens of the kingdom of heaven through the new birth; but we have been commissioned to earth as its caretakers—as those who can subdue all aspects of His creation. Prayer is a huge part of this because, in and of ourselves, we do not have the strength to subdue much at all.

Jesus Christ has command over the angels, and He is the Head of His body. Through the Holy Spirit, He tells us what to pray for. When we pray according to His leading, He sends the angelic might and strength to accomplish His will. Although we know He can do whatever He wants, it's *guaranteed* that He will do it if He's led us to pray for it.

> *Now this is the confidence that we have in Him, that if we ask anything according to His will, He hears us. And if we know that He hears us, whatever we ask, we know that we have the petitions that we have asked of Him.* *1 John 5:14–15*

The Father's business is made clear in what most refer to as The Lord's Prayer—"Your kingdom come, Your will be done, on earth as it is in heaven." The Lord's Prayer can be thought of as the bylaws of His business. In other words, His business (which is also the family of God's business) is to bring heaven onto earth—to subdue this planet and bring it under the authority of the Lord Jesus Christ. We are here in His stead to do what He has enabled us to do on His behalf. Amazingly, He has given us the authority to have dominion over the works of His hands.

The Bible says that Satan is the god of this world (2 Corinthians 4:4 KJV), which means he has successfully usurped our job. He's not going to give it back without a fight, and this is why he does everything he can to distract us from praying. When we pray with faith and authority, we are taking back what is rightfully ours. He has trespassed and we are coming to reclaim our land.

One of the lies that most American Christians have bought hook, line, and sinker is that we don't have time to pray. Even if we don't put it in those words, our actions bear witness that we have swallowed that logic. We often speed through our prayer time or feel inconvenienced in having to stop and take the time for it. We must recognize that we are here to subdue this place—that this is one of our main purposes, second only to our fellowship with our Creator (which, by the way, is another aspect of prayer).

> *So God created man in His own image; in the image of God He created him; male and female He created them. Then God blessed them, and God said to them, "Be fruitful and multiply; fill the earth and subdue it; have dominion over the fish of the sea, over the birds of the air, and over every living thing that moves on the earth."*
>
> *Genesis 1:27–28*

If we think this was only for Adam and Eve, then we need to read Psalm 8:4–8.

> *What are mortals that you should think of us, mere humans that you should care for us? For you made us only a little lower than God,*

> *and you crowned us with glory and honor. You put us in charge of everything you made, giving us authority over all things—the sheep and the cattle and all the wild animals, the birds in the sky, the fish in the sea, and everything that swims the ocean currents.*
>
> *Psalm 8:4–8* NLT

One of the major ways to bring heaven down to earth, to subdue this planet and everything in it under the rule of Jesus Christ, is through prayer. How can we not have time to do what we were born to do? It's easy to see why the god of this world would try to talk us out of this all-important mandate.

Do we want to be about our Father's business? Then, let's exercise our spiritual authority and unleash the power of God by binding evil spirits and loosing God's angels to spring into action. This not only keeps us in the race and in shape; but it's also in our job description—we are His employees, His servants, His people—and we are to be about His business. *Just do it!*

Prayer is also one of the ways we can minister to the Lord. The Lord responded to Cornelius' prayers in Acts 10:1–5 by saying that they had come up before Him as a memorial. To minister to the Lord means to give ourselves totally and wholly to Him. He loves our worship, our appreciation, and our praise of Him. It takes our minds off ourselves and puts them onto Him instead; and He can fill us up and use us in amazing ways as we do this.

The pastor of a mega church of 25,000 people in Texas was once asked the secret to his success. He shared how his time with the Lord is his first scheduled appointment every single day, no matter what else is on the agenda that day. He knows that he must first minister to the Lord in order to have what it takes to minister to His people. No matter what we are called to do, we need a strong prayer life in order to fulfill it.

Does your career have you by the throat? Are you so worn out that you don't have time for Him? If we literally do not have time to pray, then we need to realign our lives and cut out some of our nonproductive pursuits. There will be no rewards in heaven for activities that came out of our own strength and desire; the only rewards will be for what we did through and for Him.

As born-again (saved) Christ followers, we are citizens of heaven who were sent to earth to bring our country here. We are legal, *not* illegal, immigrants because we have the authority of the earth's Creator to do this. We can do this if we will focus and discipline ourselves to do the Father's will. This is why we need the Holy Spirit—He is our helper (personal trainer) to strengthen and direct us in this critical effort. He takes away our excuses not to pray.

There are times when, in the spirit realm, I have seen (as have others) angels standing around with their arms folded across their chests because they are not released to do anything. What releases them? Our prayers! Jesus said that we could bind and loose; and within that is the authority to bind evil spirits and loose God's angels to spring into action.

> *Assuredly, I say to you, whatever you bind on earth will be bound in heaven, and whatever you loose on earth will be loosed in heaven.*
> *Matthew 18:18*

Fasting and Prayer

Ministering to the Lord through prayer is sometimes accompanied by fasting, as we can see in Acts 13:2. Fasting helps to cultivate the focus of our minds upon the spiritual, rather than the physical. We are not distracted by food and the satisfaction it gives our taste buds. Fasting is not optional, according to Jesus in Matthew 6:16–18; it is expected of us.

> *Moreover,* ***when*** *you fast, do not be like the hypocrites, with a sad countenance. For they disfigure their faces that they may appear to men to be fasting. Assuredly, I say to you, they have their reward. But you,* ***when*** *you fast, anoint your head and wash your face, so that you do not appear to men to be fasting, but to your Father who is in the secret place; and your Father who sees in secret will reward you openly.*
> *Matthew 6:16–18*

There can also be great health benefits from fasting as well, when done correctly. We will be judged for our stewardship someday, including the stewardship of our earthly tabernacles. Remember the verse we read earlier about abstaining from fleshly lusts which war against the soul?

> *Beloved, I beg you as sojourners and pilgrims, abstain from fleshly lusts which war against the soul.* *1 Peter 2:11*

"Abstain" is "to hold one's self off."[2] When we fast, we hold ourselves off food. The mind becomes the boss of the body, as it should be. When the mind is disciplined to control that aspect of life, other areas will line up as well. We will discover a new level of temperance in our lives, making us less likely to fall into fleshly lusts that war against our souls.

God has probably never worked with people as weak as those in the United States. Although fasting is a great way to gain control of our bodies, most people within the western civilization would have a hard time with it. Our flesh is weak and complains about what it wants, so we have to tell it to shut up. Remember that Jesus fasted for 40 days; yet it's difficult for most of us to fast for even one day! When we are led to fast by the Holy Spirit, it is much easier because He empowers us.

From Milk to Meat—Mature Believers

As vital as fasting from physical food is, so is feasting on spiritual food. In order to train properly, we need the right nutrients. We need the protein of the Word of God to build strong muscles! Milk is essential for new-born Christians; but to really have the energy necessary to run our race to the end, we need the meat—the "solid food"—of God's Word.

> *For everyone who partakes only of milk is unskilled in the word of righteousness, for he is a babe. But solid food belongs to those who are of full age, that is, those who by reason of use have their senses exercised to discern both good and evil.*
>
> *Hebrews 5:13–14*

Milk is easier to swallow, and usually sweeter, than meat. But meat has more substance and fiber than milk. It must be chewed (meditated upon) before it can be swallowed and digested. Those who have disciplined themselves to grow and mature have developed the spiritual teeth and stomach to handle it. Meat (solid food) would consist of any spiritual truth that does not fall into the category of the elementary principles pointed out in Hebrews 6:1 and 2.

> *Therefore, leaving the discussion of the elementary principles of Christ, let us go on to perfection, not laying again the foundation of repentance from dead works and of faith toward God, of the doctrine of baptisms, of laying on of hands, of resurrection of the dead, and of eternal judgment.* *Hebrews 6:1–2*

In Hebrews 6:1, Paul says it's time to leave the discussion of these elementary principles—repentance, faith, baptisms, laying on of hands, resurrection of the dead, and eternal judgment—and move on to perfection (maturity). When we speak of leaving the milk behind, bear in mind to maintain a supply for those who still need it.

> *And I, brethren, could not speak to you as to spiritual people but as to carnal, as to babes in Christ. I fed you with milk and not with solid food; for until now you were not able to receive it, and even now you are still not able; for you are still carnal. For where there are envy, strife, and divisions among you, are you not carnal and behaving like mere men?* *1 Corinthians 3:1–3*

We may have received the new birth years ago, but if we are exhibiting the carnal characteristics of envy, strife, and divisions and behaving like "mere men," we will not be able to digest anything stronger than milk. First Peter 2:2 says that the pure milk of the word can bring us to a point of maturity, but Hebrews 5:14 says we also need to have our senses exercised to discern both good and evil. If a baby only drinks milk and does not exercise, he will not develop as he should. Just like the man in James 1:21–24 who looks in the mirror and then walks away unchanged, we cannot expect to mature if we simply listen to the "first principles of the oracles of God" (Hebrews 5:12) but continue doing things our way.

We are made in the image of Christ, much in the same way that Christ was/is the image of God. To the degree that we look and act like Him, the world will see who He is. We can bring heaven down to earth and glorify the Father, just as He did. Each of us has a portion of Christ; and as we each do our part in His body, the wholeness of who He is will be seen. For so long, western Christianity has cranked out cookie-cutter believers who do not really resemble the Christ we read about. As the Potter, our Father wants to conform us into the image of His Son. Therefore, let's make sure that we are pliable, so that He can form us in the molds He designed for each of us.

Two prevalent attitudes in our culture that block spiritual growth are self-pity and resentment. Self-pity says, "You don't understand how bad off I have it;" and resentment whispers, "You don't understand how deeply I've been hurt." These lies can easily deceive those whose spiritual senses have not yet been exercised to discern between good and evil.

By reading and incorporating the Word of God into our thought patterns and then using it to make Godly choices, we exercise our senses to discern both good and evil. We will no longer be easily seduced by the temptations of envy, strife, and divisiveness; and at this point, we will be ready to handle the meat. This is why developing a daily spiritual regimen is so vital.

For those who are ready to move on, it's time to (1) partake of the meatier truths—the more in-depth teachings on the gifts and fruit of the Spirit, and (2) walk in our callings to serve others within the body of Christ.

Resisting Temptation and Overcoming Sin

As we saw earlier, some temptations require discipline of the physical body as well. When resisting the more mental or emotional temptations of strife and divisiveness, the body is still involved since gossip, slander, and/or cursing can evolve from both of these temptations. The tongue is rumored to be the strongest muscle in the body and can stir up a mighty fire according to James 3:5–6. We have been given spiritual authority over our souls and our bodies, and a great way to exercise that authority is to control our thoughts and our tongues. We *choose* to make our bodies obey our souls, and we submit our souls to the leading of the Holy Spirit. When we are tempted to speak a word against a brother or sister that could stir up strife or divisiveness, we must submit our tongue to our souls. In other words, we keep our mouths shut. This is all determined by our choice. As we choose to do things God's way, He supplies us with the grace to help us.

We need His help. Even Paul said he could not do this on his own.

> *For I know that in me (that is, in my flesh) nothing good dwells; for to will is present with me, but how to perform what is good I do not find.* *Romans 7:18*

We need the Holy Spirit to empower us to resist temptation and overcome sin. Jesus gave us the right to call upon His name and employ His help in any and every situation. He has given us the privilege to exercise spiritual authority and to overcome this world.

> *You are of God, little children, and have overcome them, because He who is in you is greater than he who is in the world.*
> *1 John 4:4*

Developing Spiritual Perception

> *But solid food belongs to those who are of full age, that is, those who by reason of use have their senses exercised to discern both good and evil.* *Hebrews 5:14*

Solid food (meat) is for those who by reason of use have exercised (trained) their (spiritual) senses to discern both good and evil. The Greek word for "exercised" is *gymnazō*, from which we get our English word gymnasium.[3] We reach the point of spiritual discernment by reason of use—in other words, use it or lose it! We would never lose the indwelling Holy Spirit or His gifts, but rather the sensitivity to hear His voice—to make righteous decisions, to walk in our callings, to flow in what He has for us. An athlete is not going to lose his ability to walk or even run if he doesn't train, but he will not have what it takes to win the race. As we daily discipline ourselves to seek the Lord and His ways, the adeptness to discern both good and evil will be naturally cultivated.

Training to win requires discipline, as seen through Paul's own testimony in 1 Corinthians 9:26–27.

> *Therefore I run thus: not with uncertainty. Thus I fight: not as one who beats the air. But I discipline my body and bring it into subjection, lest, when I have preached to others, I myself should become disqualified.* *1 Corinthians 9:26–27*

Paul brought his physical body into subjection through discipline. This is greater than the worldly practice of "mind over matter." He exercised his spiritual authority over his body by recognizing that the Holy Spirit within him was far greater than his willpower. As we build truth within our hearts and speak and act with faith, God will do His part to give us the grace we need to surrender our bodies and our souls to the Christ in us. If we preach righteousness to others yet allow sin to reign over us, not only are we hypocrites but we also risk being kicked out of the race. Training to run our course successfully all the way to the finish requires discipline, like an athlete training for a competition. Remember that Rocky Balboa pushed himself *daily* to win the prize. Although our main focus should be our spiritual regimen, physical and mental disciplines can definitely help as well.

Those who desire spiritual growth and progression are not satisfied to simply get their "ticket" to heaven; they aren't content to sit around like spiritual couch potatoes for the rest of their lives.

According to Matthew 25:30, those who are lazy could someday hear the Lord say, "Cast the unprofitable servant into the outer darkness. There will be weeping and gnashing of teeth."

The Bible says that God is not mocked (Galatians 6:7). He knows our hearts and what He has called us to do. We cannot use the liberty that He's given us as an excuse to sin (Galatians 5:13) and neglect the talents He's given us (Matthew 25:14–30).

We are responsible to do more than simply ask for Jesus' help. Our faithfulness to the daily spiritual regimen will prepare us for His answer, sharpening our spiritual senses to hear His voice and strengthening our spiritual "muscles" (resolve) to follow through. It's always easier to be lazy, but the day is coming when He will ask us to give an account of what we did with the talents He gave us. It could be very uncomfortable at that point to explain why we buried them when we should have used them.

Sinning Not

Most (if not all) sin is based in selfishness. It's doing what *we* want—e.g., what "feels good"—instead of following the voice of the Holy Spirit and the Scriptures. Even in our earthly lives, we eventually have to give up what feels good if we want to be successful. For instance, we cannot sleep in until 11 AM when our job starts at 9 AM. We can't be content with only satisfying our flesh, or we will get nowhere. Those who are truly successful, whether Christian or not, had to learn to live disciplined lifestyles in order to attain their dreams.

For those who choose to live for more than this present world, who desire to live a pure life of "sinning not," the challenge is even greater. It begins with thinking the thoughts of God, which means putting on the Word of God to learn to discern good from evil. His living words sharpen us and keep us alert to the invasion of the enemy's influence upon our lives. This is why part of our daily spiritual regimen mandates time in the Scriptures.

Just as prayer is made up of spoken words, so is the wielding of the sword of the Spirit. The sword of the Spirit is the Word of God, and we wield it by speaking it forth with faith. As supernatural beings under the direction of the Holy Spirit, we can command (and not just ask for) things to happen. We have the authority to command when He leads us to or when it is clearly within the will of God according to the Scriptures.

Jesus is both the written Word and He is also the Spirit in us—the Word Incarnate *and* the Spirit of Truth. **The more we incorporate the Scriptures into our souls, the easier it will be to proclaim them.** This is why we need to spend time in the Bible—not just to ingest the Word, but to digest it through meditation by focusing on what we are reading and re-reading it if necessary—and asking the Holy Spirit to reveal truths to us. We should allow it to sink deep into our minds and hearts.

Reading the Scriptures and praying are two key components of our training, much like punching the bag (or frozen meat) and running were Rocky's.

Avoiding Deception

> *Therefore lay aside all filthiness and overflow of wickedness, and receive with meekness the implanted word, which is able to save your souls. But be doers of the word, and not hearers only,* ***deceiving yourselves.*** *James 1:21–22*

Those who think that Christians cannot be deceived are already deceived. James 1:21–22 tells us that it's possible to only hear God's words and not do them. If we read the Bible but justify not practicing it, we are deceiving ourselves. The word "deceive" is the Greek word *paralogizomai,* which comes from two roots: *para*—beside, and *logos*—something said, including the reasoning behind it (logic).[4] So to be deceived is to line our thinking up with something that the world says and its reasoning—as opposed to lining our thinking up with what God says and His reasoning.

When our logic is not paralleled with the Scriptures, a small compromise inevitably leads to rationalization for sin. When our logic becomes skewed one degree contrary to the logic of the Scriptures, it's like the rails of a train track that are not perfectly parallel. When one of them is turned in just ¼ inch, soon they are inoperative because of their eventual intersecting and crossing each other. We can still read what God is saying in His written Word, but since our logic is not parallel with what we're reading, we won't practice it. We will justify that it does not apply to us in our situation.

If we say that we have no sin, we deceive ourselves (1 John 1:8). However, it is possible to live a life of obedience and purity in which sin does not dominate us because we can exercise our senses to discern between good and evil. Jesus Christ is our advocate, so that when we do sin, we can confess those sins and be forgiven.

The Spirit of the World

> *Beloved, I beg you as sojourners and pilgrims, abstain from fleshly lusts which war against the soul.* 1 Peter 2:11

We are constantly bombarded by the spirit of the world; however, as believers, our regenerated spirits give us the ability to discern, fight, and overcome. The fleshly lusts that come from the spirit of the world war against our soul, but greater is He that is in us than he that is in the world (1 John 4:4).

All of us are tempted with fleshly lusts (Galatians 5:17 and James 4:1); yet, according to Galatians 5:24, those who are Christ's have crucified their flesh with its passions and desires. This becomes a reality for us as we faithfully surrender to the Lord and allow Him to increase in our lives (John 3:30).

As long as we have these earthly bodies, we will have fleshly instincts; but if those instincts are allowed to dominate us in ways that oppose God's purposes, then we have the right to spiritually overpower them. If we cannot overcome them, it could be due to one of the following: (1) demonic activity and/or influence in our lives, (2) deficient scriptural nourishment, or (3) a lackluster desire to live a Godly life.

Demons feed on the carcass of the dead old man, and they know our background and history, i.e., which buttons to push to get us to do what they want. If we are not consistently countering their words with the words of Truth (the sword of the Spirit), then we will not overcome them. Demons also have a tendency to talk to us in the first person, which makes us think that their words are coming from us.

Reading, meditating upon, and ingesting the words of life will strengthen and sharpen our spiritual senses to more readily perceive and thwart demonic attacks in our lives so that we fall less and less prey to their temptations.

The Rewards of Overcoming

The book of Revelation is filled with promises for those who overcome. We don't understand everything about all of these promises right now, but we have the witness of the Holy Spirit to know that they are greater than anything we can imagine on this earth. *They are far greater than any earthly reward a man or woman could achieve and receive in their lifetime on this planet.*

According to these verses in Revelation, overcomers will

- eat from the tree of life (2:7),
- not be hurt by the second death (2:11),
- eat the hidden manna (2:17),
- be given a white stone with a new name written upon it (2:17),
- have power over the nations (2:26),
- be given the morning star (2:28),
- be clothed in white garments (3:5),
- not have their name blotted out of the Book of Life (3:5), but
- have their name confessed by Jesus before the Father and His angels (3:5),
- be a pillar in the temple of God (3:12), from which they will go out no more,
- have the name of God written on them by Jesus (3:12),
- have the name of the city of God written on them by Jesus (3:12),
- have Jesus' new name written on them by Jesus (3:12),
- sit with Jesus on His throne (3:21),
- inherit all things (21:7),
- have the One who sits on His throne as their God (21:7), and
- be His sons (or daughters) (21:7).

Most of these promises have the admonition of, "He who has an ear, let him hear what the Spirit says to the churches," marking its significance. Those who have an ear will be the mature believers who have disciplined themselves to hear the voice of their personal trainer and obey Him.

Overcoming sin requires a maturity level that's gained through a perpetual "wrestling match" within our minds to keep our thoughts on Him and on the finish line. This repentant lifestyle of humility and patience and consistent exercise of our spiritual senses will allow us to discern evil from good. Jesus wants us to win and He's on our side. He's our "cheerleader" and advocate up in heaven who ever lives to make intercession for us (Hebrews 7:25); and He sent us the Comforter, the Holy Spirit, to help us (John 16:7).

As we discipline ourselves to exercise our spiritual senses, the Holy Spirit will grow us up in the Lord. Do we desire spiritual maturity? Do we desire to overcome? Do we desire to work in our Father's business? When we cross over the commitment line and decide we are fed up with feeling sorry for ourselves, the Holy Spirit will energize and inspire us to do the work.

There are no excuses. None of us have had it easy, though some have had a tougher time than others. We all came from the factory with faults and have dealt with challenges in our lives. So, we can either wallow in self-pity and resentment, or we can put on our Nikes and *just do it.* **In order to subdue the world (Genesis 1:28 and Psalm 8:6), we must develop a spiritual regimen.**

This spiritual regimen will also help us to more accurately "re-present" Christ on the earth, which we will discuss in the next chapter.

Related Materials at LMCI.org

- Developing Your Spiritual Sensitivity (CD- or MP3-set)
- Fellowship with Jesus Christ (CD- or MP3-set)
- Fit for the Kingdom (DVD-set)
- 40 Days of Communion in Your Home (Booklet or E-book)
- How to R.E.A.D. and S.T.U.D.Y. the Bible (CD- or MP3-set)
- Praising God (CD or MP3)
- Yahweh: the Sacred Name of God (CD- or MP3-set)

Relevant Points

1. What scripture tells us that we are to be holy as He is holy?

2. According to the different growth levels revealed in 1 John 2:12–14, write down where you presently see yourself.

3. Write down the seven armaments of the Spirit as revealed in Ephesians 6 and memorize them (Mark a check next them once you have memorized them.)

Chapter Eleven

Re-Presenting Jesus on the Earth

NOTE: I choose to call this concept "Re-Presenting Jesus" instead of "Representing Jesus," not only for the sake of pronunciation but also so it will carry an intended nuance of interpretation. To re-present Jesus is more than simply representing Him. It means to stand in His stead and replicate His purpose and passion.

Each of us in the body of Christ has been called to replicate Jesus in a particular way. No matter how insignificant we may think our purpose is, we are still a vital part of re-presenting Christ on this earth.

Within the measure that the Holy Spirit pours out on us individually, we have the potential to re-present Jesus—meaning that we can literally re-present Him in that specific area where He has gifted us. As we grow in commitment and understanding, we will re-present Him more in other areas as well. Ultimately, we should be able to say that whoever sees us has seen Him, just as He said that whoever saw Him had seen the Father (John 14:9).

This may seem a bold statement, but that's the kind of authority and spiritual faith we should walk in; our attitude should be unabashed and open in manifesting the glory of God.

> *Now the Lord is the Spirit; and where the Spirit of the Lord is, there is liberty. But we all, with unveiled face, beholding as in a mirror the*

glory of the Lord, are being transformed into the same image from glory to glory, just as by the Spirit of the Lord.

2 Corinthians 3:17–18

When we grasp our specific portion of the manifestation of Jesus Christ in our lives, we will reveal that aspect of God's glory. Each member of the body of Christ is to evidence a part of His character; and as we work together, we will collectively represent His whole being. A significant factor in re-presenting Jesus is to walk in His power and replicate His miraculous works.

Doing His Works

Most assuredly, I say to you, he who believes in Me, the works that I do he will do also; and greater works than these he will do, because I go to My Father. *John 14:12*

Jesus promised that we would do the works He did. In the early years of my zealous Christian life, I thought of this only as His works of power; but the deeper reality is that it includes His character as well.

Jesus said that the Holy Spirit would reveal the Father and the Son—their essence or character (John 15:26, 16:13–15)—and dwell in us and among us. He also spoke of how the world could know that the Father had sent Him as it saw the glory that brings us into unity and perfection in Him.

I pray for them. I do not pray for the world but for those whom You have given Me, for they are Yours. And all Mine are Yours, and Yours are Mine, and I am glorified in them.

John 17:9–10

> *And the glory which You gave Me I have given them, that they may be one just as We are one: I in them, and You in Me; that they may be made perfect in one, and that the world may know that You have sent Me, and have loved them as You have loved Me.*
>
> *John 17:22–23*

The works He did were not limited to snatching someone out of a wheelchair (because they didn't have wheelchairs then anyway) or pulling someone off a stretcher. His works were a manifestation of who He was, and they revealed His character.

Of course, healings and miracles are wonderful and we should desire to see them. None of us would mind having a collection of "trophies" like abandoned wheelchairs or stretchers. T. L. Osborn had a room where he hung up all the wheelchairs and canes and those little white- or red-tipped poles (used by the visually impaired) of people who had been healed.

I have had some trophies in the past too, *but the point is that we need to be even more concerned with having the character of Jesus in our lives, so that those who see us will truly see Him.* Although we should have both His character *and* His works of power, if I had to choose only one, it would be His character. However, the good thing about being a "spoiled" child of God is that we don't have to choose between the two; we can have both! His character and His works of power should go hand in hand, so that the works come out of who He has formed us to be.

Years ago, I was so power-crazy and wrapped up in charismatic Christianity, that I couldn't hear the Lord's voice reminding me about the fruit of the Spirit. All I desired then was the gifts; but now I desire the fruit of the Spirit, because it is God's person manifested in Christ. The Holy Spirit has brought me to the place where I would now rather hear my wife compliment me on my kindness than for a miracle brought to pass under my hand.

We can only have His character through knowing Him. However, it is possible to work mighty miracles and do amazing things in His name without knowing Him or having His character, as we can see from Matthew 7:22–23.

> *Many will say to Me in that day, "Lord, Lord, have we not prophesied in Your name, cast out demons in Your name, and done many wonders in Your name?" And then I will declare to them, "I never knew you; depart from Me, you who practice lawlessness!"*
> *Matthew 7:22–23*

These verses show us that it's possible to practice lawlessness and yet still prophesy in His name, cast out demons in His name, and do many wonders in His name. The consequence for those who do His works without truly knowing Him (thus, not reflecting Him) is that they will be commanded to depart from Him at the judgment day. I would never want to hear Him say this to me, and it should scare anyone who is operating as an undercover selfish agent in a ministerial role.

Let's make sure we get to truly know Christ through the Holy Spirit and the Scriptures and have the kind of relationship with Him that will cultivate His character in us. Christianity is not a religion; it is a relationship with the Father and His Son.

> *Truly our fellowship is with the Father and with His Son Jesus Christ. 1 John 1:3b*

The Fruit of the Spirit

Jesus' character is revealed through the fruit of the Spirit listed in Galatians 5:22.

> *But the fruit of the Spirit is love, joy, peace, longsuffering, kindness, goodness, faithfulness, gentleness, self-control. Against such there is no law. And those who are Christ's have crucified the flesh with its passions and desires. If we live in the Spirit, let us also walk in the Spirit.* *Galatians 5:22–25*

These are values that people search for all their lives: love, joy, peace, longsuffering, kindness, goodness, faithfulness, gentleness, and self-control. Yet, every born-again believer has these imbedded within their new nature along with the potential to live them. I call it our spiritual DNA (Divine Nature Attributes).

The phrase "against such there is no law" indicates that there is no Old Testament law against being God-like or Christ-like. God never pronounced a law against His people having the fruit of the Spirit in their lives. The truth is that He is very much in favor of it.

My good friend and spiritual counselor Russ Chandler gave me an interpretation of the fruit of the Spirit that needs to be written and remembered. The following is a paraphrase of what he explained to me.

> Galatians 5:22 and 23 are a figure of speech, asyndeton, meaning no "ands" or conjunctions.[1] The word "sinew" comes from the same word and means connection—sinew is the fibrous tissue that

connects muscle to bone. No "ands" connecting these indicates a process to the final end—and that is *temperance.* The Holy Spirit teaches us all these characteristics so that they mature into a nature of temperance and self-control. That is the goal of the fruit of the Spirit: to give us control and temperance that overpowers and negates the law of behavior (the flesh). The Holy Spirit will be our temperance tutor if we will yield to Him.

The Gifts of the Spirit

The gifts of the Spirit are not the end but a means to the end. The end that we should desire is to carry out our foreordained purposes in Christ (which includes having His character). All regenerated believers have the gift of the Holy Spirit within them, and with that gift comes all nine of the gifts or manifestations of that Spirit. However, God gives each of us a measure of faith that specifically activates the particular gifts that are needful for our callings.

First Corinthians 12 gives us an understanding of the gifts of the Spirit and how they work in us. Verses 4–6 show how the members of the Godhead work together to provide what we need to walk in His power.

> *Now there are diversities of gifts, but the same Spirit. There are differences of ministries, but the same Lord. And there are diversities of activities, but it is the same God who works all in all.*
>
> *1 Corinthians 12:4–6*

- The Holy Spirit is the source (verse 4);
- Jesus administrates them (verse 5);
- The Father energizes all of them in all of us (verse 6).

Our part is defined in verse 7.

> *But the manifestation of the Spirit is given to each one for the profit of all.* *1 Corinthians 12:7*

There will be a specific manifestation of the Spirit that is unique to each of us, which is why it appears in its singular form in this verse. As our unique manifestation of the Spirit is empowered by the Holy Spirit, it benefits the entire body of Christ. We are responsible to live out our portion of Jesus that will ultimately profit the other members.

> *For to one is given the word of wisdom through the Spirit, to another the word of knowledge through the same Spirit, to another faith by the same Spirit, to another gifts of healings by the same Spirit, to another the working of miracles, to another prophecy, to another discerning of spirits, to another different kinds of tongues, to another the interpretation of tongues.* *1 Corinthians 12:8–10*

The words "to one" in verses 8–10 could either refer to one profit or to one individual. If it is to an individual, it would indicate that only one particular person is endowed with the gift of wisdom, another with the word of knowledge, and so forth. This is not logical. It makes more sense that "to one" is referring to the profit spoken of in verse 7, which was for the common (one) benefit of the entire body.[2]

Jesus sent the Holy Spirit to help us fulfill our destinies, and His power can work in and through us on a daily basis throughout our lives—not just once in a while. As He energizes us, each of us will replicate Jesus in part; then, as we individually pursue our part, the body of Christ can replicate Him in whole throughout the earth.

The Lord's distribution of gifts to the members of His body is determined by their divine callings. For instance, if one has the ministry of intercession, it would benefit him/her to be especially adept in diverse kinds of tongues and discerning of spirits; if it is a healing ministry, the Lord may include a combination of the word of knowledge, the gift of faith and, of course, the gifts of healings.

> *But one and the same Spirit works all these things, distributing to each one individually as He [the Holy Spirit] wills.*
> *1 Corinthians 12:11*

The combination that He gives will enable us to fulfill our individual ministries, which benefits the entire body of Christ. We are all knit together, and each of us supplies a vital aspect of Christ that is useful to the rest of the body. Practically speaking, we can observe this with those who most closely surround us in ministry; yet the truth bears out across the entire body of Christ for the common profit of all.

> *For as the body is one and has many members, but all the members of that one body, being many, are one body, so also is Christ.*
> *1 Corinthians 12:12*

> *If the foot should say, "Because I am not a hand, I am not of the body," is it therefore not of the body? And if the ear should say, "Because I am not an eye, I am not of the body," is it therefore not of the body?* *1 Corinthians 12:15–16*

In the context of the gifts of the Spirit, we see our need for one another and how He manifests uniquely through each of us.

> *But now God has set the members, each one of them, in the body just as He pleased. And if they were all one member, where would the body be? But now indeed there are many members, yet one body. And*

> *the eye cannot say to the hand, "I have no need of you"; nor again the head to the feet, "I have no need of you." No, much rather, those members of the body which seem to be weaker are necessary. And those members of the body which we think to be less honorable, on these we bestow greater honor.* 1 Corinthians 12:18–23a

Verses 27–30 then speak of specific ministries within the body of Christ, including the five-fold gift ministries. Even though speaking in tongues is mentioned in this list, it is referring to the unique ministry of speaking in a diverse tongue rather than to individual prayer languages. I believe this is how it should be interpreted because of the question in verse 30, "Do all speak with tongues?" Whereas, Paul shares in 1 Corinthians 14:5a, "I wish you all spoke with tongues," indicating that we all have the ability to do this. Therefore, 1 Corinthians 12:28 must be referring to the *ministry* of speaking in tongues.

> *Now you are the body of Christ, and members individually. And God has appointed these in the church: first apostles, second prophets, third teachers, after that miracles, then gifts of healings, helps, administrations, varieties of tongues. Are all apostles? Are all prophets? Are all teachers? Are all workers of miracles? Do all have gifts of healings?* ***Do all speak with tongues?*** *Do all interpret? But earnestly desire the best gifts. And yet I show you a more excellent way.* 1 Corinthians 12:27–31

This ministry of speaking in tongues is vastly overlooked in even the most charismatic churches. The first time I witnessed this particular ministry was in India, and it just about knocked me down. During a meeting, a believer brought forth a diverse tongue which was then interpreted by another with the ministry of interpretation. This was followed in suit by several others; and as these believers operated their unique ministries of diversity of tongues and interpretation of tongues, several people were healed.

I discerned that these healings were not activated by revelation but by believers simply walking in their ministries and callings.

Although we may look at the last verse of 1 Corinthians 12:31 and focus on the "more excellent way" that Paul was exhorting them in (the love of God), let's not overlook the first part of that verse, "but earnestly desire the best gifts." I believe the "best" gifts will vary for each of us, depending upon our calling. My best gifts will differ from yours and vice-versa.

To covet earnestly the best gifts is to desire the combination of gifts that will make us uniquely more Christ-like. Although we each have the ability to manifest all of the gifts of the Spirit, God gives us a measure of faith for the ones we need for our ministries, enabling us to excel in those particular gifts.

We cannot will which of these gifts will be stronger in us; it is the Father who wills them for us according to our callings. Then the Lord Jesus distributes them according to His will.

> *God also bearing witness both with signs and wonders, with various miracles, and gifts of the Holy Spirit,* ***according to His own will?*** *Hebrews 2:4*

Remember that the gifts are a means to an end—to fulfill our ministries.

The Nine Gifts Categorized

The nine gifts of the Spirit break down logically into three categories: the speaking gifts, the knowledge gifts, and the power gifts.

- *Speaking gifts* are speaking in tongues, interpretation of tongues, and prophecy. These are the utterance gifts that are operated by speaking.
- *Knowledge gifts* are word of knowledge, word of wisdom, and discerning of spirits. These are the gifts that provide the information, or knowledge, that we need for a particular situation.
- *Power gifts* are faith, the working of miracles, and the gifts of healings. These are the gifts that supply the necessary power to produce miracles and healings.

The More Excellent Way

We need all of the gifts, and the indwelling Holy Spirit enables us to walk in all of them. There will be certain ones that we are to covet earnestly—the "best gifts" (1 Corinthians 12:31), meaning the ones that are necessary to fulfill our callings. Then God sets the stage for 1 Corinthians 13, the love chapter, by telling us that there is a more excellent way to walk in them.

> *But earnestly desire the best gifts. And yet I show you a more excellent way.* *1 Corinthians 12:31*

The more excellent way that we are to operate the gifts is within the *agape* love of God. When we are walking in His love, He will give us whatever we need; but when we're not walking in love, He will resist us.

> *Yes, all of you be submissive to one another, and be clothed with humility, for "God resists the proud, but gives grace to the humble."*
> *1 Peter 5:5a*

We should desire and pursue after the love of God in all its aspects, exemplified in 1 Corinthians 13 New Living Translation as being

- patient and kind, not jealous, boastful, or proud (verse 4);
- not rude or demanding its own way; not irritable or keeping record of when it has been wronged (verse 5);
- never glad about injustice, but rejoicing whenever the truth wins out (verse 6); and
- never giving up, never losing faith, always hopeful, and enduring through every circumstance (verse 7).

The more excellent way is the character of Jesus. God is love, according to 1 John 4:8; and Jesus is the express image of the Father (Hebrews 1:3). His attributes manifest themselves in power through the gifts of the Spirit and in character through the fruit of the Spirit.

A Leader Who Inspires Others

> *Shepherd the flock of God which is among you, serving as overseers, not by constraint but willingly, not for dishonest gain but eagerly; nor as being lords over those entrusted to you, but being examples to the flock.* *1 Peter 5:2–3*

A leader should be a model, a fashion, a form, a pattern or blueprint for others to see. Even if you are not specifically called as an overseer, you can inspire others to walk out their callings as you consistently live out your own.

Churches should not be religious clubs that compete with one another, but rather communities that nourish and encourage each other to have a relationship with the Lord and with each other. As we begin to recognize our unique purposes within the body of Christ, these relationships will naturally form. Let's cleave to the Lord with the desire to walk out our callings and work together, so that we can all fulfill our callings. As we encourage others to fulfill their ministries, jealousies and rivalries will fade away.

NOTE: Our e-book on *Realizing & Fulfilling Your Personal Ministry* is a great aid and resource to help in your pursuits, as are our *Christological Astronomy* materials. Seeing where we are going makes it much easier than guessing and stumbling. This is why Liberating Ministries for Christ International exists—to help others in their journey of fulfilling their God-given purposes.

When we realize our specific callings and begin to live them out, we will truly represent Jesus here on the earth—both as individuals and as the body of Christ.

The more excellent way to fulfill that representation is by cultivating His character in our lives—to have and operate not only the same power He did, but for it to flow from the love of God within us. As our roots grow deeper into the soil of His love, not only will we walk in supernatural power, but the fruit of the Spirit will be evident in everything we do. Our ultimate goal should be to reflect Him just as He reflects the Father.

Related Materials at LMCI.org

- Christological Astronomy (Workbook, E-workbook, DVD-, CD- or MP3-set)
- Fellowship with Jesus Christ (CD- or MP3-set)
- Flowing in All Nine Gifts of the Holy Spirit (Booklet)
- New Creation Realities (CD- or MP3-set)
- Realizing & Fulfilling Your Personal Ministry (E-book, CD- or MP3-set)
- Utilizing Gift Ministries (Book)

Relevant Points

1. What scripture shows us that one of the ways we can re-present Jesus is by doing the same works (and greater) than He did?

2. In what area of your life do you believe you re-present Jesus best?

3. What are the nine fruit of the Spirit?

PART FIVE

OUR AUTHORITY TO RE-PRESENT JESUS IN POWER

In Part V (chapters 12–17), the spiritual power behind our authority will be explained scripturally, as well as detailed in a practical way. A policeman represents authority because he has an arsenal to back it up. If someone was resisting arrest, he could control the situation with either his billy club, a can of mace, a Taser, or even a gun. These implements and weapons provide the force and might to back up his authority. In the same way, God's arsenal backs up the spiritual authority Jesus gave us. Our "gun," "club," "Taser," and/or "mace" are the empowering gifts of the Spirit. Our spiritual arsenal is vital to exercising spiritual authority, and that is why the chapters in part 5 are devoted to them.

The gifts of the Holy Spirit are the power behind our authority.

I have invested many years in the study of gifts of the Spirit from the Scriptures and gleaned invaluable lessons from more than a few patriarchs on the subject as well. Some of my findings are presented in a booklet entitled, *Flowing in All Nine Gifts of the Holy Spirit*,[1] which focuses on the premise that all the gifts are available for all believers and that they are meant to work together synergistically.

As mentioned in chapter 11, the three major categories of the gifts of the Spirit are (1) utterance, (2) knowledge, and (3) power. Their synergy can be summarized in the following equation.

Spiritual utterance + spiritual knowledge + spiritual faith → spiritual results

The Holy Spirit gives us the words, which can be in the form of speaking in tongues, interpretation of tongues, or prophecy; He also gives us knowledge in the form of revelation, discerning of spirits, or word of wisdom; and He provides the faith we need to bring to pass the spiritual results of signs, wonders, and/or miracles.

The chapters in part 5 are arranged to accommodate this equation. Chapters 12 and 13 deal with the utterance gifts of speaking in tongues, interpretation of tongues; and prophecy. Chapter 14 covers spiritual knowledge. Chapters 15–17 explain the power gifts.

All of these work together to yield manifestations of the Holy Spirit, and they are the power behind our authority.

Chapter Twelve

Receiving the Holy Spirit and Speaking in Tongues

When Jesus ascended into heaven, He sent the Holy Spirit down with gifts for the church, along with the empowerment, revelation, and utterance gifts.

The gifts of the Holy Spirit enable us to effectually operate and fulfill our God-given ministries—all to the end of bringing Him glory. It was not until Jesus ascended into heaven to the right hand of the Father that the Holy Spirit could descend to the earth. Although Old Testament believers were able to have His anointing upon them from time to time, we are now able to have His constant abiding within us—as well as His anointing upon us as needed. This was first evidenced on the Day of Pentecost when the twelve apostles initially received the Holy Spirit and spoke with other tongues.

Once we receive Jesus as our Lord and Savior, if we truly desire to exercise spiritual authority, our next step must be to receive the power of the Holy Spirit into our lives. He not only empowers us to produce signs, miracles, and wonders, but He also transforms us into ambassadors for Christ who speak and act fearlessly. These changes rely upon our yielding to His leading and our consistency to tap into His power. The twelve men who so boldly brought forth tongues and declared God's message on the Day of Pentecost were the very same men who, only days earlier, had hidden behind closed doors for fear of their very lives. On that great day in the temple, they boldly spoke in tongues in front of all who were gathered there on a major feast day at an hour of prayer. This newfound fearlessness was especially seen in Peter, who had shortly before emphatically denied his Lord and was now giving the speech of his life in front of people from all the surrounding nations!

In the least common denominator, words are the basic weapon of spiritual warfare and exercising spiritual authority.

The words they spoke were the most noticeable changes witnessed by those present—first they spoke in tongues and then Peter gave an empowered speech that was not the norm for him. It was evident to all present that these were not their own words and that they were from a spiritual source. The words we speak will only come from one of two sources: the world or the Holy Spirit.

Before we proceed to receiving the Holy Spirit into manifestation through speaking in tongues, let's first examine the significance of the words we speak and their impact upon ourselves and others.

Spiritual Utterance

> *You are of God, little children, and have overcome them, because He who is in you is greater than he who is in the world.*
>
> *1 John 4:4*

We need holy boldness in order to live above ourselves, to allow the almighty glory of God to shine through us. As we subjugate our souls to Him, the working of His spirit can be shown even through our bodies—starting with us speaking words that are empowered through Him.

Primarily, His power in us is released through utterance. We yield to the Holy Spirit to hear His words and then obediently speak the message. Even if we only have the beginning of the thought, as we open our mouths and start speaking, God will provide the rest. That is speaking by faith and the spirit of God. When we speak His words by faith, it brings His power into manifestation.

When I was teaching this in one of my classes, a medical doctor who was there explained to me afterwards that, from a biological perspective, we were literally built for utterance. He later showed me a chart he had put together that diagrammed the structure of the brain with its 12 major pairs of cranial nerves. This chart shows how five of the nerves are connected to the mouth. **God built us to speak.**

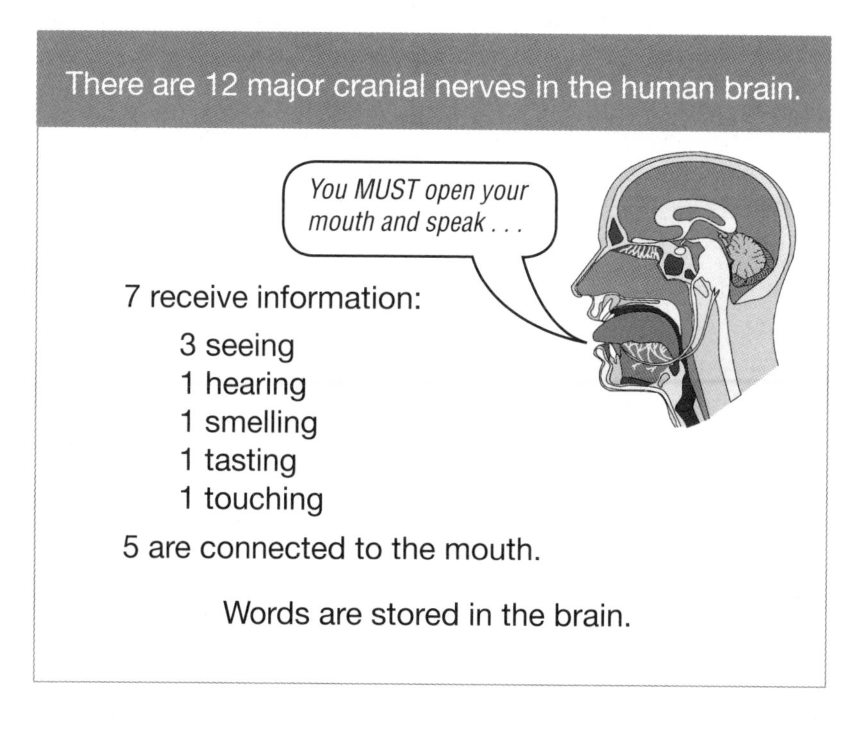

The number 12 spiritually represents government, and our bodies are governed by these cranial nerves (as well as by the spinal nerves). God designed our bodies, with Adam being the blueprint; and He designed the brain as the "head" quarters.[1]

The human tongue is the strongest muscle in the body and the only one that is connected at only one end. We were created for utterance, and our tongue is either our best friend or our enemy depending upon who we yield it to. God meant for it to be controlled by the Holy Spirit, and this is why we need to give it to Him.

It is the rudder of our ship—the wave point of our destiny. If all that pours out of us is garbage, then we need to look at what we're putting into our souls and minds. If there is junk inside us, the least we can do is keep our mouths shut so we don't pass it to others. We must set a guard by the door of our mouths. If we absolutely cannot gain control over them, there could be a spiritual reason. If this is the case, then by all means, get help and be delivered!

We can change what is inside of us by what we feed upon. If we continually eat the garbage of the world, then that's what will eventually come out. Thinking and speaking the Scriptures can become second nature to us as we discipline ourselves to consistently read, speak, memorize, and meditate upon His words that are spirit and life. The Holy Spirit can also empower us with heavenly words that set the captives free. The world is longing for heroes who will speak truth and inspire them to a higher calling, rescuing them from the lies of the devil that have torn their souls and hindered them from fulfilling their God-given destinies.

Small minds discuss people, average minds discuss current events, but great minds discuss the eternal truths of Jesus Christ. If the main content of our conversations is focused upon worldly issues, then we are living on the first or, at best, the second floor. It's time we move our furniture to the third floor and start speaking what is truthful and faith-building; and the greatest thing we can speak is the holy writ—**God's words are spirit and life.**

> *It is the Spirit who gives life; the flesh profits nothing.* ***The words that I speak to you are spirit, and they are life.***
>
> *John 6:63*

I remember an incident when I was ministering to someone with a foot problem, and I started out by speaking the truth of the Scriptures. I talked about Jesus stilling the storm and walking on the water and continued with some of His other miracles. As I spoke supernatural truths from the Word of God, I could sense this person's faith building. When I knew it was big enough to receive their healing, I ministered to their foot and it was healed. Why?—because spiritual words of life were spoken right into the situation, *and they bring faith and power.*

The power of God is greater than any of our physical circumstances. When we open our mouths and start speaking supernatural truths from His words of life, our spirits respond. This is why it is vital that we speak aloud the blessings of God over our lives. Also, there is something about the way God made us that causes our souls and our bodies to respond to the words *we* speak even more than when we hear the same truths from someone else.

The utterance gifts of the Holy Spirit allow us to speak as if we were Jesus, with His authority. Jesus was the fullness of the Godhead bodily, and now He dwells in us. Not only are the spiritual utterances He gives us impacting, but they also carry His authority to produce His works. The same Holy Spirit that worked in Jesus lives in us, so when we speak with His authority, we can produce those same works.

Spiritual utterance is a powerful tool, as we have seen during times of praise and worship. Psalm 22:3 says that He inhabits our praise, and most of us have experienced a tangible feeling of His presence during these times. We are speaking (or singing) words of truth concerning our all-powerful, all-knowing, loving, and gracious heavenly Father. These words carry power and they return to earth with even more power as He responds to them.

We should speak words of truth over our lives and the lives of others. The Bible says that angels respond to these words as the commands of God. The New King James version says in Psalm 103:20 that they are "heeding the voice of His word." For this reason, the devil will do all he can to either shut us up or to provoke us to speak lies about ourselves and others.

Ephesians 6:17 refers to the sword of the Spirit as the word of God. I like to refer to it as our "rhema rifle," since the Greek word for "word" in this verse is *rhema*, which is a spoken word or an utterance. Strong's Concordance defines it as "that which is or has been uttered by the living voice, thing spoken, word."[2] We are to use the utterances of God as a weapon. This may seem extreme, but we are constantly engaged in spiritual warfare. Whenever we speak the truth of God's Word, it will oppose the forces of this world whether we are aware of it at the time or not. It's vital that we keep our swords sharpened (or our rhema rifles loaded), and the best way to do this is to memorize scriptures. The more scriptures we have memorized, the more ammunition we have in our magazine.

> *But He answered and said, "It is written, 'Man shall not live by bread alone, but by every word that proceeds from the mouth of God.'"* *Matthew 4:4*

Jesus made it clear that we need "every word (rhema) that proceeds from the mouth of God" as much as we need physical food. This is easy to agree with, but if we are not eating (or speaking) them as much as we are eating physical food, then we probably do not really believe it. The spoken word is our weapon. We are supposed to possess our souls to the end that we habitually speak out spiritual words and release them into the physical realm.

We already saw that angels heed God's words (Psalm 103:20), but the same holds true when we speak the words of the world—except the spirit beings that heed them are the demons, principalities, and powers from the evil spirit kingdom. When we speak words against others, we legally invoke the right to a demon to go attack that person; but when we speak words of truth over people, they give angels the right to bless that person. The quantum law of observation can explain why.[3]

When we utter God's words, we release angels. It's not magical cosmic rays or auras that are sent out—it's angels. We are not necessarily commanding them, but we are speaking spiritual words of life that put them into action. Some angels are assigned only to heaven, such as cherubim, seraphim, living creatures, and worshipping spirits, who have no interaction with us unless God chooses to send one down; so they are not typically the ones who jump into action. However, the angels that are assigned to earth are different. They are the ministering spirits (Hebrews 1:14) and archangels.

These ministering spirits and archangels spring into action at the sound of His words spoken by faith—especially when the words are given directly by the Holy Spirit. When we are led by the Holy Spirit to speak the words God gives us, these supernatural beings carry them out.

NOTE: Ministering spirits minister according to the anointings that are on us, and the amount and strength of these ministering spirits will vary according to the anointing. This is why corporate anointings are so strong, because there is a combination of not only the anointings, but the angels who are assigned to all those people.

When Jesus was about to be crucified, He said, "don't you think I could ask and the Father would give me 12 legions of angels?" It doesn't mean that there are only 12 legions of angels; He was simply making it clear that He could have a multitude of angels immediately available if He asked the Father.

Receiving the Holy Spirit into Manifestation

Now that the significance of our words has been established, we can move into receiving the baptism of the Holy Spirit into manifestation through speaking in tongues. There are three utterance gifts we have through the Holy Spirit: speaking in tongues, interpretation of tongues, and prophecy.

Although speaking in tongues is also referred to as speaking in an unknown tongue, the impact of these spiritual words is just as powerful as speaking the words of life from the Scriptures or a spiritual utterance spoken in our known tongue. Even if we can't understand them, they still affect the spirit realm; and, if it is a diverse tongue, they can even be direct commands to angels in their language (1 Corinthians 13:1).

Acts 2 records that the Holy Spirit was poured out on the Day of Pentecost, and the sign that the 12 apostles had received it was that they all spoke in tongues. This was their first evidence, and so it is today.

When we first receive salvation, our spirits are regenerated by His Holy Spirit. At that point, we have the Holy Spirit in us; but most new believers do not evidence it as they did on the Day of Pentecost. The Acts 2 account is not the only one that shows speaking in tongues as the evidence of the Holy Spirit's baptism. It can also be seen in Acts 10:44–46 when Cornelius' household received the Holy Spirit and in Acts 19 when the Ephesians received.

The gift of speaking in a tongue is one of empowerment that enables us to make perfect intercession. The following is a list of some of its benefits according to the Scriptures.

- It edifies the spirit (1 Corinthians 14:4; Jude 1:20; Ephesians 3:16);
- It is speaking divine mysteries with God (1 Corinthians 14:2);
- It is perfect prayer (Romans 8:26–27);
- It speaks the wonderful works of God (Acts 2:11);
- It magnifies God (Acts 10:46);
- It is perfect praise and thanksgiving (1 Corinthians 14:17);
- It is warfare prayer (Ephesians 6:17–18);
- It burns up the chaff in your life (Matthew 3:11–12).

Paul said, "I wish you all spoke in tongues," in 1 Corinthians 14:5. By placing His gift of the Holy Spirit within us, God guaranteed us the ability to speak in a prayer language. The Bible refers to this as praying in the spirit. There are other tongues (diverse tongues) that can come upon us temporarily when the spirit leads us that way, but our individual prayer language is available at all times.[4] The primary benefit of praying in the Spirit is the direct communion it gives us with God. Our spirit speaks directly to His Spirit, and the conversation is perfect because our flesh is completely left out of it (Romans 8:27–28). We should aspire to use our prayer language consistently as Ephesians 6:18 exhorts us to.

> ***Praying always with all prayer and supplication in the Spirit,*** *being watchful to this end with all perseverance and supplication for all the saints.* *Ephesians 6:18*

Speaking in tongues is a supernatural ability. Although the spirit realm surrounds us and affects us constantly, we do not always sense it in a tangible way. It is supernatural, meaning above and beyond the natural—beyond what we may see or explain. We cannot explain how we can speak in an unknown tongue just as we cannot explain how Jesus walked on the water. Therefore, in order to receive the Holy Spirit into manifestation through speaking in tongues, we must launch out in faith. We have to believe that the Holy Spirit is within us and that He has impregnated us with the power to do this—and that He will energize it as we exercise our authority. In other words, *act on your faith.*

> *And because you are sons, God has sent forth the Spirit of His Son into your hearts, crying out, "Abba, Father!"*
> *Galatians 4:6*

> *Now He who establishes us with you in Christ and has anointed us is God, who also has sealed us and given us the Spirit in our hearts as a deposit.* *2 Corinthians 1:21–22*

> *In Him you also trusted, after you heard the word of truth, the gospel of your salvation; in whom also, having believed, you were sealed with the Holy Spirit of promise.* *Ephesians 1:13*

The Holy Spirit lives within us, and we can build our faith to manifest it by speaking this truth over ourselves: *I have the Holy Spirit. The Holy Spirit lives in me. Christ lives in me. I can do all things through Christ who strengthens me.* Remember the impact of spiritual utterance? These are all statements of truth that will build our faith; and when they are said aloud, we will feel it increase.

Since we are spirit beings, it is logical that we would have a spiritual language; and that is exactly what God has given each of us whose spirit has been regenerated by His. We have His perfect creation of Holy Spirit within us, but we have to know how to release it so that the power comes through us. This requires us *doing* something rather than passively waiting for it to happen. This is true with any of the gifts of the spirit; but, for some reason, we think it is not the case with speaking in tongues. Some believers do not speak in tongues because they have been passively waiting instead of acting on the promise.

After His resurrection, Jesus appeared to 11 of the 12 apostles, preparing them for what would occur on the Day of Pentecost. He showed them His side and feet and hands, so they would be assured that it was really Him; and then He instructed them.

> *Then Jesus said to them again, "Peace to you! As the Father has sent Me, I also send you." And when He had said this,* ***He breathed on them****, and said to them, "Receive the Holy Spirit."*
>
> *John 20:21–22*

"Breathed on" is the Greek word *emphusao*, consisting of the root *phusao* from which we get "to breathe" and the prefix *em*, meaning "in."[5] This verse is saying that Jesus breathed in and said to them, "receive the Holy Spirit." He was demonstrating what they should do when the Holy Spirit came. As we consider the mechanics of breathing, we see how this is supported by John 7:38 KJV, which also refers to receiving the Holy Spirit (Ghost).

> *He that believeth on me, as the scripture hath said,* ***out of his belly*** *shall* ***flow*** *rivers of living water. (But this spake he of the Spirit, which they that believe on him should receive: for the Holy Ghost was not yet given; because that Jesus was not yet glorified.)*
>
> *John 7:38–39 KJV*

Any singer will tell you that the diaphragm is vital for singing. It is the muscle that enables breath support, making it also what empowers speech to come forth. We typically think of the vocal chords and tongue as being the main components in speech; but the power source for speech is breath, and the strength of the air that comes from the lungs is dependent upon the diaphragm. When properly breathing, it is not the lungs that move but the diaphragm as it pushes the air out of them. When we sing or speak, we naturally take in a breath first; and then, as we release it, the utterance comes forth.

Further confirmation that this is what Jesus was referring to is found in the word "flow" in John 7:38. It is the Greek word *rheo*[6]—the root of *rhema.*[7] Jesus was teaching them how to bring forth the spiritual utterance that would occur at the time they received the Holy Spirit. Literally, this verse is saying that out of their bellies would flow spiritual utterance.

When the 12 apostles saw the cloven tongues of fire resting upon each of them on the Day of Pentecost (Acts 2:3 KJV), they knew this is what Jesus had been referring to. They breathed in like He had commanded them and were all filled with the Holy Spirit. As they released the power, they began to speak with other tongues.

We have the creative power of God in us and we just need to learn how to let it out. As we focus on speaking out of our "bellies," we will be less likely to engage our mental processes in what we are saying. There should be no forethought of what we are about to utter.

> *Trust in the* LORD *with all your heart, and lean not on your own understanding; in all your ways acknowledge* Him, *and He shall direct your paths.* *Proverbs 3:5*

The mechanism of speaking is not the supernatural part of speaking in tongues. We are in charge of that, and the spirit is not going to overtake our will. Paul said, "I will pray with my understanding, and I *will* pray in the spirit." The word "will" is emphasized to show that Paul was in control of the mechanics of speech. *The supernatural part of speaking in tongues is the language God gives us.* We are not in charge of that language—the Holy Spirit is.

Have you ever felt at a loss for words when thanking God for everything He has done for you? Paul said that speaking in tongues gives thanks well (1 Corinthians 14:17). We run out of words in our understanding to express ourselves to Him, but the prayer language He gives us can express what we cannot with our known language. Just as we give a small child money to buy us a Christmas present, so God gives us the "cash" to bless Him!

When the 12 spoke in tongues on the Day of Pentecost, they spoke as the Spirit gave them utterance. They spoke by the freedom of their will—but the Spirit gave the utterance. Speaking requires movement of the lips and tongue, rather than just opening the mouth and saying "ahhhhh" and expecting the Spirit to take us over at that point. We can certainly start with "ahhh," but then we need to start moving our lips and tongues to formulate words, just as we do with our known language. The difference is that we won't be thinking about what we are saying, nor will we understand it.

To get a better mind picture of how speech is empowered by our diaphragms, put your hand right below your ribs and then make laughing sounds, i.e., "hahaha!" Do you feel the flexing of your diaphragm? This is speaking out of your belly as John 7:38 describes. It's the vowel sounds that engage the diaphragm, so start moving through each of them audibly, holding them out one by one. After you have gone through them a couple of times this way, start engaging your lips, throat, and tongue as you would when speaking English. However, do not think about what you are saying; instead, think about the flow that is coming from your belly as Jesus said it would. Yield your tongue as an instrument of righteousness. Remember that this is done by the freedom of your will, so you can stop when you want and you can start again at will. As you become more fluent at this, however, you will begin to spiritually sense when you should stop and begin. It is a language, and your spirit will sense the beginning and ending of the phrases.

If you are still struggling with the process, try starting it off by singing a song. Sometimes in my classes, I will have the participants sing the chorus of "Oh, How I Love Jesus," since it is a familiar song to most and easy to sing.[8] Whatever song you pick, sing it first with all your heart in English until you feel comfortable. The Bible says that God will not withhold good from those who walk uprightly (Psalm 84:11). Romans 8:32 asks if He did not even spare His own son, "how shall He not with Him also freely give us all things?" Think about His desire to bless you as you sing.

> *If a son asks for bread from any father among you, will he give him a stone? Or if he asks for a fish, will he give him a serpent instead of a fish? Or if he asks for an egg, will he offer him a scorpion? If you then, being evil, know how to give good gifts to your children, how much more will your heavenly Father give the Holy Spirit to those who ask Him!* *Luke 11:11–12*

Once you begin to feel His anointing and presence, start humming instead of singing the lyrics. After you hum it through a couple of times, start going through the vowel sounds, i.e., one line through on "ah;" the next line through on "ee;" the next line through on "oh;" the next line through on "oo."

God has given you a prayer language; so as you sing, simply allow that language to flow forth. Remember that you are responsible to move your lips and tongue, but His Spirit gives you the words. Your prayer language will flow from your belly, not from your brain; so sing in the spirit from the core of your being, and think of His great love for you as He sacrificed His Son on Calvary.

When you begin to feel comfortable singing in the spirit, switch over to speaking it. Let it out like a river—let it flow like a mighty river. As you continue speaking, you will be amazed at how easy it becomes. It's easy because it was not a language you had to learn—it was already embedded within your regenerated spirit—you simply had to let it out! The more you use your prayer language, the more it will develop. Speak out the wonderful works of God and praise Him perfectly in the spirit. This is the power of God. This is where we find real intimacy with Jesus, and it is where we can experience the presence of the Holy Spirit.

The more you speak in tongues, the more you strengthen your spirit (Jude 1:20). We were born for the supernatural; *we were designed to do this!* If any believer struggles with speaking in tongues, it's because they are making it too complicated.

NOTE: For more help in the area of speaking in tongues, I suggest an LMCI audio teaching (available in CD- or MP3-format) entitled "Led by the Spirit to Speak in Tongues" that can be ordered from our e-store at LMCI.org.

We each have certain gifts that we will be stronger in and some that we will be weaker in. But this does not invalidate the need to speak in tongues to build up our spirits and our proficiency in the other gifts. The more serious our Christian walk, the more vital it becomes; and an attitude of humility and obedience will help us to receive.

At specific times when we need them, God will give us diverse tongues that are different than our prayer languages. Serious intercessors are familiar with these and will often go into them as they pray. Do not be alarmed if a diverse tongue sounds like a warlord's cry, but go with it in faith, knowing that God is using you to wage warfare in the heavens. It will be either the tongues of men or of angels, and some angels are warring angels; so you may be actually commanding angels in their own language. It is also possible to receive a diverse tongue that another person will understand. There are accounts of this in the Scriptures (e.g., Acts 2:5–11), and I also personally know individuals who have had this happen.

At the times that the Holy Spirit leads us to speak in tongues loudly and aggressively, I believe we are engaging in spiritual warfare. When He leads us to speak in tongues more quietly, I believe we are communing with the Lord. Let's yield ourselves as instruments to the Holy Spirit and allow Him to lead us. Our prayer language can be used at will and can open a floodgate for the supernatural to occur as it allows the other gifts of the Holy Spirit to flow more easily through us.

The significance of spiritual utterance was brought to a new level on the Day of Pentecost when the 12 apostles first spoke in tongues as they received the Holy Spirit. Just as Jesus had instructed them, "rivers of living water" flowed from their bellies, and it was witnessed by the thousands who had come to the temple to celebrate the day. Nothing has changed from that earliest beginning of the first-century church. To this day, the initial evidence of receiving the Holy Spirit is speaking in tongues, and God has given us the ability if we will step out in faith and speak as He gives the utterance.

Related Materials at LMCI.org

- Diverse Kinds of Tongues (Booklet)
- Led by the Spirit to Speak in Tongues (CD or MP3)
- The Physics of Faith (CD or MP3)
- Speaking by the Spirit of God (CD or MP3)
- Quantum Physics, continued: Entanglement/ Entrainment/Observation (CD or MP3)

Relevant Points

1. What is the most basic weapon of spiritual warfare and exercising our spiritual authority?

2. We can change what is inside of us by ____________________.

3. According to Psalm 103:20, what do the angels heed?

Chapter Thirteen

The Utterance Gifts of Interpretation of Tongues and Prophecy

Now that we have covered the gift of speaking in a tongue (as well as diverse tongues), we can move on to interpretation of tongues and prophecy. These three gifts—speaking in tongues, interpretation of tongues, and prophecy—are the utterance gifts.

Although God can certainly do whatever He wants and inspire an interpretation of tongues from our personal prayer language, it is usually diverse tongues that will generate an interpretation. Often, on the heels of a diverse tongue, we will sense or "hear" the beginning of an interpretation. As we speak out those words, the Holy Spirit will flow through us and give us the rest of the message.

In the previous chapter, we discussed how a diverse tongue can be used for a variety of purposes. It is called "diverse" because it will differ from our prayer language. Diverse tongues are often guttural and passionate, at times sounding like the cry of a warrior (think *Braveheart*).

Diverse tongues, as well as their interpretations, occur when the anointing comes upon us; whereas our prayer languages come from the anointing within and can be operated at any time by our will.

The Utterance Gifts of Interpretation and Prophecy

- YOU **MAY** INTERPRET
- YOU **MAY** PROPHESY

The Gift of Interpretation of Tongues

Interpretation of tongues is exactly what it says: it is the interpretation, or the making plain, of what was just spoken in an unknown language. Through the interpretation, God opens our understanding to the divine mysteries we just spoke in tongues. It can be praise (1 Corinthians 14:16 NLT), a message to God (1 Corinthians 14:2), thankfulness (1 Corinthians 14:17), speaking the wonderful works of God (Acts 2:11), or a message of warfare (Ephesians 6:18), for example.

The Holy Spirit communicates with the person giving the interpretation, who is often the same one who spoke the diverse tongue. This can come as a feeling or an impression, a word, or sometimes even a picture. As we become more adept at learning how God communicates to us, interpretation of tongues can be a primer or stepping-stone to operating the gift of prophecy, as we will discuss later.

There is a *gift* of interpretation of tongues and also a *ministry* of interpretation of tongues.

When it is the gift, the person who spoke in a diverse tongue is the one who brings forth the interpretation. When it is the ministry, it will be another person giving the interpretation rather than the one who spoke in the diverse tongue.

Interpretation of tongues is not just for the public church service; it is for private life as well. The gift can be used in circumstances where God is revealing truth to you personally; whereas the ministry would more commonly be used within a church setting.

The Old Testament accounts of Joseph's and Daniel's dream interpretations provide parallels to how interpretation of tongues works. Even though Daniel did not dream the dream, he was able to say what it was and also give the interpretation. This profiles the *gift* of interpretation; whereas, Joseph gave the interpretation of Pharaoh's dream only after Pharaoh first shared the dream with him. This was a profile of the *ministry* of interpretation of tongues.

Interpretation of Tongues (or Prophecy) in the Church

When words are brought forth via interpretation of tongues or prophecy within the church, it will be for those in that particular environment—not to bring attention to the person bringing forth the message. In our private life, speaking in tongues edifies us as individuals in our spirits; but within the church it is about what God has for all of us as a whole. The interpretation or prophecy may have more impact upon certain individuals, depending upon their callings or where they are in their walk with Christ; but overall, the message will be for the whole body of believers to be edified in their minds.

> *I wish you all spoke with tongues, but even more that you prophesied; for he who prophesies is greater than he who speaks with tongues, unless indeed he interprets,* ***that the church may receive edification.***
> *1 Corinthians 14:5*

> *Even so you, since you are zealous for spiritual gifts,* ***let it be for the edification of the church that you seek to excel.*** *Therefore let him who speaks in a tongue pray that he may interpret.*
> *1 Corinthians 14:12–13*

Our reason for seeking to excel in the spiritual gifts is to edify, or build up, our brothers and sisters. If we speak in tongues, but lack proficiency in bringing forth an interpretation, we should pray for help in that area. Interpretation will come if we ask God for it (1 Corinthians 14:13).

Also, when messages from the Holy Spirit are brought forth within a church setting, they should be done in a decent and orderly way. God is not the author of confusion, but of peace, as stated in 1 Corinthians 14:40. This indicates that there is a proper timing and structure for the release of interpretation of tongues or prophecy within the church.

Church authorities are responsible for establishing the boundaries in their own churches in such a way that the Holy Spirit is still free to reign without hindrance. We should always respect the authority of the worship leader, pastor, or elders in a church. Many churches require that someone desiring to speak get permission first from the leaders before releasing their word. Others make it clear at some point in the service that words can be released. If you are in an unfamiliar setting and believe that the Holy Spirit has given you a diverse tongue or a word of prophecy, find an elder or an usher to see what their proper procedure is.

God works through recognized authority, not unrestrained, unbridled release. The bigger the church, the more parameters are needed to keep the gifts of the Spirit flowing decently and in order.

When the Holy Spirit comes upon you, it often feels like a spiritual emotion. Ask, "Lord, is this for me or for the church?" If it is for the church, speak it out—within the parameters set by the church leadership.

How to Bring Forth an Interpretation or Prophecy

> *Pursue love, and desire spiritual gifts, but especially that you* ***may*** *prophesy.* *1 Corinthians 14:1*

> *Therefore let him who speaks in a tongue pray that he* ***may*** *interpret.* *1 Corinthians 14:13*

The word "may" in 1 Corinthians 14:1 and 13 indicates permission: a condition must be supplied. Pursue love, and desire spiritual gifts, but especially that you *may* prophesy. Therefore let him who speaks in a tongue pray that he *may* interpret. The condition to be supplied in both interpretation of tongues and in prophecy is that the Holy Spirit must come upon you to give you the words. It is an exercise in faith to interpret tongues or bring forth prophecy without premeditation because we are put into a situation where we must trust God to provide the entire message as we start speaking what He's already given us. The words are not generated from, or even filtered by, our minds; He gives them to us and we simply speak them.

James 3:4 and 5 compares our tongue to the rudder of a ship. How aggressive we are in pursuing interpretation of tongues may indicate how aggressive we are in other spiritual matters too. Shyness is not a fruit of the Spirit; it is a manifestation of rejection. The only remedy for rejection is to receive and experience the Father's love for you through a personal relationship with Jesus Christ. It won't be long before you realize how much stronger His love for you is than anyone's rejection of you, and shyness will be replaced with boldness borne out of that love.

The first step to interpreting tongues, in a practical sense, is to speak in tongues. There cannot be an interpretation without the tongue; whereas, prophecy comes as a word from the Lord not preceded by a tongue. As you get more proficient in interpretation of tongues, the Holy Spirit may begin giving you the interpretation in a picture. As you get adept in prophecy, the Holy Spirit may give you visions.

It is inspiration (in-spirit-action), not revelation. We must speak that first word in order to get the second one, and this means trusting God and not allowing our minds to get in the way. He is faithful to give us the remainder of the message if we step out in faith and speak the phrase or the couple of words that first came to us. If we hesitate because of doubt, the flow can be interrupted by our intellect. The more we step out in faith, the easier it will become to recognize when God is giving us a word to speak—and the more adept we will become at allowing the in-spirit-action to continue by speaking it.

The following is a simplified five-step procedure for interpretation of tongues. (Minus step 2, the same instructions also cover prophesying.)

1. Pray that you may interpret (prophesy).
2. Speak in a tongue or tongues (or wait for someone else to speak in tongues).
3. Watch for the first word or picture.
4. Speak what you are given—word-by-word and line-by-line.
5. Finish it!

Sometimes the interpretation may come as a picture, especially if you are a visually oriented person, but more often it will be a word or a phrase.

Speak the first word that comes to you.

Finish the interpretation (prophecy); God speaks in complete thoughts. If the interpretation does not seem complete, speak in tongues again and then add on the interpretation you receive from that in order to regain the flow and finish the message.

Always remember that the mechanics of the *ministry* of interpretation of tongues are the same as for the *gift* of interpretation of tongues—e.g., spiritual words come up and out of your spirit, which are brought forth by speaking one word at a time.

Prophecy

Prophecy is the generic term used for spiritual utterance that can be understood by men. It is used in public worship and in public service. As a gift of the Spirit (1 Corinthians 14:1), it may be given to any son or daughter of God (Acts 2:17, 21:9; 1 Corinthians 14:5) to speak words of edification, exhortation, and comfort (1 Corinthians 14:3). All believers are encouraged to prophesy (1 Corinthians 14:1), to earnestly desire it (1 Corinthians 14:39), and to not despise it (1 Thessalonians 5:20). Whereas interpretation of tongues generally comes to us word-by-word, prophecy often comes as a picture or pictures. (A prophetic utterance can also be brought forth through prophetic singing.)

NOTE: We are dealing with the gift of prophecy, not the office of a prophet. Just because someone brings forth a prophetic word does not mean he or she has the ministry of a prophet.

Misunderstanding and ignorance concerning the gifts of the Spirit and their combined usage has led to confusion concerning prophecy and revelation. When the gift of prophecy is used in combination with revelation, an individual may speak specific information to an individual or to an entire congregation. The content of a prophetic word when only the gift of prophecy is employed will be either edification, exhortation, and/or comfort (1 Corinthians 14:3). However, if a prophetic utterance contains specific revelation information, then it means that a word of knowledge is also in effect and both gifts of the Spirit are being energized.

Since prophecy is an utterance that is intelligible and the Bible warns of false prophecy and false prophets, it must be judged (1 Corinthians 14:29). The content of the message, the spirit from whence it comes, whether or not it comes to pass, and the reliability of the individual bringing it forth are all factors to be considered.[1]

Allowing the Holy Spirit to Flow through Us

The "best gifts" are those that help us fulfill our God-given ministries. For instance, if someone has the ministry of intercession, then one of their best gifts could be speaking in tongues; if it's teaching, their best gifts may be the word of knowledge to know what should be taught and also the prophetic gift for communicating it. Regardless, we need the equipping and empowering of the Holy Spirit to fulfill our ministries; and the spiritual gifts we should pursue are those that can best help us carry out God's purpose for our lives.

Whether we are interpreting tongues or prophesying, we must allow the Holy Spirit to be the one who moves through us. It's important that He doesn't just flow *to* us but that He also flows *through* us. If we get a word to speak but then we neglect to open our mouths, it doesn't profit anyone. On the other hand, if He hasn't flowed to us but we think He has and we speak a word anyway, it will be from our flesh instead of from Him. He was not the prime mover, so we would be giving a word from our own souls.

The Holy Spirit shows His willingness for us to bring forth a word from Him by bringing it to our attention. When He is willing, we must also be willing. When His anointing comes upon us, we have an obligation to respond. The primary way the Holy Spirit moves through us, or we manifest Him, is through our mouths—through utterance. It is not possible to interpret tongues or to prophesy without first opening our mouths. If we don't allow Him to move through us, we grieve Him; therefore, *we cannot allow any fear to hinder us from obedience.* Remember that His perfect love casts out fear (1 John 4:18)

Interpret Your Own/Interpret Another's

If no interpretation is given in a public service, the leader or pastor should ask if anyone there has the interpretation. If someone else is to interpret another's tongue(s), they will get the first word of the interpretation. There may be times when two people have the interpretation. This is a confirmation of the message and both should be given.

In a public worship service, you may receive a diverse tongue to speak. If the witness of the Spirit and the flow of the worship service allow you to speak it out, then you should stand up and speak it out and then wait to see if there is an interpretation from the Holy Spirit—either from you or someone else that the Spirit gives it to. The tongues and/or interpretation may also be sung, just as prophecy can be. Spiritual song is powerful and beautiful (Ephesians 5:19).

Walk in love, allowing yourself and others to grow in these gifts/ ministries of the Holy Spirit. Press into speaking in a tongue, as well as with diverse tongues, and utilizing the interpretation of tongues. Your prayer closet will never be the same—meaning it will develop to a whole new level—if you utilize these in your private life.

Becoming proficient in interpretation of tongues and in prophecy can really help you progress into understanding how to receive revelation, how to be led by the Holy Spirit, and how to walk in all nine gifts of the Holy Spirit.

Relevant Points

1. What are the three utterance gifts?

2. What is a diverse tongue?

3. Why should we desire to prophesy?

Chapter Fourteen

Receiving Spiritual Information and the Revelation Gifts

The spirit realm is a dimension of energy frequencies that are virtually invisible and undetectable by humans. Some have speculated that the reason we cannot physically operate within it is because our flesh vibrates at a lower wave length than the spirit does, and that if our bodies could vibrate faster, we *would* actually be able to function within the spirit realm.

> The basic premise of all research into the relationship between quantum reality and consciousness is that "God" and the physical universe are one, not two distinct realities. Because humans are the only self-conscious beings who are capable of contemplating their own inner divinity, they can cultivate the power of consciousness to create their own reality. This has now been allegedly proven by quantum physics because it has been established that the consciousness of the observer has the capacity to affect and shape the quantum field.[1]

Years ago, I experimented with this theory. During my early-morning hunting times, alone in a tree stand, I repeatedly (and unsuccessfully) tried to pass my hand through the tree. After I returned home from one of these adventures, my wife asked me how I was doing. I was still a little excited about the possibilities of doing the impossible and blurted out, "It's unbelievable!" Vicki asked, "What's unbelievable—did you get a deer this morning?" I said, "No—I sat in the tree stand all morning trying to pass my hand through a tree."

Without missing a beat, she responded, "Well, did you do it?" (She's been married to me long enough to know I'm a little on the zany side.) I said, "Well, no—but I'm still a relatively young man."

If I had been vibrating at that higher frequency, I believe I could have put my hand right through the tree. Even though we do not know how to speed up our bodies to the same wave length as the spirit realm, God has given us the ability to develop our spiritual perception so that we can be much more in tune with it.

Alive to the Spirit Realm

We began our lives as spirit beings dead in trespasses and sins. However, when we made Jesus our Lord and received the new birth, He regenerated our spirits and made us alive to God through the Holy Spirit; and this makes us more sensitive to the spirit realm.

> *Likewise you also, reckon yourselves to be dead indeed to sin, but alive to God in Christ Jesus our Lord.* *Romans 6:11*

> *And because you are sons, God has sent forth the Spirit of His Son into your hearts, crying out, "Abba, Father!"*
> *Galatians 4:6*

Our regenerated spirits are alive to receiving information, or revelation, from God. The Bible refers specifically to three revelation gifts of the Spirit: (1) the word of wisdom, (2) the word of knowledge, and (3) discerning of spirits. This spiritual information does not come to us by our own will but by the Spirit's will.

> *But the manifestation of the Spirit is given to each one for the profit of all: for to one is given the* ***word of wisdom*** *through the Spirit, to another the* ***word of knowledge*** *through the same Spirit, to another faith by the same Spirit, to another gifts of healings by the same Spirit, to another the working of miracles, to another prophecy, to another* ***discerning of spirits****, to another different kinds of tongues, to another the interpretation of tongues.* ***But one and the same Spirit works all these things, distributing to each one individually as He wills.*** *1 Corinthians 12:7–11*

Although spiritual information can come to us through spiritual perception and inspiration, the only time one or more of these three gifts are activated is when it comes to us via revelation. When this happens, the anointing will come *upon* us, rather than from the abiding, internal anointing that we received in our regenerated spirits. However, the anointing *within* still allows us to receive spiritual information through spiritual perception and/or inspiration. So, even if we do not receive revelation, we can have the spiritual perception we need to live above the heap—above the physical circumstances that surround us.

The Anointing Within and the Anointing Upon

The two ways the Holy Spirit empowers us is by the anointing within and by the anointing upon. We have an abiding anointing that is *in* us, which will never leave us; and this is what gives us eternal life.

> *Now He who establishes us with you in Christ and has anointed us is God, who also has sealed us and given us the Spirit in our hearts as a deposit.* 2 Corinthians 1:21–22

But there is also a function of the Holy Spirit that comes *upon* us and empowers us to do things that are beyond our normal abilities. John the Baptist saw that anointing come upon Jesus when he baptized Him.

> *I did not know Him, but He who sent me to baptize with water said to me, "Upon whom you see the Spirit descending, and remaining on Him, this is He who baptizes with the Holy Spirit."*
> John 1:33

The Holy Spirit remained *upon* Jesus because He had a perfectly purified vessel. With our corruptible bodies (and sin in our bodies and souls), we can only maintain the Holy Spirit's anointing upon us for a durational time. I believe that as we live holier and healthier lives, we will be able to increase the amount of time that we can maintain His anointing upon us.

The Holy Spirit Anointing Is ***In*** You AND ***Upon*** You

- John 14:17—"with you and will be in you"
- The anointing that is in you is to reproduce Jesus' ***character***.
  - It is for teaching, fellowship, and holiness.
- The anointing that comes upon you (and flows through you) is to reproduce Jesus' ***power***.
  - Acts 1:8; Acts 19:6

Spiritual Perception

Since we are alive to the spirit realm, we can perceive spiritual activity around us—in a sense, we pick it up with our spiritual "antennae." This is known as spiritual perception. Everyone has this, but those who receive the Holy Spirit become more spiritually powerful and perceptive. It allows us a constant awareness of the spirit realm around us; and the more cognizant we become of it, the more we will pick up on entities and activities within it.

The word "perception" comes from the Greek word *epignosis*,[2] which sounds similar to another Greek word that we are familiar with, "diagnosis." Diagnosis is made up of the prefix *dia*, which means "by way of" or "through the means of" and the root *gnosis*, which implies an experiential knowledge from its usage. When a doctor diagnoses a patient's ailment, he does it by way of experiential knowledge—either his own or others who have dealt with the symptoms. The prefix for *epignosis* is *epi*, which means "over." Spiritual perception means spiritual "over-knowledge" or knowledge that is over and above what we know by experience. When we spiritually perceive something, it is *over and above the basis of our experiential knowledge.* We cannot explain why we perceive it—we just do.

It's much easier for us to understand the physical realm since our five senses make us vividly aware of our surroundings. We have been picking up physical perceptions from the day we were born—we feel the temperature in a room, we see the colors of the furnishings, we hear the music coming from the stereo, we smell the food cooking in the kitchen, and we will soon enjoy the taste of that food. As these perceptions register through our five senses and our experience, they instantaneously dovetail to form a relatable impression.

Although a spiritual realm also surrounds us, we are not as sensitive to it as some cultures who are engrained with an understanding of this realm. Our western culture has steered us far away from it, and even Christians who have some knowledge of the Holy Spirit tend to stay away from the topic for fear they will be branded as New Agers or "holy rollers."

The truth of the matter is that all humans are spirit beings; but with the new birth and a regenerated spirit, Christians are innately more sensitive to their spiritual surroundings. However, if they ignore these impressions or shy away from them, their sensitivity to them will eventually dull.

The first step to heightening our spiritual perception is to recognize that we are spirit beings—not animals who live strictly by physical instinct or even physical faculties. *We are spirit beings who are now alive to God and the spirit realm.*

The Holy Spirit is especially alive to us within our individual callings. For instance, as a teacher, my spiritual senses enable me to read my audience, helping me to more pointedly present the Scriptures to them. Jesus was gifted in all the callings, so His spiritual awareness or perception was evident in all aspects. As we grow up in Him, our ability to perceive spiritual signals will also mature and strengthen.

> *But solid food belongs to those who are of full age, that is, those who by reason of use have their senses exercised to discern both good and evil.* *Hebrews 5:14*

The word "senses" in this verse is the Greek word *aistheterion* which Strong's Concordance defines as the "faculty of the mind for perceiving."[3] However, I believe it would be more accurately defined as a faculty of the *spirit* for perceiving since it is the spirit of God in us that enables us to minutely discern good and evil.

Have you ever been talking to someone, and you start to get a "gritchy" feeling? You might feel the need to take a step back from them, and it's not that they have bad breath or body odor. Rather, there is something coming off of them that you perceive in the spirit. It might be that the person has a demon or is full of negativity. Children are often more sensitive to this than adults who have learned to be copacetic and amenable; but young kids will tell you right out, "That guy's creepy!" Their sensitivity to the spirit realm is probably stronger since they have not yet been numbed by worldly experience.

An example of Jesus' spiritual perception can be found in the healing record of Mark 2. The scribes and Pharisees were not happy when they saw Him heal the man in the stretcher by forgiving him of his sins, and verse 8 shows that Jesus used His spiritual perception to know what they were reasoning within themselves.

> *And immediately, when Jesus* ***perceived in His spirit*** *that they reasoned thus within themselves, He said to them, "Why do you reason about these things in your hearts? Which is easier, to say to the paralytic, 'Your sins are forgiven you,' or to say, 'Arise, take up your bed and walk'?"* *Mark 2:8*

Jesus said that we can do the works that He did (and greater), so we should be able to do this as well. Just as He perceived what these people were thinking, there will be times when we will spiritually pick up people's reasoning, or their spiritual "vibes." This is not done by operating psychic powers but by being alive to the spirit realm through our regenerated spirits.

Because we are alive to God, we can pick up what's going on in the spirit realm like a Geiger counter detects radiation; and our "batteries" stay charged as we consistently use this ability. However, the challenge is to learn how to consistently exercise it while still living in a physical realm that often seems to overtake the spiritual.

I probably receive more spiritual information through my spiritual perception than I do through revelation. However, through my experiences, I have learned that we need to be cautious when we receive spiritual information this way because it is not always as accurate as revelation. At times, we may misinterpret it as revelation, which is why we should guard ourselves from such phrases as, "The Lord said this or that." If it's spiritual perception and not revelation, it can be wrong. When it's revelation from God, it's never wrong because God does not lie.

We also need to be careful when sharing with others what we believe the Lord has revealed to us. We should be known by the fruit in our lives, rather than by letting others know how much the Lord talks to us. When we believe He has spoken to us, we need to use wisdom about passing on the information. Just because He told us something does not automatically mean that He wants us to tell anyone else.

If the Lord said, and the Lord did say that you could say He said, then you can say it. But if He did not say you could say He said, then you can't say that He said. (I'm not saying that one again!)

The point is that spiritual perception is *not* the Lord saying. We need to learn to temper our vocabulary with the accuracy of the Word of God, so that we don't come across as religious punks who are always boasting that the Lord talks to us. We all have spiritual perception, but sometimes what we are "picking up" can be demonically influenced, since demons can affect spiritual atmospheres. This is why it may not be accurate. We should say that we *perceive* something rather than that God is telling it to us. This will allow us to state what we believe the Holy Spirit has shown us without misrepresenting God's integrity. We could say, "I have perceived this, and my spiritual perception is not always correct, so I want to check it with you." As God's sons and daughters, we need to walk in humility and love.

We perceive it because we are alive to the spirit realm, which is above the natural realm. That is why we need to separate spirit from soul. I served in the ministry for 20 years before I learned this. There would be times when I would pick up on spiritual rumblings; but it took a while before I began to realize that the more I lived in that upper level of my three-story house, the more I could pick up things from the spirit realm. If we can live in the higher realm of God's kingdom, we can exercise our spiritual authority over those evil spirits rather than being the victim. So let's move our furniture to the third floor and make it our *main* floor.

This means that as we go about our daily activities, let's think of accomplishing our tasks as spirit beings. The Holy Spirit wants to help us in everything we do. The greatest discipline we will ever undertake is to learn to be spirit-minded. Our spirits are the real us, and they are eternal and regenerated by God.

Some Gender Differences in Spiritual Perception

At the risk of sounding politically incorrect, I would like to point out some of the gender differences when it comes to the topic of spiritual perception. Please keep in mind that these are observations that stem mostly from hearsay, experience, and a bit of research; and they will not always hold true across the board for either gender.

Perhaps you have noticed that women tend to be more sensitive to spiritual perception than men, which is probably where the idea of women's intuition came from. However, this heightened sensitivity can also open them up more to deception as well. Although it appears that Eve was the one who found the serpent in the garden, she also was the one who was initially duped by him.

After the serpent deceived Eve and God cursed him, the devil's hatred for women began to surface. God revealed to him in Genesis 3:15 that a woman would bring the seed of the Messiah into the world; thus, he eventually dispatches the watchers to intermingle with the daughters of men in hopes of foiling this prophecy.

Perhaps it is for this reason that God gave women the physical ability to process information in a broader way than men. This has been detected by scientists who discovered that women have more brain cells connecting the right and left sides of their brains than men do.

> Women on the other hand have four times as many brain cells (neurons) connecting the right and left side of their brain. This latter finding provides physical evidence that supports the observation that men rely easily and more heavily on their left brain to solve one problem one step at a time. Women have more efficient access to both sides of their brain and therefore greater use of their right brain. Women can focus on more than one problem at one time and frequently prefer to solve problems through multiple activities at a time.[4]

This enables women to more readily utilize both sides simultaneously, while men tend to independently use the left side of their brains more. As a result, women often tap into two quadrants of reasoning within their brains and toss information back and forth between the two to reach a conclusion. This cultivates a more holistic way of thinking and a deeper view of things; whereas, because of the strong use of the left side of their brains, men are usually more analytical in their thinking and perspectives.

Husbands, listen to your wives—they will often read the spirit realm better than us because they are not as analytical. This means if your wife says she's wondering about something, bury your pride and listen up. Adam was one being before he was split into male and female; so the divine plan of husband and wife as one flesh is a precious pearl of great price—and this is one example of that.

Receiving Revelation

Revelation is a different concept than spiritual perception. The Greek word is *apokalupsis,* comprised of the prefix *apo,* a preposition that means "away from"[5] and the root *kaluptō*, which means "to hide" or "to veil."[6] So revelation means to take away the veil or to disclose, which is what the Holy Spirit does when He reveals a truth to us. It would be like pulling the drapery off of a great piece of art so the patrons could observe it for the first time—and everyone gasps with admiration (hopefully) as they see it.

When the Holy Spirit pulls the cover off a truth, your spirit becomes impregnated with that reality. It will be a new truth (or a deeper layer of that truth) to you—a concept that your heart has never really grasped before. We cannot make this happen either; it is by the will of God. But we can certainly ask for it; and then the timing of it is God's prerogative.

So although we can ask God for revelation, He will sometimes give it to us when we did not ask. We can usually recognize it more clearly when that happens, because we are not looking for it. When we do ask for it, we have to be really sharp to discern it between our own thoughts and God speaking to us. When endeavoring to exercise our spiritual authority to do the works of Jesus, we need revelation.

One of the mistakes we can make is to run ahead of God instead of waiting for His revelation. This happened to a friend of mine who quit a very successful job because he did not wait for the Lord's timing. He ran into financial ruin and it ended up costing him his marriage. It is vital that we know the difference between when God speaks to us and when He's not speaking to us.

One way to recognize revelation is that when it comes upon us, it will move us.

> *For the prophecy came not in old time by the will of man: but holy men of God spake as they were* ***moved*** *by the Holy Ghost.*
> *2 Peter 1:21*

"Moved" by the Holy Spirit in 2 Peter 1:21 is in the passive voice, which means the subject is not the one initiating the movement; rather, the subject is being acted upon. This verse says that prophecy (revelation) did not come in old time by the will of man. When we ask for revelation, the temptation is to think it into being (that would be the subject initiating the movement). Our thought processes usually work by way of association or impression, so as we focus upon what we want the Lord to tell us, a snowball effect begins as our imagination makes up our desired answer. This power of suggestion, as some would call it, is a mental process that is controlled by us and not by the Holy Spirit.

Revelation does not come by the will of man, but holy men of God spoke as they were moved by the Holy Spirit. When the Holy Spirit moves, He impregnates our spirit with a truth that intersects and cuts across the grain of our thinking—it will be a *new* thought. So when we get a thought and wonder if it was revelation, we should consider what was going on in our mind before the thought came. If what we were thinking before the thought came is associated to the thought, it may not be revelation.

As an example of an *un*associated thought, once when I was driving my pickup truck to the local county dump, I suddenly had the thought that I would be issuing a teenage publication. I knew it had to be revelation because it was not related at all to anything I was thinking. In fact, I can guarantee it was not a thought that came out of me, because the last thing I wanted to do at that time was a teen publication. (I still considered myself a teen vet and was thankful to have graduated from that era.)

On the other hand, while praying, I will often be reminded of an individual or a related situation, and I wonder if God is telling me to call or do something for that person. However, when I check my thoughts, I usually recognize that it was my thoughts, and not the Holy Spirit, that triggered the memory. It doesn't mean that I shouldn't call them or do something for them, but it wasn't necessarily God giving me revelation to do it.

One of the early books I wrote, *You Don't Have to be Smart to Walk with God*, simplifies the revelation process and breaks it down so that we realize that walking with God is not a complicated reality. None of us want to move to Stupidville (or back to it, as the case may be); so let's learn how to do this right.

Another reason we need to be sharp at discerning revelation from soulish thoughts is because it is possible to be deceived by demons who could talk us into doing goofy things that could hurt our witness. We should have a sense of peace when God is speaking to us. The carnal mind is death; but the spiritual mind is life and peace (Romans 8:6–8).

Revelation ***Must*** Agree with Scripture

- The word of the Lord ***comes***.
  - It actively arrives on the scene.
  - It can fill in the spaces between the lines in the Bible.
- Revelation must agree with Scripture and the witness of the Holy Spirit.

My friend, Randy MacMillan from Cali, Colombia, taught me a way to get confirmation from the Holy Spirit when we are already associated to the answer desired within the revelation. For instance, we might ask Him if we should move to a certain location that we are already familiar with. In a situation like this, our souls could go haywire with information and short-circuit what God is trying to tell us. The following is the five-step list Randy developed that really works for me when I have to make these kind of decisions. (In fact, C. Peter Wagner keeps this same list on his refrigerator and reads it every day.)

- Initially choose one way or the other;
- Do not change your position;
- Do not move forward or take any action;
- Wait for a confirmation (often in the form of peace) or a rejection (often in the form of unrest) from the Holy Spirit;
- Make your final decision based upon the confirmation or rejection from the Holy Spirit.

We may even have an interjection of thought that is so wild and bizarre that we think it just can't be from God. In these situations, my friend taught me to figuratively drive a stake into the ground that has "peace" written on it and stay right there tied to it. When we have an attitude of peace with Him then we know that He will give us what we need when we need it. He will either confirm the information if it was from Him or let us know that it was not from Him.

We can make a decision according to what we think God is telling us and what we know by our five senses; but in that decision-making process, we must stay tethered to that stake of peace. If we are still connected to the peace of God, then the Holy Spirit's response to our decision should be clear. The reason it's important to make a decision and then see how it sits with the Holy Spirit is because God will not honor a wishy-washy attitude; and He cannot confirm a "maybe."

There are times when the Holy Spirit will give us direct revelation and clarity; but there are also times when we must make the best decision we can, based upon the Scriptures and the physical information we have. Once we make up our minds one way or the other, God can either confirm our decision or put that "check" (uneasiness) in our spirit. Either way, He will let us know because He loves us and does not want us to walk outside His will. Patience is key, and it is rooted in that stake of peace. If we let impatience propel us into action, we run the risk of walking outside of God's will for us. Too often, a rushed action is based upon what our flesh desires and not upon what God wants us to do.

If we stay connected to that peace, we will know whether or not that decision is God's will. If we drift away from that peace, confusion will take its place and we will not receive our answer. Make the decision, and then stay in a holding pattern to see how the Holy Spirit witnesses to your spirit about it. It does work.

What is Inspiration?

> *But the Helper, the Holy Spirit, whom the Father will send in My name, He will teach you all things, and* ***bring to your remembrance*** *all things that I said to you.*
>
> *John 14:26*

The Greek word for "remembrance" in this verse is *hupomimnesko*, which is comprised of the prefix *hupo*, a preposition meaning "by" or "under,"[7] and the verb *mimnēsko*, which means "to remind."[8] Thus, the phrase, "bring to your remembrance" could read "bring from under (the surface) to remind." This third activation of spiritual information is best defined by the word "inspiration." Inspiration is often related to spiritual truths already within us that are triggered by something we hear or see, i.e., a song or a view of nature; but it is the Holy Spirit who brings that memory to the surface. That does not mean that every time you remember something that the Holy Spirit prompted it—otherwise, we wouldn't have to tie strings around our fingers.

When I teach, the Holy Spirit often pulls scriptural truths to the surface that I've studied and meditated upon. Many times, I will place my notes to the side and trust that whatever God wants me to say will be brought to my remembrance. In a sense, I put my teaching into "God gear" by laying everything out on the table and trusting Him to pick up only what He wants to use, when and however He desires to use it. He never fails to help me this way when I give it to Him in faith.

When we have a storehouse of scriptures at our disposal, the Holy Spirit will bring them back to our remembrance at just the right time. This is one of the ways the Helper helps us—by bringing truths back to our remembrance right when we need them.

One of the differences between revelation and inspiration is that inspiration comes from within us, whereas revelation comes from outside us—it comes upon us. This is often how the Holy Spirit works—when we need additional energizing to get a job done, the anointing can come upon us with the extra information (revelation) or empowerment (grace) we need at the time.

The Three Revelation Gifts

> *For to one is given by the Spirit the word of wisdom; to another the word of knowledge [these are two of the three concepts of revelation; the third one being discerning of spirits] by the same Spirit.*
> *1 Corinthians 12:8*

Word of wisdom is a "how-to" revelation. Although it is often attached to discerning of spirits and/or to word of knowledge, we can also receive a word of wisdom that is relative to biblical truths without receiving a word of knowledge or discerning of spirits. When the Holy Spirit gives us instruction on getting something done, He has delivered a word of wisdom to us.

Word of knowledge is spiritual information that is necessary to carry out God's purposes in the physical realm. An example we see in the Scriptures is Joseph's revelation of Pharaoh's dream concerning the coming ordeal in the land of Egypt. God revealed to Joseph what was necessary for the Pharaoh to understand—that there would be seven years of plenty and then seven years of famine. God then subsequently gave Joseph a word of wisdom so that he could counsel Pharaoh on how to save Egypt.

Discerning of spirits is spiritual information that is relevant to the spiritual realm—dealing with angels, demons, evil angels, or territorial influence. Ephesians 6:12 teaches us that our battle on this earth is not against physical entities but against spiritual ones; therefore, to overcome the evil of this world, we must be able to discern what is happening in the spiritual realm.

Ephesians 3:16 tells us that we have an inner man who is strengthened with might through God's Spirit. Our inner man is spiritual, and it is through the spirit that we receive spiritual information (revelation)—not through the soul or body.

> *That He would grant you, according to the riches of His glory, to be strengthened with might through His Spirit in the inner man.*
> *Ephesians 3:16*

The Holy Spirit is within us; Christ, the hope of glory, is *in* us, according to Colossians 1:27. Colossians 3:11 tells us that Christ is "all in all," and that means that *all* of Him is in all of us! Christ in us, the indwelling Holy Spirit, gives us the spiritual senses to receive spiritual information, just as we have physical senses to receive physical information. Spiritual information can even come as a "feeling" within our bodies, although it is actually coming to the inner (spirit) man. Once we grasp this concept, it will become easier to recognize it when it comes this way.

The Holy Spirit first communicates directly with our spirit.

> *The Spirit Himself bears witness with our spirit.*
> *Romans 8:16a*

Then our spirit delivers that revelation to our soul and/or body.

In the Scriptures, when word of wisdom or word of knowledge is mentioned, "word" in the Greek is *logos.* One of the meanings for *logos* is "what is declared,"[9] which does not necessarily have to come through speech or a written word—it could be a picture or even an impression. It is simply a declaration of information. This differs from *rhema*, which is also translated "word" but means a *spoken* word.[10] If we wait for a literal word, we are limiting it to something spoken. Studies show that 83% of our knowledge comes to us visually.[11] If this is true in the physical realm, then we should expect the same in the spiritual realm.

> *But blessed are your eyes for they see, and your ears for they hear.*
> *Matthew 13:16*

We were built for spiritual vision. When Jesus said, "Blessed are your eyes for they see, and your ears for they hear," He was referring to the eyes and ears of the spirit man. To become adept at receiving revelation, we must continually remind ourselves that we are spirit beings with spiritual senses. We are living on this planet in a body made of flesh; but in reality, we are spirit beings in earth suits. There will come a day, however, when these earth suits will be dissolved; and we will have a house that is eternal—made of God in the heavens (2 Corinthians 5:1).

We don't know yet what our spirit body is going to look like. Perhaps we will look similar to what we look like here; but the point is that we are really spirit beings who are *alive* to God. We need to learn how that affects our spiritual senses and what that feels like so that we recognize revelation when it comes.

A friend of mine was sharing with me about his spiritual journey once, and as he made the statement that he still had a long way to go, we felt "Holy Spirit goose bumps" on our arms. The spiritual feeling was so strong that we both felt it. We can actually *feel* the anointing of God. Sometimes it will be felt in different places in a room; so the people in one area of a room may not feel anything at all, while others are experiencing a strong spiritual sensation in another area.

The point is that the Holy Spirit will reveal truths to us through our spiritual senses, and we can learn to recognize these. There have been times when I could tell my spiritual eyes were seeing something because there were "special effects" involved, like in a movie. The way we see in the spirit is different than the way we see in the physical realm because it vibrates in a different wavelength. Sometimes the things I see in the spirit look translucent even though they also have substance. We could be fooled into thinking we are imagining these visual revelations; but in reality, they are not imaginations—they are what I like to call *image*-nations. This is how we see in the spirit, and it takes faith to walk out on what we see this way.

God has different ways of imparting spiritual information to us. Since we are spirit beings, we have spiritual senses—just as we have physical senses as physical beings. Spiritual perception happens when our spiritual senses pick up spiritual information; inspiration is an inner working of the Holy Spirit to bring something to our remembrance; and revelation occurs when the Holy Spirit comes upon us (the anointing upon) and reveals truth to us from the outside, as opposed to a truth already within us. The three gifts of the spirit that correspond with revelation are word of wisdom, word of knowledge, and discerning of spirits. The more we recognize that we are spirit beings, the easier it will be to receive the spiritual information God has for us—whether it comes through spiritual perception, inspiration, or revelation (and regardless of which gift or combination of gifts are activated).

We already have spiritual authority as given by the written Word of God; but these revelation gifts are the spiritual eyes and ears to give us specific direction on exercising it.

Related Materials at LMCI.org

- The Anointing In and On (Booklet)
- Approved of God: by Grace or by Works? (Booklet)
- Developing Your Spiritual Sensitivity (CD- or MP3-set)
- Manifesting the Holy Spirit (CD or MP3)
- Recognizing Revelation (CD or MP3)
- You Don't Have to Be Smart to Walk with God (Book)

Relevant Points

1. What are the three revelation gifts?
2. What are two other ways we can receive spiritual information?
3. What is the difference between the anointing within and the anointing upon?

Chapter Fifteen

Spiritual Faith

> *To another **faith** by the same Spirit, to another gifts of healings by the same Spirit, to another the working of miracles, to another prophecy, to another discerning of spirits, to another different kinds of tongues, to another the interpretation of tongues. But one and the same Spirit works all these things, distributing to each one individually as He wills.* *1 Corinthians 12:9–11*

So far in this section of *Exercising Spiritual Authority* we have looked at the utterance gifts of speaking in tongues, interpretation of tongues, and prophecy; and we went through the knowledge gifts of word of knowledge, word of wisdom, and discerning of spirits. These, plus the gift of faith, gifts of healings, and the working of miracles, combine in various ways to produce a manifestation of the Holy Spirit, which is the power lever to exercise spiritual authority in the journey of any Christ follower.

Of all nine gifts, faith is perhaps my favorite because it is through a deeper understanding and application of its concepts that the manifestation of the Holy Spirit can be increased exponentially. Although my favorite, it took me awhile to understand this incredible gift; and this resulted in a rather stormy relationship with the subject. It seemed the more I heard, the more confusing the whole concept became. Yet the significance of faith cannot be over-emphasized if we want to be led by the Holy Spirit and produce the miracles and wonders the Lord said would follow those who believe (Mark 16:17–18). Hebrews 11:6 says, "Without faith, it is impossible to please God." **If we want to please God, then we must understand and operate faith.**

Jesus said if we have faith the size of a grain of mustard seed we can say to this mountain, "Be removed and be cast into the sea," and it would obey us (Mark 11:23). However, there have been times when I knew I had that much faith, but that mountain just stayed right there. With such a small amount of faith, it seems we would all be moving mountains quite frequently. So why don't we?

Part of our problem, I believe, is that we don't understand that there are different kinds of faith. When the Lord opened the eyes of my understanding to this vital aspect of His kingdom, it was a major turning point in my life and a significant launching point in my ministry. I began seeing miracles with increased regularity that were of such size and magnitude, my ministry was literally catapulted from a basement operation (literally) to one that was worldwide. My prayer is that the Lord will open the eyes of your understanding concerning faith just as He did for me and that it will have a similar impact on your ministry as it did on mine.

This is what we need to know: *The Holy Spirit supplies a gift of faith that enables us to do supernatural things that we cannot do of our own accord or even by our own faith.* If we can learn how to tap into that gift of faith, we can consistently do the works that Jesus said we could. This kind of faith comes with revelation and not through guesswork.

> *Most assuredly, I say to you, he who believes in Me, the works that I do he will do also; and greater works than these he will do, because I go to My Father. And whatever you ask in My name, that I will do, that the Father may be glorified in the Son. If you ask anything in My name, I will do it.* *John 14:12–14*

Faith is the spiritual power that penetrates the veil between the real (physical) and the surreal (spiritual). Faith is supernatural.

Romans 1:17—From Faith to Faith

Years ago, I left the Methodist church I grew up in to seek the baptism of the Holy Spirit. Once I received it and spoke in tongues, I hungered for the miracles that others were experiencing. John Wimber (a founding leader of the Vineyard movement) followed a similar path. He first attended a traditional church where he got saved; but as he read his Bible and started seeing the works that Jesus did, he sought out the pastor to ask him one main question: *"When do we get to do the [real] stuff?"* [1]

His hunger for "the [real] stuff" is what led him to find out about the gift of faith, and the Holy Spirit was faithful to open his spiritual eyes. The Holy Spirit will do the same for us—He is no respecter of persons. As He opens our eyes to see the truth, we too will begin to understand how faith can work in our life and ministry. My own hunger to understand and teach others about "the real stuff" is what drew me to find all the scriptural usages of "faith" and intensely study them. The Holy Spirit opened up these scriptures to me so that I could finally grasp the concept of faith and see amazing results everywhere I utilized it in my travels—including India, Africa, South America, and all over the United States.

Eventually, I had so many notes and information on faith that I knew it was time to back up and find a starting place so I could teach it to others. Since we all come from various backgrounds, we have different learning curves. Some Christians have already been taught from the basic doctrinal tenets in the New Testament: Romans, Ephesians, and Thessalonians. However, others have very little knowledge of the basic tenets; so I prayed that the Holy Spirit would show me a fitting launch pad for a teaching on faith that everyone could grasp. The Lord provided that in the first chapter of Romans.

There were two reasons I chose the book of Romans to look for my starting point: (1) Romans has more usages of the word "faith" than any other book in the Bible (although Hebrews comes in a close second), and (2) Romans plays a vital role in laying out the basic foundation for Christians. As I began reading the opening chapter, Romans 1:17 quickly caught my attention.

> *For therein [in the Word of God] is the righteousness of God revealed* ***from faith to faith****: as it is written, The just shall live by faith.*
> *Romans 1:17*

Throughout the years, I listened to various explanations of this verse; but none of them really made sense to me. With my focus now on the concept of faith, however, the Holy Spirit started opening my eyes.

This first letter written by the Apostle Paul opens with salutations that might sound like this today: "Hello. How're ya doin'? How's your Mama? You guys in Rome are okay. I'm doing cool, man; glad you're saved!" Once he gets through the hellos, he tells them his purpose for writing the letter.

> *First, I thank my God through Jesus Christ for you all, that* ***your faith*** *is spoken of throughout the whole world.*
> *Romans 1:8*

The first thing he thanks God for is that the *faith* of these Roman believers was being talked about throughout the whole world. Suddenly, all of my studying and praying ballooned up in a big crescendo and "exploded" in my spirit. At that split second in time, I knew the Holy Spirit was allowing me to see something big about faith. I cannot communicate the sensational feeling I had in my spirit—it was as if I had swung a pickax into a rock wall and hit a vein of gold about three feet wide. The gold just started falling out of the wall, and I was catching as much of it as I could before it hit the floor.

One of the biggest pieces I caught was contained in the phrase, "from faith to faith" in verse 17. I suddenly received an epiphany when the Holy Spirit showed me that the phrase, "from faith to faith" is talking about two kinds of faith—yet they are called the same thing. He showed me that it would be like driving from one location to another that both have the same name, e.g., like leaving Charleston, West Virginia and traveling to Charleston, South Carolina. Just because they have the same name does not mean they are the same place or entity. Physical things can have variety, even when they are called the same thing; and the same holds true in the spirit realm.

This is when I saw that the righteousness of God is revealed from *our faith* to the *gift of faith*. These are two distinct kinds of faith. We often start out with our faith, but God has the option of kicking in and pouring out His faith if ours is not enough to produce a miracle. We receive the gift of faith by God's mercy; it is a *gift* from God. We end up with something much more powerful than we started with. However, our faith is not to be taken lightly, because it is what opens the door to activate the gift of faith.

Thus began my search. I looked for the phrases "your faith, thy faith, my faith, our faith, their faith, etc.," on my Bible computer program and found a fountain of truth. Through this search and from what the Holy Spirit had already shown me through the

Scriptures, I realized that we are spirit beings with spirit power—*and our spirit power is faith.*

NOTE: A deeper explanation of my study on faith is in a CD- or MP3-set entitled Foundations of Faith available at LMCI.org.

The Two Kinds of Faith

Just as there are two anointings of the Holy Spirit—*in* you and *upon* you—there are also two distinct kinds of faith: (1) your faith that comes from your spirit, and (2) the gift of faith that comes as a Holy Spirit gift and enables you to do works of power.

As we begin to differentiate between these two kinds of faith, we will see why our results are sometimes predictable and sometimes *un*predictable. The first kind of faith—our own—is off again and on again. It can be high, but it can also be low. There are times when it is strong enough to "buy from God's storehouse" and see the impossible come to pass; but then there are times when it is too weak to get anything at all. Our own faith is like spiritual cash—the more we have, the more we can purchase. But it is not reliable like God's faith; and His faith, even when it is the size of a grain of mustard seed, is powerful enough to produce miracles.

When the gift of faith is activated, it turns us into supermen (and women) who can "fly." Remember, we are spirit beings—and that makes us *supernatural.* The gift of faith is activated when we carry out a revelation from the Holy Spirit, and it spiritually enables us to do the works of Jesus. His faith is already inside of us through the gift of the Holy Spirit; and it will be activated by our faith as we walk in obedience to His revelation. However, if we do not receive revelation, then we have to rely upon our own unreliable faith—which is sometimes strong but can also be weak at times.

When I started understanding the gift of faith, my phone began to ring off the hook from about 6 AM until midnight when we would finally turn it off. People wanted me to minister healing to them because they were hearing reports of miracles from all around the country. I still minister healing to people over the phone but not in the massive amounts I did in the beginning; because, in obedience to the Holy Spirit, I taught others to do it too, rather than just keeping the knowledge of it to myself.

The Lord wants all of His people to walk with faith in their ministries; and I believe this is why He put it on my heart to establish Liberating Ministries for Christ International and teach others what He was teaching me.

With this revelation, I knew that miracles were possible—and not just in my ministry. They are possible for any believer with the right information and desire. I also discovered in 2 Corinthians 1:24 that we each have our own faith that no one else has dominion over.

> ***Not that we have dominion over your faith****, but are fellow workers for your joy; for by faith you stand.*
>
> *2 Corinthians 1:24*

For years I had relinquished dominion over my life to people in leadership positions and said, "You decide where I go and what I do." Now I know that Jesus Christ is the Lord of my life, and by my faith I stand. If my faith is weak, then I will fall. Of course, there are those within the body of Christ who help us build our faith, but it is still ultimately our responsibility to utilize the faith we have been given.

Two Kinds of Faith

- Your faith
  - Yours to operate at your choosing
  - Limited to your expectation
- The Holy Spirit's faith
  - Can use with His permission (revelation)
  - Unlimited because of the promise

The Gift of Faith—Batteries Included

Do you think God would ask us to minister healing to someone without supplying the faith to energize it? We might or might not see results with our faith; however, when God tells us by revelation to pray for someone, He also supplies the necessary gift of faith to bring it to pass. As we step out with our own faith to follow through on what He reveals to us, the gift of faith is activated. When the gift of healing and the gift of faith are combined, a miracle is the result.

When we get revelation, the gift of faith comes included within it. It's like a child getting a brand new remote-control car on Christmas morning. They push it to level four, and it does nothing. Then the parents look at the box carefully and see that it says, "Does not include batteries." And so the kids have no car to play with on Christmas morning. But when our heavenly Father gives us a gift, it always has batteries included. When He tells us to do something, He will also give us the gift of faith to do it. Remember though, that it still requires our own faith to act on what He has told us to do.

Jesus gave us authority over sickness and disease—right? We can speak with authority because sickness and disease have already been defeated at the cross. So even by my own faith, I have the authority to heal; yet by the gift of faith, it is absolute.

One experience I had after the Lord taught me about the gift of faith took place in southern California. Within a small group of believers there, we witnessed about 250 instantaneous, miraculous, bone-jolting, jaw-teeth-jarring, spine-tingling miracles inside of a few weeks!

When word got out, a particular ministry invited me to teach them how to produce such miracles. When I got there, I listened carefully to what they were teaching and could clearly see the missing elements in their belief system. In an effort to help them, I explained there were two truths that could open up their understanding of faith: (1) that man is a spirit being, and (2) that there is a gift of faith. Their immediate response was, "No, he is not" and "No, there is not." I quickly realized that there was no profit to arguing with people who were not willing to change their way of thinking. I have more important things to do for the kingdom of God then to stand around and argue.

Before I left, one of them challenged me again with, "There's no such thing as the gift of faith." I asked him if he would like to defend his statement, and he said he would love to. This was our conversation:

> I said, "So all faith is your faith?"
>
> He responded confidently, "Absolutely—there is no gift of faith."

Then I said, "Do you mind if I ask you a couple of questions?"

"Okay," he said.

"Does the gift of speaking in tongues come from you or the Holy Spirit?"

"From the Holy Spirit," he answered, and then added, "I can't do that by myself."

"What about the interpretation of tongues?"

"It also comes as an enablement from the Holy Spirit; I can't do that myself either."

"Then what about prophecy—can you do it of your own accord?"

I could tell he was growing weary of the redundancy as I went down the list of gifts of the Spirit from 1 Corinthians 12:7–10, but he still responded, "No. It comes from an empowerment and enablement of the Holy Spirit."

"What about the gift of a word of knowledge? Can you just conjure it up and make it yourself?"

"No, it comes from the Holy Spirit. What's your point?"

"I'm just giving you some rope [figuratively], and you're tying it in a noose and slipping it around your neck. And in a minute, I'm going to kick the stool out from underneath you and see your eyeballs bulge out of your head, if you keep answering my questions! What about the gift of the word of wisdom—this gift of the Spirit—do you conjure it, do you make it come yourself, or does it come from God?"

"It comes from God," he said a little impatiently. "What's your point?"

"What about discerning of spirits?"

"It comes from God."

"What about the gift of faith?"

"Well, that comes from G—," he stuttered when he realized what he was saying. As he stumbled, I "kicked the stool out" from beneath him.

The point? *There is a gift of faith that comes from the Holy Spirit that enables believers to do the works of Jesus in miraculous power—and it is not the same as our faith.*

Our Faith

For assuredly, I say to you, whoever ***says*** *to this mountain, 'Be removed and be cast into the sea,' and does not doubt in his heart, but believes that those things he says will come to pass, he will have whatever he says.* *Mark 11:23*

> *Therefore I say to you, whatever things you ask when you* ***pray,*** *believe that you receive them, and you will have them.*
> *Mark 11:24*

Mark 11:23 does not say that we are to pray, it says we are to *say*—in other words, to verbalize or speak; whereas, verse 24 says we are to *pray.* I believe these two verses show the difference between the gift of faith and our faith. The gift of faith is triggered by our command rather than a prayer; but when we do not have the gift of faith, we use our faith instead in a prayer.

This is the simplicity of operating our faith: *believe that we receive, and we will receive.* In order to receive from our faith, our spiritual consciousness must "see" the event coming to pass.

This kind of faith comes into our soul from our spirit because we are spirit beings whose spirits have been regenerated by the Holy Spirit. When our souls are submitted to our regenerated spirit, our faith will be strong. The more consistently we surrender our souls to our regenerated spirit—the indwelling Christ—the more our faith will increase. Also, the more miracles we see, the greater our own individual faith will become.

Our faith is operated by our desire, our prayers, and our expectations. Sometimes we use the word "faith" so much, it loses its impact. If we substitute the word "expectation" for faith, it can help us to regain the necessary impact. Our expectation is equivalent to our faith. We can get amazing things done with our faith if we truly expect amazing things will come to pass (Ephesians 3:20). The more we understand God's love for us and His desire to intervene in our lives, the bigger our expectations will become.

The following acronym can be used to help us remember that faith is what we expect to happen through God's intervention in our lives.

F-Forever
A-Anticipating
I-Intervention
T-Through
H-Him

The Difference between the Gift of Faith and Our Faith

There is a correlation between the gift of faith and your faith. If I asked a friend to buy me a brand new truck complete with all the extras, he would probably hesitate. On the other hand, if I asked the same friend to buy me a pack of gum, he would have no problem whatsoever. Why? Because it doesn't cost as much. That is the scenario we deal with in our walk with God; but when God asks us to do something that's outside the range of our personal faith, He does not expect us to pay for it. Instead, He gives us His faith to pay for it. It is the *gift* of faith.

As humans, we have our limitations; but God does not. His bank is a lot bigger than our accounts. If you needed to buy a car and I gave you the option of either using my gold American Express credit card or a wad of bills that only amounts to $45—which would you pick? The gold card represents the faith of God—spiritual faith that is virtually limitless. Hebrews 11:3 tells us that God made the world by faith. That's a lot of faith.

> *Through faith we understand that the worlds were framed by the word of God, so that things which are seen were not made of things which do appear.* Hebrews 11:3

He commanded it and never doubted that it would happen. The real power behind all of this is not our faith—it's God. That is why we should never worship faith, but we should worship the One who put the whole universe together with it.

Many of us remember the whole "name-it-and-claim-it" movement. That only worked when our faith was there; but when the gift of faith (spiritual faith) is activated, we can absolutely name it and claim it. However, the temptation can be to only name it and claim it when it fits into our desires. Spiritual faith is operated by revelation and will not necessarily correlate with our desire. We can pray and ask Him, but the revelation to activate our spiritual faith only comes from Him according to His will (Hebrews 2:4). At that point, we are under an order—God calls us up and tells us to go and we go—and He supplies the supernatural faith.

The following passage shows Jesus teaching His disciples the difference between these two kinds of faith. It begins with a journey to Bethany during the last week of His life when He is looking for a snack and notices a fig tree in the distance.

> *And seeing a fig tree afar off having leaves, he came, if haply he might find any thing thereon: and when he came to it, he found nothing but leaves; for the time of figs was not yet. And Jesus answered and said unto it, "No man eat fruit of thee hereafter for ever." And his disciples heard it.* Mark 11:13–14 KJV

He commanded a tree. *Yes, Jesus talked to a tree.* This is the kind of authority He walked in because of His faith. His disciples were watching and wondered what He was doing. When they returned back the same way the next morning, they passed by the same tree and saw that it was dried up from the roots.

> *And Peter, remembering, said to Him, "Rabbi, look! The fig tree which You cursed has withered away." So Jesus answered and said to them, "Have faith in God. For assuredly, I say to you, whoever says to this mountain, 'Be removed and be cast into the sea,' and does not doubt in his heart, but believes that those things he says will come to pass, he will have whatever he says. Therefore I say to you, whatever things you ask when you pray, believe that you receive them, and you will have them."* *Mark 11:21–24*

The disciples pointed out the fig tree to Jesus, amazed that it had withered away. Jesus' response to Peter's astonishment was, "Have faith in God." Technically, this sentence is in the genitive case and should have been translated, "***Have the faith of God.***"[2] If we had His faith, we would have no problem seeing miracles happen.

He went on to explain that they could even cast a mountain into the sea if they would not doubt in their hearts but simply believe that those things they say "will come to pass." This is talking about the operation of the *gift* of faith. The only way we could cast a mountain into the sea would be if we had revelation to do so.

NOTE: This may have been a reference to the prophecy in Zechariah 14:4 where it says that the Lord will split the Mount of Olives when He returns.

However, in verse 24, He talks about the operation of *their* faith.

> *Therefore I say to you, whatever things you ask when you pray, believe that you receive them, and you will have them.*
>
> *Mark 11:24*

He was teaching them the difference between the gift of faith and their faith. In verse 24, He teaches them to ask when they pray and believe (with their faith) that they will receive. As the Master teacher, He taught His disciples by word and deed; and now He is teaching us.

Even when we have the gift of faith, *our* faith also comes into play—not to bring it to pass, but to carry out the revelation. The gift of faith will be activated as we walk in obedience (with our faith) to the revelation.

When Moses stuck his rod into the Red Sea, was it his faith that made it part? When Joshua said to the sun, "Sun, stand still over Gibeon; and Moon, in the Valley of Aijalon" (Joshua 10:12), do you think it was his own faith that caused it to happen? Moses and Joshua were not that big, and neither are we. By their own faith, Moses and Joshua both obeyed the revelation they received; but it was God's gift of faith that caused the miracles to happen.

These men believed (with their faith) in God's ability, not in theirs. Spiritual faith (the gift of faith) is supernatural faith that calls things that be not as though they are; and it is operated by word of knowledge, word of wisdom, and discerning of spirits.

Operating Faith	
Your Faith	**Spiritual Faith**
Your desire	By revelation
Your prayer	By command
Your expectation	By faith in the revelation
Mark 11:24	Mark 11:22–23

The doctrine of different kinds of faith is in Romans 1:17.

The practice of operating different kinds of faith is in Mark 11:23–24.

The Faith of Those We Pray For

> *Then He touched their eyes, saying, "According to* ***your faith*** *let it be to you."* *Matthew 9:29*

When we pray for people, their faith also needs to kick in to receive the answer. Jesus did not say, "According to My faith, let it be to you." Now, this does not mean that we can be weak in our faith when we pray for people; but *their* faith needs to be there as well.

I ask people what they are expecting to happen when I minister to them and can usually predict the outcome by their response. If they say they are expecting their condition to improve a little, then that's probably what will happen—they will get a little better. But if their expectations are great, then their results will be greater.

The good news is that there are things we can do to help others increase their faith and build their expectation (and ours as well). We also need to understand that people might have more faith in a specific minister to pray for them, especially if that minister has a reputation for getting results. That is okay. God sets healing ministries in the body of Christ too.

The subject of faith can be a difficult and confusing one, but when we break it into the basic categories of our faith and the gift of faith, it becomes easier to grasp. Our faith comes from our knowledge of the Scriptures and our experience and is activated by our will. The gift of faith is given to us at the time of our salvation and is activated by the will of the Holy Spirit to empower us to do miracles. It is the fulcrum of power leverage in the spirit realm.

Relevant Points

1. Which two kinds of faith are referenced in Romans 1:17?

2. Give a brief explanation of the difference between these two kinds of faith.

Chapter Sixteen

Gifts of Healings and the Working of Miracles

We are still in part 5 of *Exercising Spiritual Authority*, which deals with the power behind the spiritual authority Jesus has given us. His power manifests itself through faith, gifts of healings, and the working of miracles that are activated as we boldly and accurately command and/or act upon the revelation He gives us. There are various categories of healing, but this chapter deals specifically with the *gifts* of healings, which are technically delivered through a revelatory word and/or act.

I chose to combine the gifts of healings and the working of miracles into one chapter since the working[1] of miracles operates in the same manner through a revelation command. Gifts of healings and the working of miracles are both the result of spiritual utterance by spiritual knowledge, accompanied with spiritual faith.

Miracles defy human logic or understanding. The *Online Etymology Dictionary* defines a miracle as "a wondrous work of God" or an "extraordinary or remarkable feat."[2] Jesus said that signs and miracles would follow those who believe, and Paul wrote that it wasn't his words or his wisdom that drew people—it was the demonstration of the Spirit and the power of God.

> *And I, brethren, when I came to you, did not come with excellence of speech or of wisdom declaring to you the testimony of God. And my*

> *speech and my preaching were not with persuasive words of human wisdom, but in demonstration of the Spirit and of power, that your faith should not be in the wisdom of men but in the power of God.*
> *1 Corinthians 2:1 and 4–5*

As believers, signs, miracles, and wonders should be daily occurrences in our lives, not just occasional ones. These baffle the world's intellect and draw people to the Lord, ultimately glorifying the Father. Soon after I received the baptism of the Holy Spirit as a college student, I ministered to a friend of mine with a broken arm, and he was miraculously healed. He immediately went over and smashed the cast off his arm on the tennis court at the school; and inside of two weeks, 250 kids came to church with me. When we all walked into the biggest Methodist church in my home town, it so shocked the minister that he couldn't even preach. Where there are miracles, signs, and wonders, revival breaks loose. At last count, more than five ministers came out of that group—and it all started with one healing.

As we rise up in faith to see signs, miracles, and wonders, people will be drawn to Jesus and He will be glorified. The poet Edgar A. Guest said, "I'd rather see a sermon than hear one any day." People need to *see* the word of God, not just hear it.

Jesus is the Word of God incarnate, and the works He did during His earthly ministry drew people to Him. **He said that whoever believed in Him would be able to do the same works and even greater.**

> *Most assuredly, I say to you, he who believes in Me, the works that I do he will do also; and greater works than these he will do, because I go to My Father. And whatever you ask in My name, that I will do, that the Father may be glorified in the Son.*
> *John 14:12–13*

"Miracles" in 1 Corinthians 12:10 is the Greek word *dunamis*, which is often translated "power."[3] The working of miracles is done through an energizing of power that produces an observable manifestation. They were abundant in Jesus' earthly ministry—from turning water into wine to walking on the water or casting out a demon. God's power is energized by a spiritual utterance according to spiritual knowledge accompanied by spiritual faith. An instantaneous healing would be considered a miracle and demonstrates God's power working through believers, as well as the authority He gave them. Miracles are proofs of His existence and power that can convince even hardened skeptics to believe.

Jesus included the authority to heal in the same context as casting out demons and sicknesses.

> *And when He had called His twelve disciples to Him, He gave them power over unclean spirits, to cast them out, and to heal all kinds of sickness and all kinds of disease.*
>
> *Matthew 10:1*

Probably the most drastic of all miraculous healings would be raising someone from the dead—especially if they have been dead for a number of days, as was the case when Jesus raised Lazarus from the dead after he had been in the grave for four days (John 11:38–44). This was considered a miracle in those days and would most definitely be considered a miracle by today's scientific and medical standards as well.

To Glorify God

The most sensational gift of healing I witnessed during my mission trips to India was the direct result of an answered prayer. Before leaving for that particular trip, I asked God for a special anointing.

When He asked me why I wanted it, I responded, "So I can heal people." He immediately convicted me that this was the wrong reason and then corrected me with the right one—*so that He would be glorified.*

I have never forgotten this truth. Healed people die. The ultimate purpose of the miracle of raising Lazarus from the dead was not for him to live forever but for those who witnessed it to see God's love and goodness and turn to Him.

On this particular India mission, the doors had opened for our team to minister at a children's polio home in Trivandrum. As I stood in the main room and listened to one of the team members preach, I felt a burning sensation in my hands and knew the Lord was giving me a revelation with a gift of healing; so I turned to my friend and explained what was happening. I knew his heart was to see the Holy Spirit heal every single kid there and that he would give me Godly advice. He said, "Well hey, put them on somebody and see what happens!" That sounded like a good plan, and that was how it started.

A little boy was sitting right in front of me, so I reached down and placed my hands on his shoulders. He didn't have any more idea of what was going on than the man in the moon. He didn't speak English—he was just sitting there like he was expecting me to give him candy or something. His little bitty legs were about as big around as my two fingers because of the polio. When I put my hands on his shoulders and picked him up, the heat went out of my hands and into his body; and in a nanosecond, his legs grew out about four or five inches longer. I exclaimed, "Wow!" This was an obvious miracle, and I knew there was no way I had the faith to do that. In that moment I knew God had done it by giving me that special healing anointing I asked Him for—along with the revelation to give it away.

It would have been easy at that point to get so excited about the miraculous healing that it could have distracted me from the anointing. But others had witnessed the miracle and their faith was already being built to the end that there could be more miracles to come; so we all needed to stay focused. (When we see a miracle take place, we cannot afford to get emotional. It's like someone making a winning shot in a basketball game with five seconds left—the rest of the team better keep their defense sharp and clean to the finish.)

Even though my hands were not hot anymore, I thought there could still be some anointing left in them. The little boy who was sitting right next to his healed friend saw what happened, so I reached down and stood him up—but he went right back down! I could have gotten discouraged and quit; but my stubbornness made me try the next kid. It seemed the special anointing was gone when I first picked him up, but when I sat him back down, his legs grew out too.

At that point, another team member began leading a parade of about 50 kids around the home who either had been, or were being, instantaneously healed. It all began with that prayer to God before I ever left for the trip, and it culminated with an obedient response to the burning sensation in my hands. I simply asked, and the Lord graciously and freely gave the necessary gifts of healings. Signs, miracles, and wonders follow those who believe.

A similar illustration can be found in a typical Benny Hinn healing service. He first prays for the anointing of the Holy Spirit to come and then he preaches and ministers in it. When the Holy Spirit gives him revelation on someone in the crowd, he utilizes the gift of faith to bring it to pass. By revelation, he speaks out the healing and the person receives it through their faith and the gift of faith. He then calls that healed person up to the stage in front of everybody and has him or her demonstrate their healing.

For instance, he might say, "Bend over and touch your toes . . . okay, now run up and down the aisle" (if they were not able to do these things before). Whatever it was that the person could not do before is what he has them do to prove that God healed them. (He learned this process from the ministries of Oral Roberts and A. A. Allen, who both operated the same way.)

Once the crowd sees that this person has been miraculously healed, they start dropping their crutches and jumping out of their wheelchairs, because that one miracle increases everyone else's faith.

This is what I believe happened: the first healing in that polio home was done by the gift of faith; the second one didn't work because this boy didn't have the faith even after seeing his friend healed; however, the third one did have the faith that was built by seeing the first healing, and both healings built the necessary faith in the remaining children to receive their gifts of healings. Not everyone will believe, but those who do will receive from God.

Receiving Revelation in a Picture

There are many ways to receive revelation for a healing or a miracle, and one of these is through pictures. A good friend of mine who is a master mechanic often receives revelation through a picture of a car part. He shared with me that the first time he received one of these visual images, he realized that God was revealing what he needed to know in a way he could understand. In that particular situation, the comparison was to throw the old part away and order a brand-new component.

I decided to apply the principle of a new part as soon as I could. While my wife Vicki and I were visiting with this master mechanic and his wife, I received a phone call from a lady who knew I was in town. She told me she had heard that I believed in praying for sick people. My response was, "No, but I do believe in *healing* sick people." She said, "Well then, I'd like to be healed." Right as she said that, God showed me a revelatory picture of her backbone. She had not mentioned at all the part of her body that needed healing or what was wrong with it; but in the picture her backbone appeared to be twisted and gnarled.

In the spirit, I "saw" a picture of a twisted and gnarled backbone, so I boldly yelled into the phone, "In the name of Jesus Christ, stand up woman! Stand up! And I command a brand-new backbone to be grown in your back right now! Stand up!" I could hear movement on the other end of the line, as if she had stood up—but then I heard a blood-curdling shriek and her phone dropped, followed by a shuffling sound and a click! I sat there shell-shocked, wondering if my boldness had killed her. I got up out of my chair and started pacing, trying to figure out what happened, and the thought flashed through my mind that I should have gotten some liability insurance.

I went downstairs where Vicki was and told her what happened, and she said, "Be cool." I thought, "That's easy for you to say—you didn't just kill a woman." About 10 minutes later, the phone finally rang again, and I picked it up. It was her husband! My first thought was that yes I had really killed her. He said, "Dale, this is so and so; you just prayed and ministered to my wife . . . ." I held my breath. He continued, "She is—" (and my mind was flying back and forth between "dead" and "healed"). Time stood still as I waited for that next word. He finally blurted out, *"completely healed!"*

I sighed the biggest sigh ever and exclaimed, "Oh praise God! Thank you, God!" Then the wife got on the other phone and said, "From the time I was 12 years old, I've had a bad back disease, and for over 25 years I have been unable to stand up straight. When you commanded me to stand up, it was just like Jesus with the man who had the withered hand. The way you said it, I was afraid not to. But when I stood up, my back changed. I have a completely brand-new back just like you said. It didn't pop, crackle, snap or anything—it simply became brand new! I stood up straight for the first time in over 25 years. It absolutely blew my mind when it happened!"

I know it was not my faith that healed that woman; however, it was by my faith that I made the proclamation. I learned from my mechanic friend that sometimes we just need a brand-new part, instead of a repair. This woman received a brand-new back from heaven's warehouse of parts.

Command Mode

As far as I know, there is no place in the Scriptures where it says Jesus prayed for the sick. That is because He always did what the Father told Him to do, which means He always healed as a result of receiving revelation; and He already had the faith of God. This is why He was able to simply command the illnesses out of people rather than praying for them.

Jesus said that if we had faith as a grain of mustard seed, we could *say* to the mulberry tree, "Be pulled up by the roots and be planted in the sea" (Luke 17:6) and it would obey us. That phrase is a command, and we are permitted to command the impossible when God gives us the revelation to do so—because He has also given us His faith to make it happen. *It only takes a small amount of God's faith to make something big happen.*

When God has not given us direct revelation to heal someone, we use our own faith to pray for them. However, when we receive revelation to impart a healing gift, we simply command the healing with the authority He has given us to do it—knowing that the gift of faith is there to bring it to pass. This is the point at which we go into the "command mode."

We see this in Acts 3:1–10 when the man at the Beautiful Gate of the temple was healed. Instead of begging God to heal him, Peter said, "Silver and gold I do not have, but what I do have I give you: In the name of Jesus Christ of Nazareth, rise up and walk" (Acts 3:6). The phrase "rise up and walk" is a command.

Peter fixed his eyes upon the lame man (by his own faith), and that's when he got the revelation. At that point Peter said, "Look on us." It says that the man gave heed to them, expecting to receive something. Peter did not say, "Father, in the name of Jesus, I ask you to heal this man." When we receive the word of God by revelation, the need is no longer there to ask—the need at this point is to demand. Peter went into the command mode once he received God's revelation.

B. G. Leonard greatly impacted my healing ministry years ago when I was a student in one of his live classes on the gifts of the Spirit and he corrected my technique. He was the one who taught me that when we have revelation, we are to command it to manifest. When we don't have revelation, we can ask (pray); however, even in these circumstances, if our faith and the person's faith are strong enough, we can still command it to come to pass.

When we receive revelation to heal someone, it's time to move from prayer mode to command mode. If we have not received revelation, we should still pray with conviction and faith rather than beg and plead with God. When we are in an authoritative mode, it sparks more faith in people than when we act like we have no authority. If we do not have the revelation, we may not see an immediate result; but if the revelation is there, get ready, because God will astound us. Remember that when miracles do happen, they are not done through our personal faith—they are energized through the Holy Spirit's faith.

Walking in Boldness

Thank God for the crucible of life, because it would certainly be dull if we had to learn everything from a textbook. I learned these truths through a lot of studying, a lot of praying, and then boldly carrying them out. We cannot pull back because of fear. The only thing I'm afraid of is being afraid; so if something intimidates me, I'm going to go bite it and see if it kills me.

We can operate from a base of our faith and pray for anybody, anytime, anywhere. We could stop in the middle of a busy downtown street in Kansas City and shout out, "Hey, I'm praying for people!" If one person gets healed and others witness it, chances are that a line will start to form behind that person because the faith of others will be built. In addition, the more miracles we see, the more our own faith will be built. Then we will start seeking out more opportunities to heal people.

We need to be courageous and speak out with faith. Mealy-mouthed prayers don't help anybody's faith. Begging God to help the person we are praying for is not going to cut it. Let's speak boldly and confidently like we are *expecting* God to do it. The person we are praying for will appreciate it, and their faith will be built. Even if we are having a bad day, we should at least act like we are in charge.

One of the excuses we might use to shrink back from reaching out in confidence is to think that healing is not our strong suit, that we do not have the calling or gift to heal. This is not really the case, however, because it is one of the nine gifts wrapped up in the Holy Spirit He gave us through the new birth. Jesus, the Master Healer, is in us; and as we begin to realize that we are walking hand-in-hand with Him, our confidence will grow. So even if it is not our particular gifting, we still have the ability and the mandate from Jesus to do it.

Another excuse that sometimes hinders us from healing others is to think that it's only for those who are in full-time ministry. Yet Jesus' only requirement was "he who believes in Me" (John 14:12). We do not need a title or to be in full-time ministry.

It's time to stop making excuses and step out in faith and confidence. If you pray for 50 people and no one gets healed, don't stop. Do not give up. Number 51 could be the first one who gets healed, and when that happens, the snowball effect will start. (And I don't believe it will take 50 people before it happens.)

Can you picture yourself doing this? God is able to do exceeding abundantly above all we can ask or think, according to the power that works in us. So, start thinking this way and looking for those open doors from the Lord. One of my goals is to pray for and/or minister healing specifically to the blind people in the villages across Africa. I've already witnessed blind people healed through the power of God, and it built my faith immensely. I am still living with the powerful memory of the Lord causing a man's eyeball to grow right beneath my hand as I ministered to him—and I want to see more healings like this. How about you?

The Reason for Healings and Miracles

Remember what the Lord taught me when He asked why I wanted that special anointing for India? **The reason we want to walk in faith and see signs, miracles, and wonders is so that God will be glorified.** This must always be our motivation and goal as we endeavor to exercise our spiritual authority on this earth.

When Peter and John were called to account for the man's healing at the Beautiful Gate of the temple, they used that opportunity to glorify Jesus and preach salvation through His name.

> *Let it be known to you all, and to all the people of Israel, that by the name of Jesus Christ of Nazareth, whom you crucified, whom God raised from the dead, by Him this man stands here before you whole. Nor is there salvation in any other, for there is no other name under heaven given among men by which we must be saved.*
>
> *Acts 4:10 and 12*

Related Materials at LMCI.org

- Biblical Health Insurance (CD or MP3)
- Covet Earnestly the Best Gifts (CD or MP3)
- Flowing in All Nine Gifts of the Holy Spirit (Booklet)
- The Foundation of Miracle Working (CD or MP3)
- How to Do Miracles (CD or MP3)
- Manifesting the Holy Spirit (CD or MP3)
- Walking in Resurrected Power (CD or MP3)

Relevant Points

1. In what common way do gifts of healings and miracles both work?

2. When do we use our own faith to pray for someone's healing?

3. At what point do we go into "command mode" and command the healing rather than praying for it?

Chapter Seventeen

Other Ways God Can Heal

Because of God's creativity and manifold wisdom, there are different ways for people to receive healing; and they may even receive healing through a combination of these. The last chapter dealt with the gifts of healings done through a revelation decree, which is reliable because it deals straight with spiritual faith. If the person has faith and we have the revelation, then that person will absolutely be healed. When we speak of "ministering" healing, we are referring to healing via a word of revelation; otherwise, we typically *pray* for the healing.

NOTE: Since God is sovereign, He can still heal even without a person's faith if He so chooses. His grace is greater than our faith and He is greater than both. This is why we must be careful not to exact a formula for healing or to put God's ways into a "box," so to speak.

The following chart lays out seven ways that I am aware of experientially and scripturally that God can heal.

Ways that God Heals

- Laying on of hands
  - The simplest way
- Anointing with oil
- Revelation word
  - The most reliable way
- Prayer of Faith
  - The combined faith of the one who prays and the one who asks for prayer
- Faith of others
- Special anointings
  - Special ways God works in certain people
- Covenant (in Holy Communion)
  - Provides healing and health

Seven Different Ways God Uses Us to Heal

From my experience and from what I have seen in the Scriptures, there are seven basic ways that God uses His people to deliver healing.

1. Laying on of hands

> *They will lay hands on the sick, and they will recover.*
> *Mark 16:18b*

This works as God transfers the current of His power from our hands to the person we are ministering to. The transference of His power is not limited to direct touch, but it is most definitely one of the ways that He set up for it to be done, as can be seen in the numerous times Jesus laid hands on the sick (Matthew 8:3, 15; 9:18, 25; Mark 1:31; 6:5; 7:32–33; 8:23, 25; 9:27; Luke 4:40; 5:13; 13:13).

> *And when the Sabbath had come, He began to teach in the synagogue. And many hearing Him were astonished, saying, "Where did this Man get these things?* ***And what wisdom is this which is given to Him, that such mighty works are performed by His hands!*** *"* *Mark 6:2*

Our hands are representative of work—and they are the instruments God uses to accomplish *His* works. When Jesus was crucified and the nails severed the median nerves that ran through His hands/wrists, His innocent blood covered all the evil deeds we have ever done with ours and purified them. As we surrender our lives to God, His power is able to flow out of our hands just as it did from His. We can confidently proclaim, "I can lay hands on the sick and they will recover."

Sometimes when we lay hands on people they may actually feel power or heat flow into their bodies. This is God's power or virtue being transferred from our hands and into the person receiving the healing. The virtue of the Holy Spirit can find that which God wants healed better than an aspirin finds a headache.

Generally speaking, before we lay hands on an individual we should ask their permission first, and this is especially the case when ministering to someone of the opposite sex. This is a good reason for married couples to minister together; the wife can lay her hands on the individual if it is a woman, and vice-versa. We do not want to do anything that could hinder someone from receiving their healing. I really believe that there's no greater ministering team than husband and wife; and the more one-flesh they are, the better they are at switching back and forth with their revelations and rhemas.

2. Anointing with oil

> *So they went out and preached that people should repent. And they cast out many demons, and anointed with oil many who were sick, and healed them.* *Mark 6:12–13*

Oil represents the anointing power of the Holy Spirit (Exodus 40:9). Anointing oil can be any type of oil, although olive oil (with essential oils added to it) is probably most commonly used. Not everyone will have faith in this delivery of healing, so be sensitive to the Holy Spirit's leading when it comes to its use. If we are inclined to use it but unsure of the person's faith in it, we can take them to James 5:14 and/or Mark 6:12–13 first to show them its scriptural basis. Often, the ones who already have knowledge of this truth (and faith in it) will come up to you with their own flask of oil, making this means of delivery an obvious choice.

3. Revelation word

> *If anyone speaks, let him speak as the oracles of God. If anyone ministers, let him do it as with the ability which God supplies, that in all things God may be glorified through Jesus Christ, to whom belong the glory and the dominion forever and ever. Amen.*
>
> *1 Peter 4:11*

When we receive a revelation word for the individual we are praying for, we should speak it aloud as led by the Holy Spirit. Speaking rhema words as well as scriptural words of truth will cause the person's faith to increase, as well as our own. Like a snowball effect, this can also bring more (or at least clearer) revelation, building our confidence to command the healing in Jesus' name.

We should not put too much stock into what the person thinks, feels, or expresses to us. Research has shown that the effects of a disease often do not manifest themselves until it is at least 70% matured. Even if the person is not feeling discomfort in that area of their body, if we believe we have received revelation on it, we should go ahead and command the healing.[1]

There are times when we might even feel the pain in our own bodies. If we were not feeling it before we laid hands on the person we are ministering to, then it is most probably revelation. Speak directly to the pain or the disease; we have authority to command it gone in Jesus' name. With the revelation comes the authority to speak right to the organ or the problem, e.g., "thyroid gland, be healed now in Jesus' name," rather than, "Lord, please heal this thyroid gland."[2]

Words are powerful, and the Creator's words have the power to heal and deliver when spoken and received with faith. This is why people can receive healing by simply listening to someone on the radio or television. A close friend of mine, Russ Chandler, was healed as a child this way when his mother was listening to Oral Roberts on the radio. Oral declared that those who were out there listening to the radio who were unable to physically attend the meeting could still claim their healing in Jesus' name. Russ' mother did just that and he was instantly healed of polio and grew up to become a healthy college football player. This is the power of spoken words of truth when they are received into a faith-filled heart. When we believe in God's power, we can call "things that are not as though they were" (Romans 4:17b NIV).

4. Prayer of faith

> *And the prayer of faith will save the sick, and the Lord will raise him up.* *James 5:15*

The context of this verse is referring to a group of elders praying over an individual, but I believe it can apply to any group of believers. When more than one believer gets together and their faith is combined, it pleases God who then throws the switch for His power to flow into the person being prayed for.

God has set up the rules of healing to operate by faith. Even He operated faith to frame the worlds (Hebrews 11:3), so this is a standard He established and exemplified from the start and expects us to adhere to. He is sovereign and can heal anytime He chooses—whether there is faith or not; however, if and when we have faith, He will absolutely honor it and perform the healing. This applies individually as well as corporately.

If someone asks for a healing and we do not receive revelation, then it will be reliant upon our faith rather than through spiritual faith. It can still happen but it depends upon our faith and/or the person's faith who asked for the healing.

5. Faith of others

> *The centurion replied, "Lord, I do not deserve to have you come under my roof. But just say the word, and my servant will be healed."*
> *Matthew 8:8, NIV*

This record does not reveal whether or not the centurion's servant had the faith to be healed, but the centurion's faith was obvious. Jesus even marveled at it in verse 10 when He said, "I tell you the truth, I have not found anyone in Israel with such great faith" (NIV).

When faith is operated, the Lord shows up—regardless of who has the faith. He can show up without faith by His choice; but He always shows up when there is faith. In this case, He healed the servant without even stepping into the centurion's home.

6. Special anointings

There are various types of special anointings. Some are upon individuals for healing certain diseases or parts of the body; e.g., I have a propensity for healing knees, while someone else may have a propensity for healing blind eyes. Some special anointings are within objects, such as the handkerchiefs and napkins used by Paul (Acts 19:11–12) or Peter's shadow that healed people (Acts 5:15). Special healing anointings can also come through a gift of the Holy Spirit, such as a diverse tongue.

This does not mean that God gave some of us a greater Holy Spirit than He gave to others. We each have the same gift of the Holy Spirit, but there will be variances to the individual gifts, or callings, within us.

7. Covenant healing in communion

Another way God can heal is through our covenant in communion. Partaking of Holy Communion is a way to claim authority over sickness and disease in our own lives.

In many ways I believe that receiving the elements of Holy Communion, when done consistently with faith, is the most effective way of exercising spiritual authority over our physical bodies—not only to heal them but also to maintain our health.

When we pray over the elements, the Holy Spirit anoints them so that they produce a physical effect when consumed. They do not actually become the blood and body of Christ but they do become empowered by the Holy Spirit. When Holy Communion is received properly, those elements become the most powerful and holy elements on the face of the earth because they contain the energy of Almighty God. When we partake of them with faith, they also energize the Holy Spirit within us.

Years ago I listened to Kenneth Hagin, Sr.'s teaching on "The Healing Anointing," and it greatly enriched my understanding of this subject. I highly recommend it.[3]

Ask God for opportunities to minister to people. It's His will for them to be healed, so He will open the doors for that to happen. Walk out in faith remembering that Jesus is ministering right there with us; signs, miracles, and wonders will follow and God will be glorified. Those who are healed will still eventually die; but when God is glorified through their healings, others can be won to Him and receive eternal life.

Relevant Points

1. Why should we be careful not to exact a formula for how God can heal?

2. What are the seven ways mentioned in chapter 17 that God can heal?

3. What should be our reason for desiring to walk in faith and produce signs, miracles, and wonders?

Epilogue

In 1977, a quest began when I saw the word "authority" (*exousia*) supernaturally magnified on the page of a Greek interlinear Bible as I was reading. After many years of studying the Scriptures and receiving revelation from the Holy Spirit, God released me to teach on the subject of exercising spiritual authority. It has been my joy and honor not only to teach it for over 20 years now, but to witness blind eyes opening, the lame walking, and the demonized delivered. What a blessed man I am.

A wise old "bird dog" taught me how to pick up the trail of birds by being downwind of them, so I used similar tactics in my hunt through the Scriptures. I gleaned knowledge from my elders to pick up the scent and then studied and applied what the Lord taught me along the way. So, tributes are due to those who went before me, as well as to many of my peers and encouragers.

Without the teaching of the late patriarch Kenneth Hagin, Sr. on spirit, soul, and body, none of my studies would have evolved to the point they have. I owe my understanding on the power of commanding to B. G. Leonard, as well as to one of his students, V. P. Wierwille, who taught me to love and study the Bible. I also owe thanks to the late Derek Prince, my all-time favorite teacher (aside from Jesus, of course). And last, but not least, the late Oral Roberts deeply impacted me as a young boy and increased my hunger for the things of God.

Many years ago, I taught about "Jesus the Teacher;" and He, of course, is *the* Man. The Holy Spirit gives power, but authority comes from the Man. Anyone who truly knows Him wants to be like Him, and that is why I dote on being the Man's man.

I believe that how we exercise our spiritual power in this earthly life will be one of the determining factors of entering the millennium kingdom of Jesus on the earth. I trust and pray that the truths in *Exercising Spiritual Authority* will help us to meet His requirements for reigning with Him.

NOTE: If you would like to have an Exercising Spiritual Authority class conducted in your area, please email me at LMCHRIST@LMCI.org or call 540-586-5813.

APPENDIXES

Appendix 1

Operating the Gift of Faith to Fulfill Your Ministry

God has planted within each of us a destiny along with the measure of faith we need to fulfill it (Romans 12:3). It will not be possible to fulfill that destiny on our own because it is a spiritual calling that requires supernatural abilities.

If we are uncertain as to what our personal calling is, then we need to ask God to reveal it so that we can write it down in a clear and plain way as Habakkuk declared in the Old Testament.

> *Then the LORD answered me and said: "Write the vision and make it plain on tablets, that he may run who reads it."*
>
> *Habakkuk 2:2*

Our desire should be to run with our destiny once we know what it is. When we write it down, we can operate faith daily to speak it aloud over ourselves, and this will help to kick in the *gift* of faith required to release that particular ministry into our lives.[1]

Write it on the tables of your heart as well as on paper and then focus on God's ability to bring it to pass rather than the time it might take. Do not be anxious, but instead be thankful for what He will do. His peace will guard our hearts and minds from worry and fear (Philippians 4:6 and 7).

Whatever ministry the Lord reveals is a promise from Him, and that means we can use the gift of faith apportioned to us for that calling. (When we get revelation, the gift of faith comes included within it.) Once He gives that initial revelation, do not wait for a release of it—*start speaking it.* As we walk in obedience to Him, He will reveal whatever details are necessary to fulfill it; but as we daily proclaim it, we start right away to activate its accompanying gift of faith. This is how we begin exercising our spiritual authority to command it to come to pass.

Our confession might sound like, "I will succeed; through God's faith it will come to pass. I will not quit; God has blessed me and called me to fulfill this aspect in my life." We may need to confess it more than once a day—anytime we begin to feel our faith weaken, we should speak it out!

> *When Abram was ninety-nine years old, the LORD appeared to Abram and said to him, "I am Almighty God; walk before Me and be blameless. And I will make My covenant between Me and you, and will multiply you exceedingly." Then Abram fell on his face, and God talked with him, saying: "As for Me, behold, My covenant is with you, and* ***you shall be a father of many nations****. No longer shall your name be called Abram, but your name shall be Abraham; for I have made you a father of many nations. I will make you exceedingly fruitful; and I will make nations of you, and kings shall come from you."* *Genesis 17:1–6*

Romans 4:20 says that Abraham "did not waver at the promise of God through unbelief, but was strengthened in faith, giving glory to God," even though it was many years before the promised birth of a son was fulfilled (Genesis 17:16). He did not stagger at the promise that said he (Abraham) would be the father of many nations. When God changed his name from Abram (exalted father) to Abraham (father of a multitude), he obediently took on the new name, which became a declaration of the promise. If we keep confessing the promise that God gave concerning our purpose, our faith will kick in the spiritual faith that enables our purposes to be fulfilled, just as Abraham's was.

> *I will stand my watch and set myself on the rampart, and watch to see what He will say to me, and what I will answer when I am reproved. [He'll show it to you.] Then the LORD answered me and said: "Write the vision and make it plain upon tablets, that he may run who reads it. [If you don't read it—you won't be running.] For the vision is yet for an appointed time; but at the end it will speak, and it will not lie. Though it tarries, wait for it; Because it will surely come, it will not tarry. Behold the proud, his soul is not upright in him [you can't do it by your soul—it's got to be by your spirit];* ***but the just shall live by his faith.*** *Habakkuk 2:1–4*

"The just shall live by his [God's] faith." We cannot accomplish the vision with our own faith; but if we write it plainly so that we can read and believe it, God's faith will empower us to run to the finish line. The race will be over when our ministry is accomplished.

Exhortation

If we do not know what God has called us to do, now is the time to get down on our knees and implore Him to find out what it is. Once we get His revelation, we then write it down plainly and stay focused on it. As we verbalize and command it, we are exercising our spiritual authority over our ministry to bring it to pass. *Though it tarries, it will come, because the just will live by faith.*

Keep the faith.

Appendix 2

Exercising Spiritual Authority to Strengthen Church Government

To be thorough in covering the subject of spiritual authority (*exousia*), we need to consider how it is used in reference to leadership in the body of Christ, according to Romans 13:1–6. I believe the powers and rulers referred to throughout this section are those given by God to the church.

> *Let every soul be subject to the governing authorities [exousia]. For there is no authority except from God, and the authorities that exist are appointed by God. Therefore whoever resists the authority resists the ordinance of God, and those who resist will bring judgment on themselves. For rulers are not a terror to good works, but to evil. Do you want to be unafraid of the authority? Do what is good, and you will have praise from the same. For he is God's minister to you for good. But if you do evil, be afraid; for he does not bear the sword in vain; for he is God's minister, an avenger to execute wrath on him who practices evil. Therefore you must be subject, not only because of wrath but also for conscience' sake. For because of this you also pay taxes ["tribute" in the KJV], for they are God's ministers attending continually to this very thing.* Romans 13:1–6

No man is an island—especially if he is a Christian. As believers, we are intricately connected to one another in the body of Christ, so it is important to know how church government works and how we can exercise our spiritual authority to help it function properly.

These verses from Romans 13 contain truths concerning this, even though many Christians believe that it is referring to secular governmental authorities rather than those within the church.

Some of the more contemporary translations render these verses in such a way that the authorities mentioned begin to sound like civil leaders rather than those appointed by God to the church. I believe this subtly deceives believers into submitting to the world's authority rather than to those God intended—those He has placed within the body of Christ.

We may have doctrinal differences about church government and structure, but most Christians would agree that God has placed certain men and women in the church to lead and instruct. They are gifts from Him to benefit His people. When we read these verses with this understanding, we see that those who are "ministers attending continually" should be paid tribute for their labor. They are overseers given by God to shepherd His church that He purchased with His own blood.

> *Therefore take heed to yourselves and to all the flock, among which the Holy Spirit has made you overseers, to shepherd the church of God which He purchased with His own blood.*
>
> *Acts 20:28*

"Overseer" is the Greek word *episkopos,*[1] which means to oversee, to look over, and to make sure the affairs of everyone are covered—to make sure that people are fed and nourished and cared for.

When we view our overseers in the proper light, as gifts from God to the church, we will be more apt to take care of them. This means praying for them, encouraging them, and providing financial support. As our leaders, they are in the frontlines of spiritual battle and take the first shots. This is why they need our prayers. *Praying for the leaders in our church is all a part of exercising our spiritual authority.*

> *Let the elders who rule well be counted worthy of double honor, especially those who labor in the word and doctrine. For the Scripture says, "You shall not muzzle an ox while it treads out the grain," and, "The laborer is worthy of his wages."*
>
> *1 Timothy 5:17–18*

These are great words of exhortation and instruction to all of us: to count those who rule well worthy of double honor and to recognize that they are worthy of his/her wages. It should be our joy to take care of them—and not just financially. Think of ways to bless and encourage them, perhaps even take them out for a meal or treat them to something special to show your appreciation of them. It's important that they know they are valued, because the enemy is constantly working to discourage them.

Ordination

Those ministers/overseers/rulers who attend continually to this end should be recognized properly within the church; and those who have gift ministries should be publically ordained so others may embrace what God has given them through these gift ministries. With the laying on of hands by revelation, ministries are conferred, transferred, and given to those individuals as appointed by the Lord. When done under the direction of the Holy Spirit, an enduing power from on high comes upon them as that gift to the church.

This is readily seen in the book of Acts. As Paul and Barnabas traveled throughout the region to encourage the churches, they recognized the need for leadership and ordained elders in each of them.

> *And when they [Paul and Barnabas] had preached the gospel to that city, and had taught many, they returned again to Lystra, and to Iconium, and Antioch, Confirming the souls of the disciples, and exhorting them to continue in the faith, and that we must through much tribulation enter into the kingdom of God. And when they had ordained them elders in every church, and had prayed with fasting, they commended them to the Lord, on whom they believed.*
>
> *Acts 14:21–23*

Once the gift of God is received, it must be stirred up by the recipient; however, the mutual faith and exhortation of the people and their leaders are also pivotal.

> *Therefore I remind you to stir up the gift of God which is in you through the laying on of my hands.*
>
> *2 Timothy 1:6*

With the combination of this empowerment *and* the support of the members of the body of Christ, these leaders have the necessary latitude to fulfill their ministries and carry out their offices in the church.

The Next Generation

As the Head Administrator of the church, Jesus is continually ordaining and installing ministries because His church is constantly growing and expanding. Not only that, but our earthly bodies are corruptible and the leaders we have now will eventually go home.

The younger generations will be called upon more and more to come forward and publicly proclaim that they are giving their lives away in service to His body. **That is the true gift of any ministry in the church—to give up (dedicate) their lives in service.**

> *Therefore He says: "When He ascended on high, He led captivity captive, and gave gifts to men." And He Himself gave some to be apostles, some prophets, some evangelists, and some pastors and teachers, for the equipping of the saints for the work of ministry, for the edifying of the body of Christ, till we all come to the unity of the faith and the knowledge of the Son of God, to a perfect man, to the measure of the stature of the fullness of Christ; that we should no longer be children, tossed to and fro and carried about with every wind of doctrine, by the trickery of men, in the cunning craftiness by which they lie in wait to deceive, but, speaking the truth in love, may grow up in all things into Him who is the head—Christ.*
>
> *Ephesians 4:8, 11–15*

The gift ministries are distributed to help us grow up in Christ. They are to furnish and help the members of the body of Christ to fulfill their own ministry functions that they have been called to.

Exhortation

Let's all rise up and start exercising spiritual authority within our spheres by praying for and supporting those that God has put in our lives to help us grow up in Christ. God intended there to be order in the Church—not rebellion, heresies, or false doctrines that destroy people. These ministries are there not only to help us grow up in Him but to also protect us from the wolves and the onslaughts of the enemy.

Appendix 3

Exercising Spiritual Authority over Personal Finances

Regardless of varying cultural economies and geographical differences, the topic of exercising spiritual authority over personal finances has made a positive impact wherever I have taught it. It is of such significant importance that I have written a booklet on the subject called *Devil, Give Me Back My Money!*[1] In the realm of material resources, the rule is that if we don't claim authority over our finances, the devil will; and, as in every other aspect of our lives, we are not to give place to the devil (Ephesians 4:27).

Claiming our financial promises has nothing to do with greed. Money is a spiritual thing when it comes to serving in God's kingdom, and I am continually amazed at how many people are not fulfilling their ministries to the fullest degree because of the lack of it. In fact, there are very few believers I know (at least in the US) who do *not* need some financial therapy.

The Spiritual Perspective of Money

There are three perspectives from which we can view money: the spirit, the soul, and the body. The body perspective says, "Give me more," and is never satisfied. The soul reasons that the more you have, the more successful you are. *The spiritual perspective of money is that it is given by God.*

There are two main questions we should ask ourselves in light of our stewardship of His resources: (1) Do we have what we are supposed to have? (2) Are we maintaining what we have received and guarding it from the thievery of the devil?

Spiritual warfare requires courage, even when it comes to warring for our resources. God wants us to prosper. When I teach the message on "Devil Give Me Back My Money!" in foreign countries, I sometimes run into problems. The reason is that our American tendency is to preach the prosperity message from a material perspective rather than from a spiritual perspective. Money can be a real test for most of us, and the more we have, the harder the test. A good friend of mine from India said, "I think life was a lot simpler whenever I had two shirts and two pairs of pants . . . . Now that I have all these clothes, I have to make a decision about which ones to wear and I have to keep all of them clean."

The spiritual perspective of money is that all we have actually belongs to God. That's why the tithe is a test of submission and obedience—it proves our recognition of Him as Lord. Remember also that ten percent is all that He *requires* back, according to the Old Testament law. The greater law that we're under now is to be led by the Holy Spirit in regard to the utilization of what we have. Most of us would have no problem with tithing or giving more if we had what we are supposed to have. That's why we should exercise spiritual authority over this area of our lives. The enemy is a thief, and the Scriptures say that when a thief is caught, he is supposed to restore and give back seven times over.

> *People do not despise a thief if he steals to satisfy himself when he is starving. Yet when he is found, he must restore sevenfold; he may have to give up all the substance of his house.*
>
> *Proverbs 6:30–31*

Not only would we have an abundance to give above and beyond the tithe, but we would also have more to give to others who have need. Ephesians 4:28 says that we are to labor so that we can have something to give to those who have need. To fight for what is ours is not just a warrior mentality, it is also a servant mentality if we keep things in the proper perspective of giving to those who have need. This servant attitude of obtaining so that we can help others will also guard our hearts from greed—the devil's number one problem that ultimately caused his fall.

Lucifer's Greed Problem

Contrary to popular belief, Lucifer's first problem was not pride, but greed. This is why we should not be surprised that he wants our money. Ezekiel 28:16 talks about his trading ("merchandise" in the KJV).

> *By the abundance of your trading [merchandise] you became filled with violence within, and you sinned; therefore I cast you as a profane thing out of the mountain of God; and I destroyed you, O covering cherub, from the midst of the fiery stones.*
>
> *Ezekiel 28:16*

It appears that Lucifer was greedy for worship because he was not content with all that God had already given him. We can see him using this ploy throughout mankind's history, and he uses it today on you and me. Way back in the beginning he planted a greedy thought in Eve to want more than she had, even though God had given her freedom to eat of all that was in the garden except for one tree—and that was the one tree Lucifer brought to her attention. He does that today with us, whispering in our ear and reasoning with us to desire or lust after something we are not supposed to have. He is tempting us to open the door to greed.

When Satan tempted Jesus in the wilderness, he tried the greed ploy on Him by offering Him the kingdoms of this world and the glory of them. This record also implies that those had been delivered to him, which happened when Adam and Eve gave up their rights in the garden.

> *The devil led him up to a high place and showed him in an instant all the kingdoms of the world. And he said to him, "I will give you all their authority and splendor, for it has been given to me, and I can give it to anyone I want to."* *Luke 4:5–6*

We know from the Scriptures that it was not delivered to the devil from God; it was from Adam. He tricked Adam and Eve into forfeiting these things. The devil has everything that he has because he is greedy and has stolen it from people. As God's children, we have the authority in Christ to take back what has been stolen, just as Abraham did from the confederation of kings in Genesis 14:1–16.

If you are sitting here today hurting financially, it's because you have been beaten up and robbed. This hurts us not just in our wallet, but in our souls also because we know we are bigger than the bully who took our money.

In Ephesians 1:3, God says that our blessings are in the heavenly places.

> *Blessed be the God and Father of our Lord Jesus Christ, who has blessed us with every spiritual blessing in the heavenly places in Christ.* *Ephesians 1:3*

However, Ephesians 3:10 reveals what else is hanging out in those heavenly places.

> *To the intent that now the manifold wisdom of God might be made known by the church to the principalities and powers in the heavenly places.* *Ephesians 3:10*

There are a couple of maniacal groups called "principalities and powers" that are in the same place as our blessings—could they be blocking them from coming down to us?

Why Gold?

When searching out the subject of finances in the Scriptures, I decided to look up the usages of "gold" rather than "money." Gold is the backing of any real money, whereas the term "money" is often used in a generic sense. The first usage of gold is found in Genesis 2:11.

> *Now a river went out of Eden to water the garden, and from there it parted and became four riverheads. The name of the first is Pishon; it is the one which encompasses the whole land of Havilah, where there is gold. And the gold of that land is good.*
>
> *Genesis 2:10–12a*

When I read that there was gold in the Garden of Eden, I wondered why God put it there. There weren't any grocery stores for Adam and Eve to shop at—no local 7-11 or "Stop-n-Rob" for them to run to and buy an over-priced quart of milk. Yet it is clear that the gold in the Garden of Eden was meant for them because they were given the specific location of where it was in the garden—in the land of Havilah, which was encompassed by the Pishon River.

However, if you go to that location now, there is no gold. We know from what Jesus told us in John 10:10 that Satan is a thief; therefore, it stands to reason that he would have stolen it and used it for his purposes against God.

> *The thief does not come except to steal, and to kill, and to destroy. I have come that they may have life, and that they may have it more abundantly.* *John 10:10*

We will be held accountable for our stewardship of all that He put here for His people, including the material and financial realm of life. He is the One who put gold into the earth, and it was used in intricate detail in the temple according to His directives. From its last biblical usage in the book of Revelation, we see His final purpose for it. The purity of gold depicts the Creator's holiness and lends itself to worshipping Him.

> *And he carried me away in the Spirit to a great and high mountain, and the twelve gates were twelve pearls: each individual gate was of one pearl.* ***And the street of the city was pure gold, like transparent glass.*** *Revelation 21:10 and 21*

Gold may be pavement in heaven, but here on earth it was meant to help us build His kingdom—to supply the physical resources that His people would need. In order to regain what was originally meant for His good, we must exercise the spiritual authority He has given us.

Rules of Warfare

In order for us to fulfill our ministries, we need three main categories of blessings, or what I call the three R's of ministerial success: Resources, Revelation, and Relationships. In this appendix, we are dealing with the first one. We need to exercise spiritual authority in order to bring in the resources we need for our ministries. This means engaging in some spiritual warfare to get back what is rightfully ours.

Remember that one of the rules of warfare when it comes to exercising our spiritual authority over our personal finances is that if we don't claim what is ours, the devil will. Other vital rules in this warfare are "all's fair in love and war," or "follow the money, find the thief," and "if you starve your enemy, you will not have to actively engage them."

Cutting off supply lines is a primary war strategy. Generally speaking, an army's ability to move quickly can be determined by how long it takes to get supplies. In World War II, had General Rommel not run out of fuel in the North African desert, we might have been flying a Nazi flag today. Supply lines are vital to warfare and to our ability to fulfill our ministry.

Moses and the Children of Israel

The way Moses brought the children of Israel out of captivity from Egypt was by breaking the backs of the principalities and powers that were in that nation. By the power of God, he was able to break ten principalities and powers and free the children of Israel. At the end of this battle, God told Moses to tell the children of Israel that the Egyptians were to give them their gold and silver.

> *Speak now in the hearing of the people, and let every man ask from his neighbor and every woman from her neighbor, articles of silver and articles of gold.* *Exodus 11:2*

> *Now the children of Israel had done according to the word of Moses, and they had asked from the Egyptians articles of silver, articles of gold, and clothing.* *Exodus 12:35*

Here is the spiritual warfare rule: "To the victor, go the spoils." If we are lacking, it's because we have been beaten, and the victor got all the good stuff. If we were in a foxhole, taking strafing fire all around us, and all of a sudden we discovered that the whole time there was a little cart next to us that held a superior weapon and unlimited ammunition, what would we do? If we were smart and courageous, we would load that weapon and shoot back!

A lot of the lies and fiery darts of the wicked have deceived us and made us think we are weak and defenseless, and therefore hopeless.

All the while, the Holy Spirit is telling us to stand up and proclaim who God has made us. Whatever our ministries are, we have the right to proclaim them fulfilled—and that means we have the right to the resources as well.

Before his first leading role in *Ace Ventura: Pet Detective* (1994) and his subsequent prominent roles, Jim Carrey would often go at night into the Santa Monica mountains and yell out affirmations. Here it is in his words:

> When I wasn't doing anything in this town, I'd go up every night, sit on Mulholland Drive, look out at the city, stretch out my arms, and say, "Everybody wants to work with me. I'm a really good actor. I have all kinds of great movie offers." I'd just repeat these things over and over, literally convincing myself that I had a couple of movies lined up.[2]

This was not just a psychological means by which he grew to believe in himself—*he was calling those things that be not as though they were!* He may not have understood this from a biblical perspective (Romans 4:17 KJV), but he still understood the principle. In addition, in 1984, he postdated a check to himself for 10 million dollars (postdated for 10 years later), and just before the postdate came due in 1994, he signed the contract for the role of the Riddler in *Batman Forever*, for which he was paid 5 million dollars.[3] When we add this to the 7 million he was paid for *Dumb & Dumber* earlier that year (1994), he was well over his postdated check of 10 million.[4]

Money is spiritual, and we are spirit beings who can call those things that be not as though they were. When we do this for the glory of God, we further His kingdom and please Him.

Stealing Your Enemy's Weapons

If we can steal our enemy's weapons, we don't have to worry about being shot. The truth of calling those things that be not as though they were from Romans 4:17 came from God but is being used by Satan (the god of this world) to take away resources that were meant to be used for God's glory and kingdom. If we allow the enemy to steal this truth, we will lose our means to gain the advantage and fulfill our ministries. We are not to use this principle for the purpose of becoming selfishly rich; we are to use it for God's glory. And, if we have a ministry of liberality, then we not only will resource our ministry but also the ministries of others.

If we are working our fingers to the bone and stressing ourselves out in the process, something is not right. Remember what Jesus said in Matthew 6 about this.

> *No one can serve two masters; for either he will hate the one and love the other, or else he will be loyal to the one and despise the other. You cannot serve God and mammon. Therefore I say to you, do not worry about your life, what you will eat or what you will drink; nor about your body, what you will put on.* *Matthew 6:24–25a*

> *Therefore do not worry, saying, "What shall we eat?" or "What shall we drink?" or "What shall we wear?" For after all these things the Gentiles seek. For your heavenly Father knows that you need all these things. But seek first the kingdom of God and His righteousness, and all these things shall be added to you.*
>
> *Matthew 6:31–33*

It is good to work, but it is not good to be a workaholic. We work to fulfill our ministry, and for most that means secular work; however, it is still for the purpose of resourcing God's kingdom.

Proportionately, there will be more who work secularly than those who make their living of the Gospel. We see this clearly from the twelve tribes of Israel—eleven of them worked secularly, and only one tended exclusively to spiritual matters.

Regardless of our ministries, we still need our rightful portion of money to fulfill it. We have God's promise concerning this.

> *And my God shall supply all your need according to His riches in glory by Christ Jesus.* *Philippians 4:19*

This promise eliminates the excuse of saying that God did not supply us with the means to fulfill our ministries. The truth is that the Lord gives, but the devil steals.

God has blessed us with *all* spiritual blessings in heavenly places in Christ Jesus. Right now we are learning to war in those heavenly places for our finances in order to fulfill our ministries. Our purpose is not to be rich, retire early, and move to Florida (unless God wants us to witness to Floridians!).

The amount of money each of us needs to fulfill our specific ministries will vary. For instance, the financial needs of an intercessor would probably be less than those of a pastor; and those of a pastor might be less than those of an evangelist. But whatever it is, God has proportioned the amount. When it comes to exercising spiritual authority over what is needed to resource our ministry, our job is to declare, proclaim, and profess that it will come to us, and to do it with faith that God will supply all we need.

Our proclamations in the spirit realm must be according to revelation, and this can be from the Scriptures or directly from the Holy Spirit. The revelation that God will supply all our needs according to His riches in glory by Christ Jesus is one that comes from the Scriptures. Therefore, we can confidently voice this aspect of God's will into the spirit realm, knowing that it is by revelation from Him. The pleasure of God works within us as we do this; and the angels that excel in strength carry out those orders.

> *Bless the LORD, you His angels, Who excel in strength, who do His word, Heeding the voice of His word. Bless the LORD, all you His hosts, You ministers of His, who do His pleasure.*
>
> *Psalm 103:20–21*

Loosing the Resources for Our Ministries

That hole beneath our nose is our spiritual weapon, our *rhema* rifle; it's our ship's rudder and dictates where we go. The Bible even refers to our tongue as a rudder on a ship, emphasizing the power that such a little member of our body can render.

> *Look also at ships: although they are so large and are driven by fierce winds, they are turned by a very small rudder wherever the pilot desires. Even so the tongue is a little member and boasts great things. See how great a forest a little fire kindles!*
>
> *James 3:4–5*

We can use our *rhema* rifles to loose the resources for our ministries; but, in order to avoid shooting wild rounds into the atmosphere, we need to know our targets. We should understand which spiritual powers are preventing our ministries from succeeding, so we can be specific with the scriptures we use. The angelic hosts are poised and ready to make our ministries function and bear fruit; and they will spring into action through our faith-filled words to loosen the finances, as well as the revelations and relationships we need from the heavenly realm to earth.

To find out more specifics about warring against the principalities and powers that are preventing us from getting our resources, I recommend my book, *Devil, Give Me Back My Money!,* which is available through the e-store on our website at LMCI.org.

In *Devil, Give Me Back My Money!*, I teach how we are to demand back from the devil what he has stolen from us. God already put resources on the earth for us, so it should not be necessary to ask Him for them—instead, we should go after the thief who has stolen them. I taught this one time to a man who worked for the post office. He and his wife began warring for their finances, and the United States Post Office gave him a $10,000 bonus! As far as I know, that is not a common practice of the Pony Express.

God wants us to fulfill our ministries. This is not the prosperity gospel of "name it and claim it." This is exercising our spiritual authority to fulfill our ministries, which includes warring in the heavens where spiritual powers are blocking our resources.

As regenerated spirit beings, we are working in conjunction with the Holy Spirit to speak into the heavenly realm. The following is an example of how to pray for your finances, your life, and your ministry. Reading this aloud will help you to get your *rhema* rifle aimed at the right target. Faith comes by hearing, and hearing by the Word of God (Romans 10:17). If Jim Carrey can stand on a hill and speak out words of success and get results, then we can talk into the spirit realm as regenerated children of God to fulfill His kingdom on the earth.

> *In the name of Jesus Christ, I am a blood-bought child of the Almighty God. I have been paid for by the blood of Jesus, and I have been commissioned by Almighty God to fulfill my ministry. I have a right under the covenant blessings of God Almighty to fulfill what I've been called to do, and I have a right to demand all my needs to be*

> *met. In the name of Jesus Christ, I command my resources to come to me. In the name of Jesus Christ, I command the spiritual powers and principalities that are blocking my resources to bow down at the foot of the cross. Luke 10:19 says Jesus gave me authority to trample on serpents and scorpions and over all the power of the enemy. I have authority over all of you; I am making you obey. You spiritual powers that are marshaled over my ministry, in the name of Jesus Christ, I remind you that you were defeated at Calvary; you will bow down; you will bow down; you will get out of my way and release my finances to me. Amen. Ministering spirits who are assigned to me, in the name of Jesus Christ, go get my resources, my revelations, and my relationships, and bring them to me!*

When you speak this out, do it with passion and use your body as well as your mouth. Remember that Jim Carrey spread his hands out, and he may not have even known why he did that. Our hands communicate our attitude. Our attitude and stance should be that of a warrior, so our hands will be clenched into fists and raised in victory. When I did this in India, some of the individuals there were first-generation Christians who were low-class Hindus. They had been so defeated all their lives, that they couldn't even raise their hands in the air and make a fist. What about you? Can you raise your hands in the air and make a fist and put on that game face?

> *In the name of Jesus Christ, I am purchased by the blood of the Lamb. Jesus is the Lamb. He is the Lion. He is the King and I am His servant. I am ordained by God with a ministry to the world to fulfill. I demand as a child of God with spiritual authority the right and the resources to fulfill my ministry. This includes the revelations and the relationships that I need. Spiritual powers that are hindering these from coming to me—you are my enemies. Ministering spirits that are assigned to me, draw your sword and make them glittering with blood. Chase my enemies; run them away and bring me my*

> *resources. Money come! Money for my ministry, come to me by the blood of Jesus. I receive what's mine. Money come. Angels go to the north and south, east and west; go get my money and bring it to me in Jesus' name. I will use it to build the kingdom of God; it's mine; I demand it. I am God's child; I will have it; resources come to me in Jesus' name.*

The devil would love to steal this information from you. He will not do it by coming in and taking it out of your mind, but by coming in and putting something else on top of it (like works) and causing you to lose it. I couldn't find my wallet a couple of weeks ago and I looked everywhere. I finally found it underneath a piece of paper on my desk. That's what he does with truth. He loves to hide the truth by cloaking it beneath legalism or lies.

A good friend of mine was going to India and needed $10,000. When he asked my advice, I said, "Brother, I'd go to Wal-Mart and buy one of those watches that has five alarms on it; and I'd set those alarms, and every time one of them goes off, I'd go outside and shake my fist in the devil's face and demand him to give me the money." I saw him less than a month and a half later, and he walked up to me and handed me a check for $1,000. I said, "What's this check for?" He said, "It's my tithe." I said, "I thought you were looking for money to go to India." He said, "I got it. I got it. Here's my watch to prove it."

Do this. Don't be surprised if you hear those little imp demons saying "What is this? I've never heard this stuff before." Hey. Just try it. I mean all you've got to do is look like a fool out there shaking your fist in the air! The Bible says we are already fools for Christ's sake anyway, so what do you have to lose? You will see it work. I just recently had to repent for not doing it enough. I'm at war even now for the finances for my ministry. Praise God, it is a war. My wife said to me the other day, "It's a violent kingdom and the violent take it by force." I said, "Okay. That's my call—I'm ready to go!"

Let's all respond and move forward *with faith* to do what the Lord has told us and with what we know from the Scriptures. Let's be vocal and bold in our proclamations as we exercise spiritual authority over our finances with faith and anticipate a return for God's blessing to be upon us. In order to fulfill our destinies, we need to exercise spiritual authority over all areas of our lives, including the provisions God has for us.

Notes

Chapter One—The Realm of Spiritual Authority

1. Usage of "God" throughout this book refers to the person of Yahweh, the Father of Yeshua (Jesus). This is not meant as a universal nomenclature of an ethereal being but of the person of the Father of Jesus Christ.
2. Definition of the Greek word *exousia,* Bible Hub, accessed January 23, 2014, http://biblehub.com/greek/1849.htm.
3. Explanation of the term "Almighty God," PROZ.com, accessed January 23, 2014, http://www.proz.com/kudoz/hebrew_to_english/poetry_literature/1236615-el_shaddai_el_yonna_adonai_er_kam_ka_na_adonai.html.
4. Definition of the Greek word *paradidomi,* Bible Study Tools, accessed January 23, 2014, http://www.biblestudytools.com/lexicons/greek/nas/paradidomi.html.
5. Definition of the Greek word *Elohim*, Bible Gateway, accessed January 23, 2014, http://www.biblegateway.com/passage/?search=Psalm+8%3A4-6&version=NKJV.
6. Definition of the Greek word *nicolaitan, Strong's Greek Lexicon*, accessed January 23, 2014, http://www.eliyah.com/cgi-bin/strongs.cgi?file=greeklexicon&isindex=3532.
7. Dale M. Sides, "It Takes Faith to Be a Believer," *Dr. Dale Blog* (blog), November 29, 2012, http://drdaleblog.blogspot.com/2012/11/it-takes-faith-to-be-believer.html.

Chapter Two—Who Am I?

1. Literal translation of the Greek word *exousia* derived from root and prefix meanings, Blue Letter Bible, accessed March 22, 2013, http://www.blueletterbible.org/lang/lexicon/lexicon.cfm?Strongs=G1849&t=KJV.
2. Definition of the Hebrew word *'adam,* Bible Study Tools, accessed January 23, 2014, http://www.biblestudytools.com/dictionary/adam/.
3. Sides, "I Believe in the Godhead (but I'm Not So Sure about the Trinity)," accessed January 23, 2014, http://www.lmci.org/articles.cfm?Article=78.
4. Definition of the Greek word *boulemai,* Bible Study Tools, accessed January 23, 2014, http://www.biblestudytools.com/lexicons/greek/nas/boulomai.html.
5. Biblically speaking, the new birth refers to being "born again." Jesus discussed being born again with Nicodemus in the Gospel of John, and the Apostle Paul explained it further in the book of Romans:

   > *Jesus answered and said to him, "Most assuredly, I say to you, unless one is born again, he cannot see the kingdom of God." Nicodemus said to Him, "How can a man be born when he is old? Can he enter a second time into his mother's womb and be born?" Jesus answered, "Most assuredly, I say to you, unless one is born of water and the Spirit, he cannot enter the kingdom of God. That which is born of the flesh is flesh, and that which is born of the Spirit is spirit. Do not marvel that I said to you, ' You must be born again.' For God so loved the world that He gave His only begotten Son, that whoever believes in Him should not perish but have everlasting life. For God did not send His Son into the world to condemn the world, but that the world through Him might be saved."* *John 3:3–7, 16–17*

   > *If you confess with your mouth the Lord Jesus and believe in your heart that God has raised Him from the dead, you will be saved. For with the heart one believes to righteousness, and*

> *with the mouth confession is made to salvation. For the Scripture says, "Whoever believes on Him will not be put to shame." For "whoever calls upon the name of the Lord shall be saved."*
>
> *Romans 10:9–11, 13*

6. Definition of the Greek word *nous*, Bible Study Tools, accessed February 14, 2014, http://www.biblestudytools.com/lexicons/greek/nas/nous.

Chapter Three—The Spirit Nature of Man

1. Definition of the Greek word *phuo*, Bible Study Tools, accessed February 14, 2014, http://www.biblestudytools.com/lexicons/greek/nas/phuo.html.
2. The return of the Adamic covenant of dominion can be seen in the phrase "more than conquerors" in Romans 8:37 as it pertains to Christ followers.
3. Definition of the Greek word *palin*, Bible Study Tools, accessed February 14, 2014, http://www.biblestudytools.com/lexicons/greek/nas/palin.html._
4. Definition of "orgy," Dictionary.com, accessed January 24, 2014, http://dictionary.reference.com/browse/orgy.

Chapter Four—Exercising Spiritual Authority over the Soul

1. Michael Hall, *Emotions: Sometimes I Have Them/Sometimes They Have Me* (n.p.: Good-News Encounters, Inc., 1985).

Chapter Five—Exercising Spiritual Authority over the Body

1. "Two-thirds of U.S. adults are overweight or obese," according to the Food Research and Action Center (FRAC) who say that 68.8% are obese or overweight with 35.7% being obese and 33.1% being overweight. FRAC's report,

"Overweight and Obesity in the U.S.," accessed January 23, 2014, http://frac.org/initiatives/hunger-and-obesity/obesity-in-the-us/.

Chapter Six—The Authority of a Disciple

1. Definition of the Greek word *dunamis,* Bible Study Tools, accessed January 23, 2014, http://www.biblestudytools.com/lexicons/greek/nas/dunamis.html.

Chapter Seven—The Authority to Re-Present Jesus

1. Definition of the Greek word *suntribo,* Bible Study Tools, accessed January 24, 2014 at http://www.biblestudytools.com/lexicons/greek/nas/suntribo.html.
2. Definition of the Greek word *metron,* Bible Hub, accessed January 24, 2014, http://biblehub.com/greek/3358.htm.
3. Definition of the Greek word *prothesis,* Blue Letter Bible, accessed January 23, 2014, http://www.blueletterbible.org/lang/lexicon/lexicon.cfm?Strongs=G4286&t=KJV.
4. An introductory article on Christological Astronomy is available at http://www.lmci.org/articles.cfm?Article=413. Since discovering Christological Astronomy, I have learned to read the messages that we each have in our birth sky and have taught others to read them as well. To find information on a particular birthdate, see http://www.lmci.org/ca.cfm?Start=Yes. A class on Christological Astronomy is also available in workbook, e-workbook, and DVD-, CD-, or MP3-set at http://www.lmci.org/showcategories.cfm in the e-store of LMCI.org.
5. Definition of the Greek word *symmorphos,* Blue Letter Bible, accessed January 27, 2014, http://www.blueletterbible.org/lang/lexicon/lexicon.cfm?Strongs=G4832&t=KJV.
6. "The Teacup," Motivate Us, accessed January 27, 2014, http://www.motivateus.com/stories/teacup.htm.

7. Definition of the Greek word *epiphaneia*, Eliyah, accessed January 27, 2014, http://www.eliyah.com/cgi-bin/strongs.cgi?file=greeklexicon&isindex=5316.
8. Definition of the Greek word *kardia*, Bible Hub, accessed January 27, 2014, http://biblehub.com/greek/2588.htm.

Chapter Eight—Overcoming the Power of the Enemy

1. Definition of "peace," The Refiner's Fire, accessed January 27, 2014, http://www.therefinersfire.org/meaning_of_shalom.htm.
2. Definition of the Greek word *phimoo,* Bible Study Tools, accessed January 27, 2014, http://www.biblestudytools.com/lexicons/greek/nas/phimoo.html.
3. Definition of "generations," Blue Letter Bible, accessed January 27, 2014, http://www.blueletterbible.org/lang/Lexicon/Lexicon.cfm?strongs=H8435&t=KJV.
4. The Greek word *daimonion* ("demons") occurs 60 times in the New Testament, while the Greek word *daimon* ("demon") occurs 5 times.
5. Definitions of the Greek words *dia* and *ballo*, Bible Hub, accessed February 21, 2014, http://biblehub.com/greek/1223.htm and http://biblehub.com/greek/906.htm, respectively._
6. Definition of the Greek word *daimonizomai,* Bible Study Tools, accessed January 27, 2014, http://www.biblestudytools.com/lexicons/greek/nas/daimonizomai.html.

Chapter Nine—Closing Portals of Demonic Entry

1. Definition of the Greek word *hamartia,* Bible Study Tools, accessed January 27, 2014, http://www.biblestudytools.com/lexicons/greek/nas/hamartia.html.
2. Definition of the Greek word *metanoeo,* Blue Letter Bible, accessed January 27, 2014, http://www.blueletterbible.org/lang/lexicon/lexicon.cfm?Strongs=G3340&t=KJV.

3. Through my study of quantum physics, as well as the truths I have gleaned from deliverance ministers who have applied these laws in their ministry, I have learned about the reconciliation of past mental injuries with the quantum law of entanglement. I have put together several audio teachings on quantum physics, one of which is *Quantum Physics, Continued: Entanglement/Entrainment/Observation*, that cover this topic. This teaching applies the law of confession to make polarity of incidents align and achieve harmony. I also recommend a book on quantum physics, written from a Godly perspective, entitled *Quantum Glory* by Phil Mason.
4. If you would like to have an Exercising Spiritual Authority class conducted in your area, please email us at LMCHRIST@LMCI.org or call 540-586-5813.

Chapter Ten—Developing the Character of Christ

1. Definitions of the Greek words *nikao* and *nike,* Bible Study Tools, accessed February 24, 2014, http://www.biblestudytools.com/lexiconsgreek/kjv/nikao.html and http://www.biblestudytools.com/lexicons/greek/nas/nike.html, respectively.
2. Definition of "abstain," Bible Study Tools, accessed February 24, 2014, http://www.biblestudytools.com/lexicons/greek/kjv/apechomai.html.
3. Definition of the Greek word *gymnazō,* Study Light, accessed January 28, 2014, http://www.studylight.org/lex/grk/gwview.cgi?n=1128.
4. Definition of the Greek word *paralogizomai*, Bible Hub, accessed January 28, 2014, http://biblehub.com/greek/3884.htm.

Chapter Eleven—Re-Presenting Jesus on the Earth

1. Explanation of the figure of speech "asyndeton," Changing

2. Minds, accessed January 28, 2014, http://changingminds.org/techniques/language/figures_speech/asyndeton.htm.
3. Sides, *Flowing in All Nine Gifts of the Holy Spirit*, is a booklet that is used in the Liberating Ministries for Christ International's Discipleship Program at LMCI.org. It offers a different perspective on the nine gifts of the Holy Spirit by showing how they work together (rather than independently) to produce an energized manifestation of God's power.

Part V—Our Authority to Re-Present Jesus in Power

1. Sides, *Flowing in All Nine Gifts of the Holy Spirit* (Bedford, VA: Liberating Ministries for Christ International, Inc., 2005).

Chapter Twelve—Receiving the Holy Spirit and Speaking in Tongues

1. J. Crimando, PhD—Gateway Community College, "Cranial Nerves: Review Info," accessed June 17, 2013, http://www.gwc.maricopa.edu/class/bio201/cn/cranial.htm. Chart of the 12 main nerve centers of the brain.
2. Definition of the Greek word *rhema*, Bible Hub, accessed June 27, 2013, http://biblehub.com/greek/4487.htm.
3. The quantum law of observation is discussed in an audio teaching available at LMCI.org entitled, "Quantum Physics Continued: Entanglement/Entrainment/Observation," LP169.
4. Sides, *Diverse Kinds of Tongues* is a booklet that explains the differences between speaking in a tongue and having the gift of tongues (plural). It is especially beneficial for intercessors.
5. Definition of the Greek word *emphusao,* Bible Study Tools, accessed January 28, 2014, http://www.biblestudytools.com/lexicons/greek/nas/emphusao.html.
6. The definition of the Greek word *rheo*, Bible Hub, accessed May 16, 2014, http://biblehub.com/greek/4482.htm, meaning "flow, overflow with."

7. The root of the Greek word *rhema* is Strong's number 4483 (*rheo*), Bible Study Tools, accessed May 19, 2014, http://www.biblestudytools.com/lexicons/greek/nas/rhema.html.
8. Lyrics and video of the song, "Oh, How I Love Jesus," accessed April 17, 2014, can be found at https://www.youtube.com/watch?v=5DZR2Ky_hlc.

Chapter Thirteen—The Utterance Gifts of Interpretation of Tongues and Prophecy

1. Sides, *Flowing in All Nine Gifts of the Holy Spirit* (Bedford, VA: Liberating Ministries for Christ International, Inc., 2005) 16–17.

Chapter Fourteen—Receiving Spiritual Information and the Revelation Gifts

1. Phil Mason, *Quantum Glory* (Maricopa, AZ: XP Publishing, 2012) 43-44.
2. Definition of the Greek word *epignosis*, Gospel Hall, accessed January 30, 2014, http://gospelhall.org/bible/bible.php?search=epignosis&dict=vine&lang=greek#A3.
3. Definition of the Greek word *aisthētērion*, Lexicon-Concordance Online Bible, accessed February 25, 2014, http://lexiconcordance.com/greek/0145.html.
4. Michael G. Conner, Psy.D, Clincal and Medical Psychologist, "Understanding the Difference between Men and Women," accessed May 20, 2013, http://oregoncounseling.org/ArticlesPapers/Documents/DifferencesMenWomen.htm.
5. Definition of the Greek word *apo*, Bible Hub, accessed May 21, 2014, http://biblehub.com/greek/575.htm.
6. Definition of the Greek word *kalupto,* Study Light, accessed February 26, 2014, http://classic.studylight.org/lex/grk/view.cgi?number=2572.
7. Definition of the Greek word *hupo*, Study Light, accessed

February 26, 2014, http://classic.studylight.org/lex/grk/view.cgi?number=5259.

8. Definition of the Greek word *mimnesko*, Bible Study Tools, accessed February 26, 2014, http://www.biblestudytools.com/lexicons/greek/nas/mimnesko.html.
9. Definition of the Greek word *logos*, Bible Study Tools, accessed January 31, 2014, http://www.biblestudytools.com/lexicons/greek/nas/logos.html.
10. Definition of the Greek word *rhema*, Bible Study Tools, accessed January 31, 2014, http://www.biblestudytools.com/lexicons/greek/nas/rhema.html.
11. Hewlett-Packard Development Company, LP, "The Power of Visual Communication," accessed January 31, 2014, http://www.hp.com/large/ipg/assets/bus-solutions/power-of-visual-communication.pdf.

Chapter Fifteen—Spiritual Faith

1. John Wimber's biography, accessed January 31, 2014, http://www.wimber.org/john-wimber/.
2. Peter Smythe, "The Faith of God (God-Kind of Faith)," accessed November 21, 2012, http://hopefaithprayer.com/word-of-faith/the-faith-of-god-god-kind-of-faith-smythe/.

Chapter Sixteen—Gifts of Healings and the Working of Miracles

1. The Greek word for "working" in the gift of the working of miracles is *energemata*, the word from which we get "energy." The prefix is *en* and the root word is *ergon* which means "work" or loosely, "getting something done." *Erg* is a measurement of expended effort in physics. Working basically means an activation of energy that can be seen.

2. Definition of "miracle," Online Etymology Dictionary, accessed May 20, 2014, http://www.etymonline.com/index.php?term=miracle.
3. Definition of the Greek word *dunamis*, Bible Study Tools, accessed May 23, 2014, http://www.biblestudytools.com/lexicons/greek/nas/dunamis.html.

Chapter Seventeen—Other Ways God Can Heal

1. Sides, "Keys to Ministering Healing," *Exercising Spiritual Authority: Level 3*, Bedford, VA: Liberating Ministries for Christ International, Inc., 2013. CD- or MP3-set.
2. I knew about ministering healing long ago, but I did not know about commanding body parts and diseases directly through revelation until I got involved with Brother B. J. Leonard's ministry, Christian Training Center, http://www.ctcoftexas.com/.
3. Kenneth Hagin, Sr.'s teaching "The Healing Anointing," accessed May 27, 2014, can be viewed online at https://www.youtube.com/watch?v=14_4kYtkjqw.

Appendix 1—Operating the Gift of Faith to Fulfill Your Ministry

1. Sides, "Having Faith to Finish," Liberating Ministries for Christ International, 2000. Audio CD or MP3 format, available in the e-store at LMCI.org.

Appendix 2—Exercising Spiritual Authority to Strengthen Church Government

1. Definition of the Greek word *episkopos* derived from Bible Study Tools, accessed March 23, 2014, http://www.biblestudytools.com/lexicons/greek/kjv/episkopos.html.

Appendix 3—Exercising Spiritual Authority over Personal Finances

1. Sides, *Devil, Give Me Back My Money!*, 2nd ed. (Bedford, VA: Liberating Publications, Inc., 2004).
2. Brad Stanton, "Affirmations," accessed January 4, 2013, http://bradstanton.com/2012/08/10/affirmations/.
3. Wikipedia Answers, accessed January 4, 2013, http://wiki.answers.com/Q/How_much_money_does_Jim_Carrey_make_per_movie.
4. Jim Carrey's biography, Internet Movie Database, accessed January 4, 2013, http://www.imdb.com/name/nm0000120/bio.

Answer Key

Chapter One

1. Matthew 28:18; John 1:12; John 14:12
2. Answers will vary.
3. The word "angels" was an improper interpretation of the Hebrew word *elohim*, which should have been translated into the English word "God." He has made us (mankind) a little lower than Himself.

Chapter Two

1. A spirit being
2. Answers will vary between spirit, soul, and body.
3. Answers will vary on how reader's perspective would change if he/she identified more as a spirit being.

Chapter Three

1. It became regenerated, made new through the power of God. I have been reborn into the image of God. My spirit is holy and pure just as He is. (Any answer along these lines is good.)
2. The spirit of man I had before was not holy and pure; neither did it have a direct contact with the Holy Spirit in order to readily receive revelation. Now I have a regenerated holy spirit that is Christ in me, the hope of glory:
3. Answer will vary, as well as scripture references.

Chapter Four

1. The soul (mind) is where our thoughts take place—it is composed of our intellect, imaginations, and emotions.
2. Answers can vary but should include basic disciplines that have been specified for the individual, such as: memorize a scripture every day; limit a specified time on the Internet or in front of the television (or eliminate one or both of them altogether); read a Bible chapter every day; listen to audio scripture while driving; whenever the mind begins to wander away from the truth, speak aloud a memorized scripture; pray daily for meekness in order to receive the engrafted Word more readily; meditate for a determinate amount of time upon one scripture every day; intentionally exercise spiritual authority over a weak area of the soul by confessing scripture over it/applying the blood of Jesus over it/binding or loosing in Jesus' name—in order to crucify the flesh with its "passions and desire;" confess the truth of the Scriptures for a specified amount of time each day, etc.
3. Answers will vary.

Chapter Five

1. The body is simply our flesh, the least important part of our three-part makeup. It is our earthly tabernacle that temporarily houses our soul and spirit.
2. The practical way to overcome our fleshly desires is to become alive to the spirit realm, and this is best done through focusing upon the life and light of God's Word. Therefore, any practical way listed similar to the example answers given on chapter 4 question #2 will work. Any answer given along the line of avoiding/fleeing/resisting fleshly temptation would also be correct; however, it should be connected with the introduction of the light and truth of Scripture rather than an attempt to rein in the flesh without help from God.
3. Goals will vary but will be similar to the sample answers given for chapter 4 question #2.

Chapter Six

1. A disciple is a believer who is willing to discipline him/herself to follow after Christ. Every disciple is a believer, but not every believer is a disciple.
2. If "yes," there should be a description of the calling. If 'no," there should be a follow-through of reading the e-book and then writing down the insights gained from it.
3. Disciple, level, authority

Chapter Seven

1. Our spiritual jurisdiction is determined by the areas God has assigned us to—our callings, our personal lives (for example, our bodies, our souls, our finances, etc.), our families, our geographical regions, etc. He may also assign temporary or other specific areas, such as a country to minister within or a person to pray for. The short answer is whatever or whoever God assigns to us.
2. Answers will vary, but it could be as a teacher, a healer, an apostle, etc., or one of His characteristics, such as His love, mercy, grace, forgiveness, etc.
3. A brief synopsis of your Christological Astronomy profile should be written.

Chapter Eight

1. Luke 10:19; 1 John4:4; Psalm 8:4–6
2. "It is written"—He spoke the Scriptures to overcome the temptations.
3. Scripture references will vary. All three should be checked off after memorizing.

Chapter Nine

1. Trauma, Rejection, Unforgiveness, Curses, Occult practices, Physical objects, Sin
2. Sinful, doorway or portal
3. The delivered man was sitting at Jesus' feet, indicating that Jesus was teaching him how to keep and maintain his deliverance. The person who receives deliverance must learn how to do the same from someone who can disciple him/her.

Chapter Ten

1. 1 Peter 1:15–16
2. A little child, a father, or a young (wo)man.
3. The belt of truth, the breastplate of righteousness, the shoes of the preparation of the gospel of peace, the shield of faith, the helmet of salvation, the sword of the spirit, constant prayer (these may be in any order)

Chapter Eleven

1. John 14:12
2. Answers may vary.
3. Love, joy, peace, longsuffering, kindness, goodness, faithfulness, gentleness, and self-control

Chapter Twelve

1. Words
2. What we feed upon
3. The voice of His Word

Chapter Thirteen

1. Speaking in tongues, interpretation of tongues, and prophecy
2. A diverse tongue comes upon us from the anointing of the Holy Spirit in specific times of prayer. It can be recognized because it will sound different than our prayer language and will often be intense and warlike, although in can also be softer and worshipful
3. According to 1 Corinthians 14:1–6, we should desire to prophesy in order to strengthen, encourage, and comfort others.

Chapter Fourteen

1. The word of wisdom, the word of knowledge, and discerning of spirits
2. Through spiritual perception and inspiration
3. The anointing within is the residing presence of the Holy Spirit, received with the new birth, which will never leave us and gives us eternal life. The anointing upon is when the Holy Spirit comes upon us to empower us to do things that are extraordinary and beyond our normal abilities.

Chapter Fifteen

1. Our faith and the gift of faith
2. Our faith is what comes from our spirit and can be high or low; the gift of faith is a Holy Spirit gift—it is the faith of Jesus and is activated by obedience to revelation
3. Forever Anticipating Intervention Through Him

Chapter Sixteen

1. Gifts of healings and the working of miracles are both the result of spiritual utterance by spiritual knowledge, accompanied with spiritual faith.

2. When we have not received direct revelation to minister healing
3. When we receive revelation to impart a healing gift

Chapter Seventeen

1. Because of God's sovereignty, He can heal someone even without their faith or our faith. Also, because of His creativity and ingenuity, He can heal in many different ways or a combination of ways. (Either or both answers are acceptable.)
2. The laying on of hands, anointing with oil, revelation word, prayer of faith, faith of others, special anointings, covenant healing in communion
3. So that God will be glorified

Index

Page numbers are italicized. Following a page number, "n" indicates an endnote.

Abraham, as example of faith, *308–309*
Abram, *308–309*
Acts
- 1:8, *77*, *240*
- 2 (chapter), *214–215*
- 2:3, *218*
- 2:5–11, *222*
- 2:11, *215*, *226*
- 2:17, *231*
- 2:17–18, *168–169*
- 2:38, *49*
- 3:6, *287*
- 3:1–10, *287*
- 4:10 and 12, *290*
- 5:1–11, *134*
- 5:15, *299*
- 10:1–5, *175*
- 10:44–46, *215*
- 10:46, *215*
- 11:22–23, *110–111*
- 11:24, *111*
- 13:2, *176*
- 14:21–23, *314*
- 19 (chapter), *215*
- 19:6, *240*
- 19:11–12, *299*
- 19:18–20, *153*
- 20:28, *111–112*, *312*
- 21:9, *231*
- 26:18, *1*, *21*, *120*

'adam, *22*

Adam and Eve
- authority of, *7*, *18–19*
- consequences of sin, *37–40*
- created in God's image (Genesis 1:27–28), *174*
- and Luke 4:5–6, *320*

Adamic covenant, *335n2 (chap. 3)*
agape, *201*
aggression, spiritual, *15–16*
Aijalon, *274*
aistheterion, *242*
Allen, A. A., *284*
Ananias (and Sapphira, New Testament believers), *134*
angels
- *elohim* mistranslated as (Psalm 8:4–6), *17*
- fallen (watchers), *127–130*
- heeding spiritual utterance, *212–214*
- ministering spirits, *213–214*
- as sons of God (Job 38:4–7), *23*
- warring (Psalm 103:20–21), *138*, *328*

anger (iniquity), *147–151*
animals
- as a habitation of nephilim, *130*
- mankind is not, *26–28*
- and physical objects in deliverance, *151–153*

Anna (prophetess), *102–103*
anointing
- oil, *294, 296*

anointing (*continued*)
special (to glorify God), *281–284*
within and upon, *239–240, 349n3 (chap. 14)*
Antioch, *110–111*, *314*
apo, *247*
apokalupsis, *247*
Apollos, *132*
appearing. *See* epiphany
arche, 81
armor of God
prayer and, *172*
putting it on, *171–172*
war rules and, *119–121*
asyndeton, *195*

Balboa, Rocky, *167–168*, *182*, *184*
ballo, *131*
baptism of the Holy Spirit, *214–222*
Barnabas, *110–112*, *313–314*
battle
armor of God as equipment for, *171–172*
Moses and the children of Israel and, *324*
spiritual, *1–3*, *81–84*
See also warfare, spiritual
battlefield of the mind (soul), *58–61*
Bethany, *272*
birth, new
alive to spirit realm, *238–239*
how to receive, *334–335n5 (chap. 2)*
what part of man gets born again, *40–43*
blood of Jesus
covenant healing in communion and, *299–300*
occult practices and, *153–155*
sin and, *144*

boldness
spiritual utterance and, *208*
walking in, *288–289*
bondage (and war rules), *120–121*
boulemai, *25*

calling, *87–112*
gifts of the Spirit and, *196–203*, *307–309*
maturing into, *178–180*
special anointings and, *299*
spiritual perception and, *181–182*, *241–245*
writing it down, *307*
See also purpose
Calvary, *11*, *120*, *221*
Capernaum, *123*
Carrey, Jim, *325*, *330*
Cephas. *See* Peter (apostle)
Chandler, Russ, *195*, *297*
chapter
questions. *See* points, relevant
resources. *See* materials, related
Christological Astronomy (Sides), *336n4 (chap. 7)*
See also under Sides, Dale M., works of
1 Chronicles 4:9–10, *79*
Colossians
1:13–14, *120*
1:15–16, *9*
1:27, *41*, *61*, *254*
2:10, *83*
2:15, *118*
3:3–4, *66*
3:11, *254*
commitment
crossing threshold of, *79–81*
spiritual battle and, *81–83*

Communion, Holy, *294*, *299–300*
conscience, *47–48*
control, limits of, *11–12*
1 Corinthians
  2:1 and 4–5, *280*
  2:9–14, *60–61*
  2:11, *44*
  2:13, *109*
  2:14, *106*, *110*
  3:1–3, *179*
  3:21–23, *132*
  6:19–20, *132*
  6:20, *160*
  7:23, *160*
  9:18, *17*
  9:24–27, *68*
  9:25, *68*
  9:26–27, *182*
  9:27, *31*, *69*
  12:4–5, *89*
  12:4–6, *23*, *196*
  12:7, *197*
  12:7–10, *268*
  12:7–11, *239*
  12:8, *253*
  12:8–10, *197*
  12:9–11, *259*
  12:10, *281*
  12:11, *25*, *198*
  12:12, *198*
  12:14–21, *93*
  12:15–16, *198*
  12:18–23, *198–199*
  12:27, *92–93*
  12:27–30, *199*
  12:27–31, *199*
  12:28, *199*
  12:31, *200*, *201*
  13 (chapter), *201*, *202*
  13:1, *214*
1 Corinthians (*continued*)
  13:4–7, *202*
  13:9 and 12, *2*
  14:1, *229*, *231*
  14:1–16, *349n3 (chap. 13)*
  14:2, *215*, *226*
  14:3, *231*, *232*
  14:4, *215*
  14:5, *199*, *215*, *228*, *231*
  14:12–13, *228*
  14:13, *228*, *229*
  14:14–15, *32*
  14:16, *226*
  14:17, *215*, *219*, *226*
  14:29, *232*
  14:33, *88*
  14:39, *231*
  14:40, *228*
2 Corinthians
  1:21–22, *124*, *216*, *240*
  1:24, *265*
  2:11, *81*
  3:17–18, *192*
  3:18, *51*
  4:4, *174*
  4:18–5:5, *29*
  5:1, *255*
  5:10, *25*, *33*, *48*, *58*
  5:17, *46*, *150*
  5:20–21, *18*
  10:4–5, *136*
  10:5, *55*, *60*
  10:8, *17*
  10:13, *93–94*
  10:14–18, *94*
Cornelius (Roman centurion), *175*, *215*
covenant
  Adamic, *40*, *335n2 (chap. 3)*
  healing in communion, *299–300*

curses
deliverance from, *155–156*
from occult practices, *153–154*
on physical objects, *151–153*
as TRUCOPS portal, *143–144*

daimon, *131*, *133*, *337n4 (chap. 8)*
daimonion, *131*, *337n4 (chap. 8)*
daimonizomai, *131*, *133*
Damascus, *1*
Daniel (prophet), *227*
daughters. *See* sons; sons of God
David (shepherd, psalmist, king), *8*, *97*, *146*
deception, avoiding, *184–185*
defense (in spiritual aggression), *15–16*
degenerate
definition, *38*
human race as, *129*
spirit, *38*, *42*, *44–45*
deliverance, *141–163*
demons
authority of a disciple and, *75–76*
casting out as a type of miracle, *281*
category of evil spirits, *81–83*
closing portals of entry, *141–163*
expelling, *121–124*
fasting and, *52*
functions of, *131*
maintaining deliverance from, *162–163*
nephilim and, *126–130*
possession, *131–135*
seducing spirits, *135–139*
TRUCOPS and, *143–162*
unclean spirits, *124–126*
war rules and, *119–121*
desire. *See* will
destiny. *See* calling; purpose
Deuteronomy
6:5, *30*
7:25–26, *152*
18:10–12, *154*
28:1–14, *40*
32:10, *138*
devil
lies of, *27*
worthy opponent of believers, *12–15*
See also Lucifer
Devil, Give Me Back My Money! (Sides), *317*, *318*, *329*
dia, *131*, *241*
diabolos, *131*
discerning of spirits
being alive to spirit realm and, *238–239*
as a gift of the Spirit, *196–201*
as revelation gift, *253–256*
Discerning of Spirits and Casting Out Demons (Sides), *163*, *164*
See also under Sides, Dale M., works of
discipline
to avoid deception, *184–185*
over body, *65–70*
to develop prayer life, *172–176*
to develop spiritual perception, *181–183*
fasting and, *176–178*
to follow Jesus, *75–78*
to put on armor of God, *171–172*
to resist temptation and overcome sin, *180–181*, *183–184*, *185–186*
rewards and, *187–188*
over soul, *55–63*
for spiritual battle, *81–84*
spiritual maturity and, *78–81*, *168–170*, *178–180*

DNA (and fruit of the Spirit), *195*
dominion
  over faith, *265*
  man's jurisdiction, *17–19*
  overcoming power of the enemy, *115–139*
  prayer and, *172–176*
doors (of demonic entry). *See* portals
dunamis
  ability to do, *77*
  miracles, *281*
  power, *76–77*

Ecclesiastes
  8:8, *16*, *32*
  10:8, *161*
  12:7, *65*
  12:13, *116*
Eden, garden of, *18*, *321–322*
Egypt, *253*, *324*
Egyptians, *324*
ek, *21–22*
El Shaddai, *8–9*
elohim, (Psalm 8:5), *17*
em, *217*
emotions
  accountability at judgment seat of Christ and, *33–34*
  forgiveness and, *158*
  interpretation of tongues (or prophecy) in the church and, *227–228*
  and not being animals, *26–28*
  as part of the soul, *55–58*
  resisting temptation/overcoming sin and, *180–181*
  trauma and, *160–162*
Emotions: Sometimes I Have Them/ Sometimes They Have Me (Hall), *56*
emphusao, *217*
en, *341n1 (chap. 16)*
energemata, *341n1 (chap. 16)*
enforcers. *See* kingdom
Enoch (book), *127*, *128*
Ephesians
  1:3, *321*
  1:4, *87*
  1:6, *138*, *159*
  1:13, *216*
  1:17, *60*, *106*
  1:17–18, *60*, *107*
  1:18, *89*, *107*
  2:1, *39*, *44*
  2:2–3, *37*, *45*
  2:4–5, *45*
  2:5–6, *19*
  2:8, *46*, *58*
  2:10, *12*, *95*
  3:10, *125*, *321*
  3:16, *215*, *254*
  3:20, *270*
  4:1–2, *101*
  4:7, *91*
  4:8, 11–15, *315*
  4:14–16, *83*
  4:24, *42*, *48*
  4:27, *317*
  4:28, *319*
  5:1, *43*
  5:8, *50*
  5:19, *234*
  6 (chapter), *14*
  6:10–18, *171*
  6:11–17, *120*
  6:12, *171*, *212*, *253–254*
  6:13, *171*
  6:13–18, *171–172*
  6:17, *212*
  6:17–18, *215*
  6:18, *215–216*, *226*
epi, *105*, *241*

epignosis, *241*
epiphaneia, *105*
epiphany, *105–110*
episkopos, *312*
erg, *341n1 (chap. 16)*
ergon, *341n1 (chap. 16)*
esti, *21–22*
eternal life. *See* life, eternal
Eve
  gender differences in spiritual perception and, *245–247*
  Lucifer's greed problem and, *319–320*
  See also Adam and Eve
Exodus
  3:2, *40*
  11:2, *324*
  12:35, *324*
  13:21, *40*
  34:6–7, *147–148*
  40:9, *296*
exousia
  definition, author's practical, *vii*, *21–22*
  exercised strength, *81*
  governing authorities, *311*
  jurisdiction, *87–88*
  power/authority, *1*, *8*, *10*, *21*, *75*, *76–77*, *121–124*
  powers, as category of evil spirits, *81–82*
  right to do, *77*
Ezekiel
  28:15, *13*
  28:16, *319*

FAITH, acronym of, *271*
fasting, *51–52*, *176–178*
fear (iniquity), *147–151*
figure of speech. *See* asyndeton
flesh, *65–67*
Flowing in All Nine Gifts of the Holy Spirit (Sides), *205*
  See also under Sides, Dale M., works of
Foundations of Faith (Sides), *264*
  See also under Sides, Dale M., works of
fruit of the Spirit
  doing His works and, *192–193*
  as Jesus' character revealed, *195–196*
  love and the more excellent way, *201–202*
  patience and exercising spiritual authority over the soul, *61–63*

Galatians
  4:6, *216*, *238*
  5:1, *67*
  5:13, *183*
  5:16, *67*
  5:16–17, *25*, *60*
  5:17, *186*
  5:19–21, *63*, *66*
  5:22, *61*, *195*
  5:22–23, *47*, *195–196*
  5:22–25, *59*, *195*
  5:24, *186*
  6:7, *183*
Gate, Beautiful, *284*, *290*
generations
  Genesis 6:8–9 and, *129–130*
  iniquity and, *147–151*
  of next leaders, *314–315*
  worthy opponent and, *12–15*
genesis, *42*
Genesis
  1:26, *18*, *22*, *23–26*, *31*
  1:27–28, *174*

Genesis (*continued*)
1:28, *18*, *40*, *188*
2:1, *321*
2:7, *22*, *32*, *65*
2:10–12, *321*
2:11, *321*
2:17, *44*
3:1, *27*
3:8, *38*
3:15, *129*, *246*
3:17, *18*
5:3, *38*
6 (chapter), *130*
6:1–2, 4, *126–127*
6:5–7, *128–129*
6:8–9, *129*
7:1, *130*
9:7, *40*
14:1–16, *320*
17 (chapter), *40*
17:1–6, *308*
17:16, *308*
31:19, *153*
37:2–5, *102*
Gethsemane, garden of, *137*
giants. *See* nephilim
Gibeon, *274*
Gideon, *152*
gifts of the Spirit, *196–202*, *205–300*
ginosko, *170*
gnosis, *241*
goals
authority to re-present Jesus and, *87–88*
of fruit of the Spirit, *195–196*
of healings and miracles, *290*
of leaders who inspire others, *203*
pressing toward, *103–104*
God, Almighty. *See El Shaddai*
Godhead
and gifts of the Spirit, *196*
Godhead (*continued*)
members of, *23–24*
gold, *321–323*, *324*
Goliath, *8*
grace
made alive by, *44–47*
saved and called by, *104–105*
Greek words. *See listings of individual words*
growth process, *75–84*, *87–112*, *167–188*, *191–203*
Guest, Edgar A, *280*
gymnazo, *181–182*

Habakkuk
2:1–4, *309*
2:2, *307*
Hagin, Kenneth Sr., *300*, *303*
Hall, Michael. *See Emotions: Sometimes I Have/Sometimes They Have Me*
hamartia, *144*
Havilah, *321–322*
Healing Anointing, The (Hagin), *300*
Hebrew words. *See listings of individual words*
Hebrews (book), *262*
Hebrews
1:3, *202*
1:14, *213*
2:4, *25*, *200*, *272*
2:11, *159*
2:16, *25*
3:4, *12*
4:12, *31*
4:15, *137*, *151*, *159*
5:12, *179*
5:13–14, *178*
5:14, *179*, *181*, *242*
6:1, *179*
6:1–2, *178–179*

Hebrews (*continued*)
- 6:12, *62*
- 7:25, *188*
- 7:25–26, *48*
- 9:22–26, *18*
- 9:27, *16*
- 10:7, *110*
- 10:36, *62*
- 10:38–39, *57*
- 11:3, *271–272*, *298*
- 11:6, *259–260*
- 12:2–4, *15*
- 13:5, *39*

hell (Tartarus), *127*
Herod, *87*
Hinduism, *29*
Hinn, Benny, *283–284*
humility, *34*, *98–101*
hupo, *252*,
hupomimnesko, *252*

identity, of mankind, *21–34*
image
- of Adam, *38*
- conformed to His Son, *14*, *48*, *97–102*
- from glory to glory, *191–192*
- of God's spirit, *37*
- made alive, *44*
- made in His (God's), *23–24*
- personal epiphany of Christ, *105–108*
- physical object, *151–153*
- revelation picture, *284–286*
- spiritual maturity and, *178–180*

impatience, as enemy of peace, *62–63*
iniquity
- demonization and, *131–135*
- found in Lucifer (Ezekiel 28:25), *13*
- as a kind of sin, *144–151*

inspiration (in-spirit-action)
- defined, *252–253*
- interpretation of tongues or prophecy and, *230*

Isaiah
- 14:13–14, *25–26*
- 14:16, *2*
- 46:9–10, *95*
- 46:10, *11–12*
- 53:3–7, *158–159*
- 53:5, *150*
- 53:7, *14*
- 64:8, *100–101*

Israel, children of
- Moses and, *324*
- worthy opponent of, *12–13*

Jabez (Old Testament believer), *79*
James
- 1:4, *62*
- 1:17, *120*
- 1:21, *57*
- 1:21–22, *184–185*
- 1:21–24, *179*
- 3:4–5, *230*, *328*
- 3:5–6, *180–181*
- 4:1, *186*
- 4:6–7, *171*
- 5:14, *296*
- 5:15, *298*

Jeremiah 29:13, *76*, *80*
Jesus the Teacher (Sides), *304*
Job
- 1:6, *127*
- 2:1, *127*
- 17:11, *116*
- 32:8, *33*
- 38:4–7, *23*
- 38:7, *23*

Job (Old Testament believer), *116*

Joel (book), *168*
John
1:4, *44*
1:12, *10*
1:33, *240*
3:3–7, *41, 334n5 (chap. 2)*
3:30, *186*
3:34, *92*
4:24, *24*
5:30, *92*, *150–151*
6:63, *211*
7:38, *219*
7:38–39, *217*, *218*
8:28–29, *92*
8:44, *27*
10:10, *119*, *141*, *322*
11:38–44, *281*
14:9, *191*
14:12, *3*, *11*, *121*, *192*, *289*
14:12–13, *280*
14:12–14, *260*
14:17, *240*
14:18, *162*
14:21, *108*
14:26, *145*, *252*
15:26, *192*
16:7, *188*
16:7–8, *145*
16:13, *16*
16:13–15, *192*
16:33, *8*
17:9–10, *192*
17:22–23, *193*
20:21–22, *217*
John (apostle), *122*, *290*
John (the Baptist), *122*, *240*
1 John
1:3, *194*
1:8, *46*, *170*, *185*
1 John (*continued*)
1:8–10, *170*, *185*
2:12–14, *169–170*
2:27, *124*
4:4, *80*, *83*, *90*, *117*, *181*, *186*, *208*
4:8, *202*
4:18, *233*
5:14–15, *173*
Joseph (interpreter of dreams), *102–103*, *227*, *253*
Joshua
6:18, *152*
10:12, *274*
Joshua (successor to Moses as leader of children of Israel), *274*
Jubilees (book), *127*, *128*
Jude
1:6, *25*, *129*
1:20, *215*, *221*
Judges
3:1–4, *12–13*
8:4–27, *152*
judgment seat of Christ, *33–34*
jurisdiction
as authority granted, *77–81*
of mankind, *17–19*
as specific sphere, *9–10*, *87–94*

kalupto, *247*
kardia, *107*
King of the Mountain (or Hill), *7*
kingdom enforcers, *10–11*, *141–163*
1 Kings 18:38, *40*
knowledge, word of
being alive to spirit realm and, *238–239*
as a gift of the Spirit, *196–201*
as revelation gift, *253–256*

Lazarus (Jesus' friend), *281–282*
leaders
in church government, *311–315*
curses and, *155–156*
overseeing interpretation of tongues (or prophecy) in the church, *227–229*
See also overseers
Led by the Spirit to Speak in Tongues (Sides), *221*
See also under Sides, Dale M., works of
Leonard, B. G., *287*, *303*, *342n2 (chap. 17)*
life, eternal, *48–51*
See also birth, new; salvation
likeness
made in Adam's, *38*
made in His (God's), *24–26*
logos, *152*, *185*, *254–255*
Lucifer
as spirit being with free will, *25–26*
greed problem of, *319–321*
See also devil
Luke
2:36–38, *103*
2:49, *78–79*
4:5–6, *320*
4:6, *10*
4:13, *137*
4:40, *295*
5:13, *295*
8:26–39, *162*
8:35, *162*
9:1, *21–22*
10:19, *115*, *119*, *329–330*
11:4, *157*
11:11–12, *220*
13:13, *295*
16:10, *69*
Luke (*continued*)
17:6, *286*
21:19, *31*, *32*, *61*
23:6–7, *87*
lust (iniquity), *147–151*

makeup of man (spirit/soul/body), *28–33*, *65*, *303*
MacMillan, Randy, *250*
man (mankind)
first usage in Bible (Genesis 1:26), *22*
jurisdiction of, *17–19*
Mark
1:23–25, *123–124*
1:31, *295*
2 (chapter), *243*
2:8, *50*, *243*
5:1–20, *162*
6:2, *295*
6:5, *295*
6:12–13, *296*
7:32–33, *295*
8:23, *295*
8:25, *295*
9:27, *295*
10:42–43, *17*
11:13–14, *272–273*
11:21–24, *273–274*
11:22–23, *275*
11:23, *260*, *269*
11:23–24, *269–270*, *275*
11:24, *270*, *274–275*
16:17–18, *259*
16:18, *123*, *294*
Mason, Phil, *338n3 (chap. 9)*
materials, related (chapter resources)
for part 1 (chapters 1–5), *20*, *35*, *53*, *64*, *71*
for part 2 (chapters 6–7), *84*, *112*

materials, related (chapter resources) (*continued*)
for part 3 (chapters 8–9), *139*, *164*
for part 4 (chapters 10–11), *189*, *204*
for part 5 (chapters 12–17), *223*, *234*, *257*, *276*, *291*, *300*
Matthew
3:11–12, *215*
4:4, *212*
4:25 and 5:1, *77*
6 (chapter), *51*
6:12, *157*
6:16–18, *51*, *177*
6:24–25, *326*
6:31–33, *326*
7:22–23, *194*
8:3, *295*
8:8, *298*
8:10, *298–299*
8:15, *295*
8:30–31, *26*
9:18, *295*
9:25, *295*
9:29, *275*
10:1, *18*, *75*, *78*, *121*, *281*
11:12, *122*
12:43–45, *124–126*
12:45, *162*
13:16, *255*
17:21, *52*
18:18, *176*
18:32–35, *157*
21:22, *89*
22:37, *116*
24:12, *150*
25:14–30, *183*
25:21, *69*, *102*
25:21 and 23, *10*, *101*
25:30, *183*
Matthew (*continued*)
28:18, *10*, *76*, *83*, *124*
maturity, spiritual, *78–79*, *168–170*, *178–180*
measure, *91–94*, *191–192*, *196–200*, *307–309*
See also portion
meros, *92–93*
metanoeo, *146*
metron, *91–92*
Midianites, *152*
mimnesko, *252*
mind, battlefield of, *58–61*
See also soul
money, *317–331*
morphē, 97
Moses (leader of children of Israel), *13*, *274*, *324*
Mount of Olives, *273*

Nathan (prophet), *146*
nature
battlefield of the mind and, *58–60*
definition, *37*
DNA (Divine Nature Attributes) and the fruit of the Spirit, *195–196*
as not animals, *27–28*
as not flesh, *65–66*
See also regeneration
necromancy, *153–155*
Nee, Watchman, *25*
nephilim, *126–130*
Nicodemus (New Testament believer), *40–41*
Nicolaitans, doctrine of, *17*
nikao, *170*
Nike, *170*, *188*
nike, *170*

Noah (Old Testament believer), *40*, *129–130*
No-Purposeville, *103*, *112*, *116*
nous, *335n6 (chap. 2)*

obedience, test of, *12–15*
objects, physical
  deliverance and, *151–153*
  special anointings and, *299*
  as TRUCOPS portal, *143–144*
occult
  deliverance from, *153–155*
  practices as TRUCOPS portal, *143–144*
offense (in spiritual aggression), *15–16*
Oh, How I Love Jesus (song), *220*
oil. *See* anointing
Online Etymology Dictionary, *279*
opponent, *12–15*
orge, *45*
Osborn, T. L., *193*
overseers
  purpose of heart and, *111–112*
  See also leaders

paliggenesia, *42*
palin, *42*
para, *185*
paradidomi, *10*
paralogizomai, *185*
patience (exercising spiritual authority over our souls), *61–63*
Paul (apostle)
  commission of, *1*
  developing spiritual perception and, *181–183*
  new birth and, *334n5 (chap. 2)*
  ordination and, *313–314*
Paul (apostle) (*continued*)
  resisting temptation and overcoming sin, *180–181*
  special anointing of, *299*
  staying within limits of authority, *93–94*
peace
  confirmation of revelation and, *250–251*
  exercising spiritual authority over our souls and, *61–63*
  as fruit of the Spirit, *195–196*
  through superior power, *117–119*
  in whole armor of God, *171–172*
Pentecost, Day of
  and growing up, *168–169*
  and receiving the Holy Spirit, *207–208*, *214–222*
perception, spiritual
  developing, *181–183*, *241–245*
  gender differences and, *245–247*
Perfect Redemption (Sides), *144*
  See also under Sides, Dale M., works of
Peter (apostle)
  on Day of Pentecost, *168*, *207–208*
  healing lame man at Beautiful Gate, *287*, *290*
  special anointing of, *299*
  withered fig tree (Mark 11) and, *272–273*
1 Peter
  1:15–16, *168*
  1:18–19, *132*, *160*
  1:19, *151*
  1:23, *43*
  1:23–25, *83*
  2:2, *179*
  2:11, *177*, *185*
  2:21–23, *15*

1 Peter (*continued*)
4:11, *296*
5:2–3, *202*
5:5, *201*
5:5–6, *98*
5:8, *118*, *141*
2 Peter
1:1–15, *64*
1:2–3, *2*
1:4, *46*, *60*
1:21, *248*
2:4, *127*
phaino, *105*
Pharaoh (king of Egypt), *227*, *253*
Pharisees (religious leaders), *109–110*, *243*
Philippians
2:15, *82*
3:14–15, *103*
4:6–7, *307*
4:19, *327*
phimoo, *123–124*
phuo, *37*
phusao, *217*
phusis, *37*, *45*
physics, quantum
law of entanglement, *338n3 (chap. 9)*
law of observation, *339n3 (chap. 12)*
reality and consciousness, *237*
pictures
interpretation of tongues or prophecy and, *226–232*
personal epiphany of Christ, *105–108*, *109–110*
revelation, *284–286*
Pilate, Pontius *87*
Pishon, *321–322*
plan
of the ages, *7*
plan (*continued*)
of God for believers, *13–15*
master, *12*
points, relevant (chapter questions)
for part 1 (chapters 1–5), *20*, *35*, *53*, *64*, *71*
for part 2, (chapters 6–7) 85, *112*
for part 3, (chapters 8–9) *140*, *164*
for part 4 (chapters 10–11), *190*, *204*
for part 5 (chapters 12–17), *223*, *235*, *257*, *277*, *291*, *301*
portals
closing, *141–163*
and demonization, *133–135*
portion
authority and, *7–10*
individual lanes within body of Christ, *93–94*
iniquity and, *147–151*
money and, *317–332*
possessed vs. demonized, *131–135*
See also measure
powers
category of evil spirits, *81–83*, *124–130*
church authorities, *311*
prayer
of faith, *298*
with fasting, *51–52*, *176–178*
for healing, *293–294*
importance of, *172–176*
of Jabez, *79*
language (speaking in tongues), *214–222*
language versus diverse kinds of tongues, *225–226*
Lord's, *173–174*
our/your faith (Mark 11) and, *269–271*, *275*

prayer (*continued*)
as part of armor of God, *171–172*
versus command mode, *286–288*
predestination, *95–102*
pride
curses and, *155–156*
gender differences in spiritual perception and, *245–247*
as iniquity, *147–151*
Prince, Derek, *303*
principalities, as category of evil spirits, *81–83*, *124–130*
Principalities, Powers, and Demons (Sides) (article), *126*
See also under Sides, Dale M., works of
proclamations (for loosing resources), *328–332*
profiles
Christological astronomy and, *96*, *107*
Old Testament types (foreshadowing) of interpretation tongues, *226–227*
prothesis, *95–96*
protithemai, *96*
Proverbs
3:5, *218*
4:23, *118*
6:30–31, *319*
15:4, *160*
20:27, *33*, *44*
23:2, *68*
25:2, *22*
25:28, *149*
Psalms
8:4, *17*
8:4–6, *17*, *116*
8:4–8, *174–175*
8:6, *188*
17:8, *138*
Psalms (*continued*)
22:3, *212*
23:3, *56*
24:1, *142*
31:15, *32*, *97*
84:11, *88*, *220*
91 (chapter), *82*
103:13–14, *67*
103:20, *138*, *212*, *213*
103:20–21, *328*
118:6, *88*
119:9–11, *147*
119:23, *156*
136 (chapter), *148*
139:14, *65*
144:1, *82*
psychikos, *110*
purpose
crossing the threshold, *79–81*
defining yours, *88–90*
the gift of faith and, *307–309*
to glorify God, *281–284*
God-given, *12–14*, *87–88*, *203*
gold and, *321–323*
of heart, *110–112*
opposition and, *13–14*, *115–117*
personal epiphany, *105–108*
predestined, *95–103*
pressing toward the goal, *103–104*
representing Jesus, *87–88*, *191–203*
saved and called, *104–105*
spiritual maturity and, *78–79*
word of knowledge and, *253*
See also calling

quantum. *See* physics
See also under Sides, Dale M., works of
Quantum Glory (Mason), *338n3 (chap. 9)*
questions (chapter). *See* points, relevant

Realizing & Fulfilling Your Personal Ministry (Sides), *80*, *203*
  See also under Sides, Dale M., works of
Red Sea, *274*
regeneration, *40–47*
  See also nature
rejection
  deliverance from, *158–160*
  trauma and, *161–162*
  as TRUCOPS portal, *143–144*
repentance
  deliverance and, *141–143*
  developing the character of Christ and, *167–170*
  sin and, *145–146*
  spiritual maturity and, *178–179*
resources (chapter). *See* materials, related
Revelation
  1:5, *18*
  2:6, *17*
  2:7, *187*
  2:11, *187*
  2:17, *187*
  2:26, *8*, *187*
  2:28, *187*
  3:5, *187*
  3:12, *187*
  3:21, *187*
  9 (chapter), *128*
  11:7, *128*
  12:4, *125*
  12:9, *131*
  20:10, *13*, *27*
  20:11–12, *48*
  21:7, *187*
  21:10 and 21, *322*
rewards of overcoming, *187–188*
rhema, *212*, *218*, *255*, *296–297*
rhema rifle, *212*, *328–331*
rheo, *218*
Roberts, Oral, *284*, *297*, *303*
Romans (book), *261–262*
Romans
  1:8, *262*
  1:17, *261–264*, *275*
  2:14–15, *47*
  3:23, *148*
  4:17, *297*, *325*, *326*
  4:20, *308*
  6:4, *49*
  6:6, *46–47*, *60*
  6:6–7, *65*
  6:11, *39*, *49*, *60*, *238*
  6:23, *49*, *148*
  7 (chapter), *57*
  7:18, *181*
  8:1–9, *66*
  8:6, *62*
  8:6–8, *249*
  8:9–10, *12*, *50*
  8:16, *254*
  8:26–27, *215*
  8:27–28, *215*
  8:28, *97*
  8:28–29, *13–14*
  8:29, *48*, *97*, *124*, *159*
  8:31, *83*
  8:31–32, *88*
  8:32, *220*
  8:37, *170*, *193n2 (chap. 3)*
  8:37–39, *139*
  10:9–10, *41*, *49*, *75*
  10:9–11, *13*, *334–335n5 (chap. 2)*
  10:17, *329*
  12:1–2, *70*
  12:2, *55*
  12:3, *307*
  12:3–9, *91*
  13:1–6, *311–312*
  14:12, *104*

Romans *(continued)*
15:5, *62*
16:20, *90*
Rommel, General Erwin, *323*

salvation
helmet of, as part of armor of God, *171–172*
of soul, *55–58*
See also birth, new; life, eternal
2 Samuel
12:1–12, *146*
22:2, *163*
Sapphira (and Ananias, New Testament believers), *134*
séances (occult practices), *153–155*
shalom, *117*
Sides, Dale M., works of
Angels in the Army, *139*
The Anointing In and On, *53*, *257*
Approved of God by Grace or by Works, *257*
Be a Proactive Warrior—Swing First, *20*
Biblical Health Insurance, *291*
The Cancer Answer, *71*
Christological Astronomy, *35*, *112*, *203*, *204*, *336n4 (chap. 7)*
Closing Gates of Hell, *139*
Covenant Healing in Communion, *300*
Covet Earnestly the Best Gifts, *291*
Developing Your Spiritual Sensitivity, *53*, *189*, *257*
Devil, Give Me Back My Money!, *317*, *318*, *329*
Discerning of Spirits and Casting Out Demons, *163*, *164*
Diverse Kinds of Tongues, *223*, *234*, *339n4 (chap. 12)*

Sides, Dale M., works of *(continued)*
Exercising Spiritual Authority for Yourself and Your Ministry, *84*, *139*
Exercising Spiritual Authority: Level 3, *300*
Exercising Spiritual Authority over Principalities and Powers, *84*
Exposing Sons of Belial, *139*, *164*
Fit for the Kingdom, *71*, *189*
Flowing in All Nine Gifts of the Holy Spirit, *204*, *205*, *234*, *291*, *339n2 (chap. 11)*
40 Days of Communion in Your Home, *189*, *300*
The Foundation of Miracle Working, *291*
Foundations of Faith, *264*, *276*
The Gift of Faith, *276*
God Damn Satan, *139*, *164*
The Gospel of the Kingdom, *64*
Having Faith to Finish, *276*
Healthy Living, *71*
How to Do Miracles, *291*
How to R.E.A.D. and S.T.U.D.Y. the Bible, *189*
I Ain't Takin' Acid Anymore, *71*
I Believe in the Godhead (but I'm Not So Sure about the Trinity (article), *334n3 (chap. 2)*
Interpretation of Tongues, *234*
It Takes Faith to Be a Believer, *333n7 (chap. 1)*
Jesus the Teacher, *304*
The Law of Conscience, *53*
Led by the Spirit to Speak in Tongues, *221*, *223*
Manifesting the Holy Spirit, *257*, *291*
Mending Cracks in the Soul, *35*, *139*, *164*

Sides, Dale M., works of (*continued*)
New Creation Realities, *20*, *53*, *204*
The Old Man Is Dead, *53*
The 1,000 Year Reign of Jesus Christ on the Earth, *71*, *84*
Overcoming Addictions, *71*
Overcoming Depression, *64*
Patience: Bearing Up, *64*
Perfect Redemption, *139*, *144*, *164*
The Physics of Faith, *223*, *276*, *300*
Principalities, Powers, and Demons (article), *126*, *139*
Quantum Physics, Continued: Entanglement/Entrainment/Observation, *164*, *223*, *338n3 (chap. 9)*
Realizing & Fulfilling Your Personal Ministry, *80*, *112*, *203*, *204*
Recognizing Revelation, *257*
Re-GENE-erated, *53*
The Satanic Deception of Knife & Fork, *71*
Second Peter 1:1–15: Character after Salvation, *64*
Speaking by the Spirit of God, *223*
Speaking by the Spirit of God (part 2), *234*
Spirit, Soul, and Body: Saving the Whole Man, *35*
Spiritual Boot Camp, *20*, *53*, *84*
Temperance: the Fruit of the Spirit, *64*
To Rejoice Is a Choice, *64*
T.R.U.C.O.P.S., *164*
True Confessions of Spiritual Warriors, *20*, *112*
Understanding & Breaking the Schemes of the Devil, *139*, *164*
Utilizing Gift Ministries, *112*, *204*
Victory over Iniquity (article), *164*

Sides, Dale M., works of (*continued*)
Walking in Resurrected Power, *291*
You Don't Have to Be Smart to Walk with God, *249*, *257*, *276*
Sides, Vicki, works of
Fellowship with Jesus Christ, *189*, *204*
Praising God, *189*
Why Should We Forgive?, *64*
Yahweh: the Sacred Name of God, *189*
sin
as portal of demonic entry, *141–151*
resisting temptation and overcoming sin, *180–181*
sinning not, *183–184*
sons
of man (mankind), *17*, *116*
maturing spiritually, *78–84*
sons of God
as angels, *126–130*
growing up, *168–169*
as kingdom enforcers, *10–11*
nephilim and, *126–130*
as reward of overcoming, *187*
soul
composition, *55*
example of exercising spiritual authority over, *61–63*
salvation of, *55–58*
See also mind
sphere
of authority, *9–10*
church government and, *315*
curses and, *155*
staying within, *93–94*
See also purpose
spirit of man (mankind), *28–31*
spirit, regenerated
alive to the spirit realm, *238–239*

spirit, regenerated (*continued*)
made alive, *44–48*
ruling over soul and body, *31*, *58*
spirit, soul, and body. *See* makeup
Stupidville, *249*
suntribo, *90*
sword of the Spirit
armor of God and, *171–172*
to combat the spirit of the world, *185–186*
in deliverance from occult practices, *153–155*
peace through superior power and, *117–119*
as rhema rifle (Ephesians 6:17), *212–213*
sinning not and, *183–184*
war rules and, *119–120*
symmorphos, *97*
syn, *97*

Tartarus, *127*
Teacup, The (Anonymous), *99–100*
temptation
resisting, *180–181*
rewards of overcoming, *187*
seducing spirits and, *135–139*
of spirit of the world, *185–186*
test
money as, *317–319*
of obedience, *14–15*
on stewardship of our sphere of authority, *9–10*
worthy opponents for, *11–13*
1 Thessalonians
5:5, *50*
5:20, *231*
5:23 *28–30*, *65*
2 Thessalonians 2:7, *150*
1 Timothy
2:5, *vii*
2:14, *18*
4:1–2, *47*, *134*
5:17–18, *313*
2 Timothy, *105*
1:6, *314*
1:7, *59*, *83*
1:8–9, *104–105*
1:9, *95–96*
1:9–10, *105–107*
2:19, *146*
3:12, *122*
Titus
3:4–5, *42*
3:5, *39*
tongues, diverse kinds of, *222*, *225–226*, *329n4 (chap. 12)*
transgression
impact of Adam & Eve's, *37–40*
as a kind of sin, *144–151*
trauma
deliverance from, *160–162*
as TRUCOPS portal, *143–144*
Trivandrum, *282*
TRUCOPS, *143–163*

unforgiveness
deliverance from, *156–158*
as TRUCOPS portal, *143–144*
utterance, spiritual, *208–213*, *350n1 (chap. 16)*

Vine's Expository Dictionary of New Testament Words, *97*
visions
fulfilling personal destiny and, *307–309*
growing in revelation and, *168–169*

visions (*continued*)
the three revelation gifts and, *253–256*

Wagner, C. Peter, *250*
warfare, spiritual
aggression, *15–16*
expelling demons, *121–124*
functions of demons, *131*
nephilim, *126–130*
peace through superior power, *117–119*
possession versus demonization, *131–135*
rules of, *119–121*, *323–324*
seducing spirits, *135–139*
unclean spirits, *124–126*
words (spiritual utterance) as weapons of, *208–214*
worthy opponent and, *13–15*
See also battle
watchers (and the nephilim), *126–130*
Wierwille, V. P., *303*
Wimber, John, *261*
will
and accountability at judgment seat of Christ, *33*
as part of being made in His likeness *24–26*
wisdom, word of
and being alive to spirit realm, *238–239*
as a gift of the Spirit, *196–201*
as revelation gift, *253–256*
witchcraft, man's jurisdiction and, *17*
words. *See under* warfare, spiritual
works (doing His and greater), *192–194*
world, spirit of, *185–186*
World War II, *323*
wrath
children of, *37*, *45*
as definition of *orge*, *45*
as a work of the flesh, *66*

You Don't Have to Be Smart to Walk with God (Sides), *249*
See also under Sides, Dale M., works of

Zechariah
2:8, *138*
14:4, *273*

Selected Resources Available at LMCI.org

by Dale M. Sides

Abaddon (a.k.a Apollyon)

Dr Dale has unraveled another Bible mystery in uncovering the secret of Abaddon. By comparing scriptures with apocryphal records, he has discovered the identity, inhabitants, and the prophesied opening of this ancient prison, as well as hints of its location. Learn about this pit and the authority you have over the evil that will be loosed out of it. More importantly, discover how those who are here during the great tribulation can be protected from its inhabitants. Available format: booklet

Angels in the Army: How to Release the Heavenly Host in Spiritual Warfare

This book discloses new information from the Dead Sea Scrolls that verifies age-old principles from the Bible—that mankind has been given the authority to release angels into spiritual warfare. Learn how to aim and shoot your "rhema rifle" and how to release the heavenly host into spiritual battle. Available format: book

The Anointing In and On

Many Christians are confused about the work of the Holy Spirit. What does it mean to have the abiding, indwelling presence of the Holy Spirit? How does that differ from the Holy Spirit coming upon someone to accomplish His will on the earth? What is the believer's responsibility when the Holy Spirit moves? These questions and others are answered through the detailed, yet concise, documentation of God's Word. Available format: booklet

Christological Astronomy

Christological Astronomy is *not* astrology but the study of the Word of God written in the heavens, which offers an amazing picture of Yeshua our Redeemer and King. Also contained within these starry messages are the potential destinies of God's children who He foreordained to represent Christ upon the earth. The workbook gives students a basic foundation of this fascinating topic and then builds upon it so that they can interpret these messages and be encouraged to rise up to the high calling of Christ in their lives. *Christological Astronomy* is well suited for individual or group study, and a Certificate of Completion is available for those who complete all assignments. Available formats: workbook, e-workbook, DVD set, CD set, MP3 set

Circle on the Face of the Deep

Far above the North Pole and visible against the night sky, there is a star-studded circle that has perpetually declared revelation and beckoned mankind to read and interpret its prophetic message since its creation. Although it has been virtually ignored since ancient times, the need to understand what it is saying is even more urgent now, since we are on the brink of its fulfillment. Find out for yourself what the Creator of the universe wants every man, woman, and child to read and understand. Available format: e-book

Closing Gates of Hell

No subject is as crucial in strategic level spiritual warfare than identifying and closing gates of hell. Jesus gave authority to the church to build the kingdom of God on the earth—including the authority to close these gates. When we operate in this manner we "blow up the communication system" of demons and wicked spirits from the heavenlies, which sows confusion and chaos into the kingdom of darkness. The truths revealed in this study are destined to become fundamental spiritual mapping strategies to help the church prevail over the evil kingdom and build the kingdom of God on the earth. Available format: booklet

Devil, Give Me Back My Money!

A despicable thief has robbed God's children. Whether he's stolen your money, your health, or even your family, it's time for God's people to develop an attitude and reclaim what rightfully belongs to them. This book will give you the truths necessary to do just that. Are you ready to take back what the devil has stolen from you? (Hard copy is also available in Spanish.) Available formats: book, e-book

Diverse Kinds of Tongues

Delve into questions that have puzzled the church for centuries: What is speaking in tongues all about? Is diverse kinds of tongues the same as prayer in the Spirit? What role does diverse kinds of tongues play in the ministry of intercession? Be prepared to see your prayer life brought to a much higher level as you glean the truths in this timely book. (Spanish version is also available.) Available format: booklet

Exposing Sons of Belial: Identifying and Overcoming Children of the Devil

Sons or daughters of Belial are dedicated, committed children of the devil, traceable throughout the Bible like a black thread that interweaves wickedness, destruction, and intended evil. Identifying and exposing them are among the highest priorities for intercessors and warriors of the spirit realm in these latter days, and one of the church's primary responsibilities is to stand in the way of their wicked schemes. Discover the identifying traits of sons or daughters of Belial and a powerful revelation of how to pray against them. Available format: booklet

Flowing in All Nine Gifts of the Holy Spirit

The Holy Spirit gives every Christian nine gifts of spiritual power in order to produce exactly the manifestation needed, according to His will. Learn how to flow in all of these nine gifts so that you can be more effective as a witness and minister for the Lord Jesus Christ. Available format: booklet

40 Days of Communion in Your Home

A powerful primer designed to aid individuals and families in receiving the full benefits available through the partaking of the Lord's Supper. Featuring daily Bible verses accompanied by short devotional passages, this booklet is designed to strengthen the reality of covenant living in your home and to enhance your intimacy with the Lord. Available formats: booklet, e-book

God Damn Satan: Subduing the Evil Kingdom through the Power of Biblical Cursing

The biblical curse is a major, powerful tool in the Christian's arsenal. This startling revelation, documented throughout the Bible, can add power to your prayer life and create terror and chaos in the satanic kingdom. Learn how Satan stole this weapon and how you can reclaim it to help build the kingdom of God. Available format: book

Interpretation of Tongues

Building upon a foundation of the baptism of the Holy Spirit, speaking in a tongue, and diverse kinds of tongues, this CD set then delves into the "meat" of interpretation of tongues through dynamic biblical instruction and hands-on practice groups. This revolutionary class teaches how interpretation of tongues can be a steppingstone to prophecy and revelation. It also differentiates between the *gift* and the *ministry* of interpretation of tongues, and instructs believers in its utilization within their private lives as well as within the church. Available formats: CD set, MP3 set

Mending Cracks in the Soul

Powerful and delivering, this material covers the subject of memory healing through the ministry of the Holy Spirit. Strongly grounded in biblical documentation and practical experience, Dr. Dale teaches how a soul can crack due to trauma, how the Holy Spirit can reveal the truth, and how that crack can be forever mended. This is an invaluable resource to those seeking freedom from the past and to those who minister healing. Available formats: book, CD audiobook, MP3 audiobook, CD set, MP3 set

The 1,000 Year Reign of Jesus Christ on the Earth: Will You Make It or Miss It?

Jesus Christ is returning soon to reign as King for 1,000 years on the earth. Will you find a place of honor in His kingdom, or will you miss it? What you do *today* determines the answer to that question. Rulership with Jesus is part of the inheritance that God wants to give to His children who have been diligent about their Father's business, building up His kingdom. Your entire life is a qualifying round for the millennial kingdom of Christ and will determine your position in it. Don't miss out! Available format: book

Perfect Redemption: The Purpose of His Passion

Jesus bled seven ways . . . how can blood shed 2,000 years ago deliver us now? Jesus Christ suffered for a reason—to redeem us. He bled seven different ways to free us from bondage, break off curses, and empower us for a life of victory. This comprehensive and practical material provides a deeper understanding of the total freedom that is available to all believers. Learn the purpose for His passion. Discover your rights—Jesus paid for them with His own blood. Learn how to embrace and live out your perfect redemption. Available formats: book, DVD set, CD set, MP3 set

Studying War: They Continually Gather Together for War

Warmongers really do exist, and their methods and schemes even go far beyond instigating wars. The Bible clearly identifies these children of darkness who line their pockets with blood money. In *Studying War* (the sequel to *Exposing Sons of Belial*), discover how these evildoers, with their goal of world domination and control, are unwittingly fulfilling end-time biblical prophecy. What the warmongers have meant for harm, God (Yahweh) can use to usher in His end-time plans. Available formats: booklet, e-book

True Confessions of Spiritual Warriors

This devotional-style booklet contains "true confessions" (testimonies) of various biblical characters: Joseph, addressing the topic of strength of character; Daniel, on prayer and wisdom; David, on patience; Joshua, on following orders; John, on victory, and many others. They are by no means "a word" from these great men and women of the Bible, but personified insights to help us all become better warriors for the Lord Jesus Christ. This enjoyable booklet is full of life's valuable lessons from a biblical worldview. Available format: booklet

T.R.U.C.O.P.S

Jesus came to set the captives free, but many Christians feel inadequate to minister deliverance to those who need it. *TRUCOPS* (pronounced "tru cops") is a deliverance manual made simple. It offers a no-nonsense approach to deliverance, employing the acronym TRUCOPS to represent the major portals of demonic entry. Read this practical deliverance guidebook and build your faith to step out into the field of deliverance and boldly help yourself and others to be freed from demonic bondage. Available format: e-book

Turning Churches into Armies

The Holy Spirit is calling the church to *war*. The time has come for us to "shed our wool" and put on the whole armor of God to be bold soldiers of Yeshua the Warrior. If we are going to take our cities, states, and countries for the Lord Jesus Christ, we must unleash the warrior inside us and exercise our spiritual authority to carry out the Great Commission of *discipling* the nations. Available format: booklet

Understanding & Breaking the Schemes of the Devil

This powerful and equipping booklet has the potential to change your life. Discover and identify the particular scheme that the devil has perpetrated against you personally. Then, armed with solid biblical and practical understanding of how the scheme works, learn how to break that scheme with the sword of the Spirit. Available formats: booklet, e-book, CD set, MP3 set

Utilizing Gift Ministries

Delve into the revolutionary truth found in the Word of God concerning the relationship of para-church provisions and revival. The workbook format is easy to embrace for individual study or for group use among church leaders. Available format: book

Where Are the Apostles?

Where are the apostles? This question begs to be answered not only by potential apostles but by every Christ-follower. This provision of leadership has been questioned, denied, and ignored; but as it properly reenters the contemporary church scene, great growth could result. Discover the long lost truths of this ministry and reactivate this vital provision to help equip the saints and edify the whole body of Christ. C. Peter Wagner, founder of the International Coalition of Apostles, said of *Where Are the Apostles?* "This is a highly readable book—it makes a long story short! In my opinion, there is no better entry-level book on apostles and apostolic ministry available today." Available format: e-book

Where Do You Go When You Die?

This booklet examines the Scriptures and other ancient texts to discover where the spirit of man goes after the demise of its physical body. The ancient book of Enoch agrees with the Bible while offering more specifics of the places a departed spirit can go. Will your destination be Paradise, where righteousness reigns? Or will it be among the deep recesses of Sheol (Hell), where darkness and separation from God is guaranteed? Do not wait to discover your eternal fate. Find out now the choices you have for your eternal destination. Learn how the decision you make on this earth will determine which place will be yours. Available format: booklet

Who Do You Think You Are?

Does the image you hold of yourself line up with the truth of who God has made you to be? This is not a self-help book filled with cheap psychological tricks; instead, it is a Bible-based book to help build your confidence in what the Creator thinks and says about you. Discover the person God made you to be and walk in confidence and true boldness. Love yourself the way God loves you; change the way you think about yourself. Available format: booklet

You Don't Have to Be Smart to Walk with God

Do you want to recognize the voice of God speaking to you? Do you desire an intimate relationship with your Heavenly Father? How about increasing the power of God in your life? This powerful and profound book focuses on these very issues. The keys revealed to walking and talking with God are easy to apply and eternally profitable. Any Christian can use them, because you really don't have to be smart to walk with God. Available format: book